Mom –   1988

   Happy Birthday – Love

      John & Shirley

FREEDOM'S CHILD

FREEDOM'S CHILD

A Courageous Teenager's Story
of Fleeing His Parents —
and the Soviet Union —
to Live in America

WALTER POLOVCHAK
with Kevin Klose

Random House 🏠 New York

Library of Congress Cataloging-in-Publication Data

Polovchak, Walter.
Freedom's child.

1. Polovchak, Walter—Trials, litigation, etc.
2. Custody of children—Illinois—Chicago.
3. Emigration and immigration law—United States.
4. Emigration and immigration law—Soviet Union.
5. Ukrainian Americans—Biography. I. Klose, Kevin.
II. Title.
KF228.P64P64 1988   346.7301'7   87-32249
ISBN 0-394-55926-6   347.30617

Manufactured in the United States of America
24689753
First Edition

Contents

1. MY ARREST   *3*
2. ROOTS IN THE USSR   *10*
3. GROWING UP SOVIET   *21*
4. HELP ARRIVES   *31*
5. MY AUNT FROM AMERICA   *41*
6. THE MAN WHO DEFENDED ME   *52*
7. THE FIRST HEARING   *67*
8. AFTER THE HEARING   *80*
9. GOODBYE, SOYUZ . . .   *91*
10. HELLO, AMERICA!   *102*
11. THINGS FALL APART   *114*
12. OUTSIDERS ENTER   *128*
13. THE JULY 30 HEARING   *140*
14. THE THIRD HEARING—PART I   *162*
15. THE THIRD HEARING—PART II   *172*
16. THE JUDGE'S DECISION   *184*
17. LEGAL UPS, LEGAL DOWNS   *197*
18. DEPARTURES—BUT NO GOODBYES   *213*
19. AMERICAN CITIZEN!   *232*

FREEDOM'S CHILD

To: Supervisor, Youth Division
From: Sergeant Leo G. Rojek
Subject: Unreported Missing: Walter Polovchak M/W 3 Oct 67

On 18 July 1980, the undersigned was requested by Commander Paul Jankowski, 014th District, to assist a Mr. Michael Polovchak M/W 13 June 1938, 3624 W. Fullerton Avenue, in locating his son Walter Polovchak.

Mr. Michael Polovchak stated his daughter Natalie enticed Walter Polovchak (son) to run away from home rather than to return to Russia with the family and she was hiding him in the home of their cousin, Walter Polowczak M/W 20 May 1956.

After learning that Walter Polovchak lived at 5025 W. Byron, the undersigned along with Y.O. [Youth Officer] Martin Flynn and Beat Representative Helen Greco arrived at the location, whereupon Walter Polovchak was taken into custody as an unreported runaway and brought to Area 5 Youth Division. The daughter Natalie Polovchak was at the address at the time. . . .

chapter one
MY ARREST

One afternoon in July 1980, a twelve-year-old immigrant Ukrainian kid was sitting in his cousin's backyard in Chicago, getting ready to take a bike ride.

The kid was me. It was a great day—sunny, quiet, and everything was more or less okay with the world. Nobody was bothering me. And I wasn't bothering anybody. I was minding my own business, polishing up my bike and thinking about taking it out for a spin.

I was sure I was safe. So I wasn't worried about anything. Most important, I wasn't afraid anymore about being taken back to the Soviet Union. My parents wanted to go back there, but not me. No way.

So a few days before, I had walked out of the Chicago apartment where my family lived and come to stay with my older cousin, who had a small place a few blocks away.

My big sister, Natalie, had done the same thing at the same time. We'd just gathered up our clothing and left my parents. My mother hardly said a word to us when we walked out right in front of her eyes. She didn't care that much. Besides, she would follow my dad wherever he took her, and after barely six months in the United States, where he wanted to go was back to Ukraine, which is how Ukrainians call our homeland, just the way it's Ireland to the Irish.

And Natalie and I didn't. We had fought with our parents

plenty about this, especially with my dad. When my parents refused
to agree to let me stay in Chicago if they went back to the Soviet
Union, we did the only thing we knew: we fled.

It was that simple. That was the whole thing: I didn't want to
go back to Ukraine.

But my parents insisted I had to come with them, which caused
all the trouble that came later, years and years of trouble. Fights,
lawyers, courtrooms, television and newspaper guys buzzing around.
International headlines. Denunciations from Moscow of me and the
people who helped me. And lots of fear. Natalie and I were never
sure whether the next day would bring defeat. If it did, they'd have
to carry me off kicking and screaming to the Soviet Union.

But all that lay ahead. Now I was just working on my bike. In
the couple of days since we moved out, I'd gotten used to the quiet.
I didn't know whether my parents even cared or not that I had left.
We'd never called them and they had never tried to find us. Life
was pretty peaceful, and I was about to take off on my bike.

I tell you, I loved that bike. It had shiny chrome fenders, big
flaring handlebars, and a sturdy frame. It was a real American bike,
as real to me as the stars and stripes of the American flag.

My cousin, Big Walter, had dug the bike out of his basement a
few months before. Years ago he had won the bike on a Chicago
television show called *Bozo Circus*. Honest. He'd used it himself as
a kid, but when he got old enough, he bought a car. The bike spent
quite a long time in the cellar. When he gave it to me, it was a
mess. I rescued it. I fixed it up—got the rust off the fenders, oiled
and tightened up the chain, fixed the brake, got the wheels to run
straight.

Even though I'd only had it a few months, I'd already had plenty
of adventures. The bike was my best friend. I couldn't speak English at all, or read a street sign, but the bike had been my passport
and ticket to America.

The west side of Chicago, where we had settled in January 1980
after coming from Ukraine, was a small part of America, mostly
small apartment buildings, stores, some churches, schools, factories. Just neighborhoods. But what neighborhoods! I'd never seen
anything like them before.

There was nothing like them in Ukraine—colorful signs on the
shops, well-painted little houses and bungalows with separate fam-

ilies living in them, all kinds of different people like Mexicans and
blacks, as well as my own Ukrainian countrymen.

Even though I couldn't read the signs at first, I had a good
memory and good sense of direction. As I rode along, I memorized
some of the intersections and streets, and I always found my way
back home. As the weeks passed, I got to know my surroundings
pretty well—better than my parents, for sure. And slowly, pain-
fully, I began to speak some English.

I rode the bike everywhere, and I saw so much of life—stores
crammed with food and clothing, shopkeepers out in front of their
stores carefully sweeping their sidewalks, people dressed up in their
best and going to church without police watching, people loading
up their cars with groceries. I knew this place was for me. I hadn't
been here very long, but I sure felt right at home. America.

I was adjusting the bike's chain and sprocket when I noticed
something out of the corner of my eye.

Four people were running down the sidewalk toward me.

My father!

My father, his face red, shouting at me. He'd come to take me
back!

I stared at him. I couldn't move. I was numb with fright. Where
was Natalie? My mind was a blank.

My father was yelling at me, words ripping out of his mouth. I
was too scared to understand him.

Another guy was shouting some kind of half Polish, half Ukrainian at me. Who was he?

And here came two more guys. No question who they were:
police.

One of them pulled out a badge big enough and shiny enough
to be a gun. He flashed it at me and started saying something in
English. I couldn't understand a word.

They stood looking at me, and then the man with my father
began repeating in Ukrainian with a lousy accent what the cop had
said.

"We're police. You're coming with us."

Scared as I was, I didn't even wait a second to answer. "I'm not
going anywhere with you!"

The guy translated this back to the cops. They moved in on me
and rattled in English at the translator. "Yes, you are," he said.

The hell I am, I thought. I grabbed the handle of the house's back door with all my might.

They were real strong. They just pulled me loose like you'd pull a suction-tipped arrow off the wall. I weighed eighty-two pounds and was four feet tall, but they carried me out of the backyard and down the sidewalk as if I were a ten-pound sack of potatoes.

Damn! Where was Natalie? Okay, maybe we hadn't gotten along all that well before, but I sure needed her now. Last I knew, she had been inside, washing the floors. As they hustled me down the sidewalk, I saw the front door open. Natalie must have heard the commotion, because she suddenly came out.

Natalie's small, but a bundle of energy. Stubborn as can be, too. And a real temper. I know all about *that*. She hesitated approximately a tenth of a second, then tore into them:

"What's going on! What do you think you're *doing*?"

They stopped and started flashing their badges at her. "Police. He's coming with us."

"Don't you dare! You can't take him away! *This is private property!*"

She was furious, and scared, too. I could hear it in her voice, kind of trembling. But they ignored her. My father pretended she didn't exist.

The cops weren't rough, but they didn't fool around, either. They were all business. Real cops. "Get in the car, one of them ordered."

I struggled. But these guys were big and I was just a little kid in short pants and a T-shirt. They threw me in their car without even trying.

I looked past them to find out what Natalie was doing. But there wasn't really anything she could do. She didn't have a car, and she didn't even know where they were taking me. Neither did I.

A guy got in on each side of me, squeezing me in between them just like a sandwich, so I wouldn't jump out. Fat chance. I'd have to climb over their laps to even get to a door.

My father was sitting there too, watching me. Maybe he tried to say something to me—I don't remember. What I do remember is that I turned away from him. I didn't want to look at him or say anything to him. I was so mad!

And he had me now. I was a child with no rights, and my father had the rights any parent has over his children. He had the cops on his side. I could barely speak a few sentences of English. It looked like the end of the line for me, just a little kid from the Soviet Union who wanted to be an American.

The cops started the car and we drove off. I didn't know where we were headed, but I was real worried I would end up back in the USSR.

It wasn't meant to be this way for my family, the Polovchaks, of Sambir, USSR, when we made the long trip from Ukraine to our new home in the United States.

Life in America was supposed to be very different. Instead of cops and trouble, there was supposed to be peace and freedom. Maybe the streets wouldn't be paved with gold in America, but we were pretty sure there weren't going to be long lines for food, or an outhouse in the backyard of our home, or political indoctrination in school, or disapproval of going to church, either—none of the things that were part of our lives in Sambir.

We came because my parents, Anna and Michael Polovchak, said they wanted a better life, in every way. When I think about that first moment when our plane flew over New York in January 1980, I can still remember how it felt—wonder, fear, and hope, all wrapped together inside me.

I was so excited, staring out the windows of the plane as we came down. It was night, and it was like you'd never seen so many lights in your life. That's what I was telling myself.

We knew this was New York and next would come Chicago and our relatives there and a new home. Even more than that, a new life for us all. I remember thinking that, and also thinking how eager I was—how eager we all were—to begin learning.

As we taxied toward the terminal at Kennedy Airport, there was movement in the darkness everywhere—planes out on the runways, little tractors pulling carts loaded with luggage and cargo, and trucks running around hauling gas or something. On our way here, I'd been in some big cities, like Moscow and Rome. But this was already the most exciting place ever.

One runway out there in the darkness pointed back the way we'd come. Of all the things I knew that night, I remember one especially: I didn't ever want to go back down *that* runway. Not back out over the ocean and beyond to the place I'd grown up. Never. That was finished for me. I wanted to check out this place, see who lived here, what kind of people they were, friends I could make.

Just for starters, they probably had more lights in this one terminal in New York than in all of Sambir. At night there, you'd see maybe one streetlight every block, and some dim little glimmers in houses along the dirt roads. Sambir was a city, but it was small and pretty far away from other cities. So at night it was real dark, and almost all the time, it was real quiet. For example, most people in Sambir didn't own cars. My parents had friends with cars, but we didn't own one.

My father was a bus driver for the city's transportation enterprise. (They don't have companies in the USSR the way they do here. There they call them enterprises instead, and they're not run for profit.) His specialty was driving all kinds of long-distance trips. He would be gone a lot of the time on these trips with the bus, three, four days at a time most weeks. When he was gone, he was gone, and when he was home, he was tired out or running around with his buddies. It seemed like he hardly ever had time for us.

We had lived very quietly in our town, and also had lived apart among ourselves. I didn't need to be a genius to sense that my life in Ukraine was pretty different from the way people seemed to live in America, with all their movement, their coming and going all the time. This was a place of excitement, I could see by looking out the windows of the New York airport. I could see from all the headlights on the roads that *every* American must have a car. This was just what our relatives in the States had told us in letters that came to Sambir, and when one of my aunts who lived in America came to visit us once there, she had said the same thing. We couldn't believe it then, but now, even after an hour in this country, it looked like maybe what they told us was true.

I could see my father was taking in all these differences the same way I was. There was so much happening, so much brightness and so many people moving around, it almost seemed to scare him, I thought.

Most of the time, my father liked to talk a lot and put on a show for people, talk loud, get himself noticed. This was a way he had of getting what he wanted, and he usually succeeded, too. But now he was silent, watching the Americans with an odd expression on his face. He looked amazed, but kind of as if he wanted to hide it. His face had a covered look, keeping his thoughts from showing.

My mother's face was the same, quietly scanning the scene. But this was her natural way.

I couldn't read their minds, but I knew what they were thinking: It's so different here from what we're used to—how are we going to fit in? I'm sure that's what they were thinking, because I was thinking the same thing. Nobody who came to America from a place like Sambir, backward and isolated, could think much else.

Over the decades, plenty of Ukrainians had come to America and made out okay, settling down, getting good jobs, buying houses, cars, the usual things Americans have. We'd heard plenty of stories about all this. People from countries all over the world had come here and done the same thing—millions of them.

So my hopes were high. I guess I just assumed the rest of us felt the same way: maybe we would all be happy here, a family together, getting ahead in America like other immigrant families. I had no idea that just six months later, I'd be under arrest for running away from my own family.

chapter two
ROOTS IN THE USSR

When the Chicago police grabbed me, I was just a nobody kid. No one knew I was as tough as I turned out to be—no one except me, that is. When I make up my mind, I'm like a bulldog. You aren't going to shake me loose. That's not boasting, it's just the way I am. To me, this is natural because my people are Ukrainians and I'm one of them. They are tough people who have survived war, starvation, terror, invasion, and a lot of other horrible things. They've even had their nation taken away from them, and they've survived that, too.

You mention Ukraine and most Americans think right away of Russia, or the Soviet Union. Some people don't have a clue there's any difference at all. I didn't understand this at first, but now I realize that ninety-nine Americans out of a hundred think that *anyone* who comes from the USSR has got to be a Russian. They don't know that the language, traditions, and culture of Ukraine are entirely different from Russia's.

I was born in Sambir, a city in western Ukraine, on October 3, 1967. My ancestors were nothing fancy, just peasants off the farm, people who knew what hard work and no money are all about.

Family history isn't a big part of my life, but my older cousin, Walter, who came to America more than ten years before I did, and who has helped me the most here, has told me some interesting things about my ancestors that may explain the way I am, my personality and conduct, and why I did what I did.

My father's father, who was named Lev, or Leo in English, was a soldier in the Austro-Hungarian army and marched all over Europe for a couple of years during World War I. Then he came back and settled down where he had grown up, a little farming village called Volosinova. He had nine kids, and my father, Mykhailo, or Michael, was the youngest. He was born in 1938.

My father was real young when the Nazis invaded the Soviet Union in World War II. They occupied Ukraine for more than three years, and they killed millions of people, women and children as well as soldiers serving in the Red Army. The Nazis also sent thousands of Ukrainians to Germany, where they were forced to work in slave labor factories and where many died.

My uncle Ivan was taken to Germany, where he vanished, and my aunt Anastasia was sent to Germany as a slave laborer. My grandfather's family might all have been killed, except that Grandfather remembered some German from his army days and was asked to translate for the occupation troops. He couldn't read or write, but he was clever and managed to save my father's life and the lives of the other children living at home.

Grandfather Leo was important for another reason: he was a religious man. His small house happened to be next door to a Ukrainian Catholic church, and he attended masses there and served as its caretaker. Some of my cousins were baptized in that church, and religion has been a strong force in my family, especially to my mother and my sister, Natalie, and to Cousin Walter.

Although my grandfather died a few months after I was born, some of his stories about what he had seen of life as a young soldier traveling outside our country became family legends. My relatives knew from his adventures that there was something more to life than what we were told by teachers or Soviet television. Some great-uncles lived in Czechoslovakia, and there was even a distant cousin who lived in Canada. All these things helped my cousin Walter and his mother, Aunt Maria, decide to come to the United States after Grandfather Leo died. That had a big impact on my life.

So there was knowledge of other countries in my family. In addition, we came from a town with a strong Ukrainian tradition.

For example, Cousin Walter has told me that quite a few people from Voloshynovo, or Daisytown, have come to the States, and when Natalie got married in Chicago in 1986, five or six people from the village who now live in America came to the wedding.

Because the place is close to the Polish border, there was pretty strong anti-Russian feeling. After the war, many villagers were sent to Siberia as punishment because they favored an independent country for Ukrainians. I've been told that something like seventeen men from the village were killed in the postwar Resistance and about thirty were exiled to Siberia.

Sambir is an hour or so by train from Lviv, as Ukrainians call it, or Lvov, as Russians and foreigners call it. Lviv is real big, with lots of stores, streets, and people. There was a zoo, a big sports stadium, and other attractions. We went there a couple of times when I was a kid, but I never got to spend much time there.

Sambir, though, isn't anything special—just a small city where people work in factories. There were some stores, an amusement park (where you had to push most of the rides by yourself), a farmers' market—the usual things you'd find in a small town out in the Soviet provinces. Like long lines and people waiting for things to buy, and plenty of bare shelves in the stores. If things came in, they came in, if they didn't, they didn't. And no explanations.

For example, sometimes the bread in the bread stores would start turning yellower. Then everyone knew that the harvest had been lousy, even though the newspapers said it had been a real good one. If a truck drove up on a street and they started selling oranges from crates right there, a huge line would form instantly. It was something you might talk about later in school, to see who had an orange. But we were lucky compared to people who lived way out in the countryside—they never saw oranges or a lot of other things at all.

In fact, I think one of the reasons my father married my mother was so he could move out of Voloshynovo and come into Sambir to live with my mother's mother. Who could blame him? Out there, there were only dirt roads that turned into mud up to your knees in the spring and fall. If you wanted to get to Sambir and no bus came, you might hitch a ride with a farm truck, or in a real pinch, try to ride in on a horse-drawn wagon passing by from some collective. Even so, most of the time there wasn't much of anything in the Sambir stores. Not so much as in America. Nothing like here at all.

The first time I went to an American supermarket, I couldn't believe my eyes. Aisles of food everywhere, whole counters with different kinds of meat. I found an aisle where they had nothing but food for dogs and things like collars and bones for them, and I remember thinking, They have dog aisles here! The dogs eat better food here than some of the people in the Soviet Union.

When I was very young, we lived in a small house on a gravel road on the outskirts of Sambir. My grandmother owned it and we lived with her. There were two stores a few blocks away where you could buy bread, cookies, cheap candies, and cigarettes. But people still farmed, and most families had their own gardens around their houses.

We had a garden, too, right in the front yard and around the side of the house. My grandmother's brother would come by with his horse and plow in the spring and help us get the garden ready. He had a small wagon—narrow and sort of like a casket without the top. We used to load it up with potatoes and the horse would pull it off to market.

We also had an orchard, with pear and apple trees. So we had everything—onions, potatoes, tomatoes, cherries, cucumbers, cabbages, peas, beets, carrots, apples, you name it. We had to do it this way, because you couldn't buy fresh fruit or many vegetables in winter at the market. My grandmother kept the garden weeded, and each fall she would preserve food for the winter—jars and jars of vegetables and fruit. Beets and carrots and things like that were stored in the basement under the house. There were bags and bags of potatoes; it seemed like they took up half the space down there.

My grandmother was named Julia. Her husband, my maternal grandfather, was killed in the Great Patriotic War (Americans call it World War II), so I never knew him. She never talked about him or told me anything much about her early life. There were no photo albums or old letters or things like that—just ancestors who had worked on farms or in factories and had families that did the same thing in their time. As far as I know, Gran had lived in that house since after the war.

Her life had been very hard. As a child, she had to quit school after a few grades and go to work, and she'd worked ever since.

But she was always sweet and gentle with me. She took care of me from the time I was a baby, and of all the people in the family, I felt closest to her.

She had long dark hair and during the day wore it tucked up under a dark scarf. When she let it down at night, it almost reached the floor. A year or two before we left Sambir, we were told the Soviets would not allow her to come with us to America. Her hair suddenly began turning gray very fast.

Gran was a churchgoer, a Christian who practiced her faith as openly as she wanted. Many old people there are believers. They came from the time before the Revolution, when the Russian Empire was still a God-fearing country. People were free to go to church back then, but under the Soviets, churchgoing got to be very dangerous.

Gran taught the basic prayers, like the Hail Mary and Our Father, to Natalie and me. We said them every night before we went to sleep. On the walls were pictures of Jesus, Mary, Joseph, and the saints; Gran told us about their lives, and they meant something special to us.

Gran went to church every Sunday—she was a real religious person. There was a Ukrainian Catholic church nearby, and she had gone there almost all her life. Many Sundays we went with her. It was a big church with tarnished domes on top, and in the yard out behind, people gathered at Eastertime to get their baskets blessed by the priest.

Although it was a Catholic church, officially we were not allowed to call it that because Stalin had outlawed the Ukrainian Catholic Church after the war. He wanted to do away with the church; he was afraid of it because the church meant so much to Ukrainian patriots, who opposed Soviet power.

I went with her about once a month. We'd take the bus three or four miles, walk up the path, and enter the dark church, where there were paintings of saints and old writing on the pictures that I couldn't read. There were big lamps and candles clustered in front of a table for donations, and candles in other spots everywhere. The priests who led the service wore robes with rich pictures of Mary and Jesus on them.

The crowd was mostly old women like Gran, in black dresses and black scarves, saying prayers to themselves or following along with the service. People's grandmothers and even great-grandmothers would come in from villages out in the country. The candles flickered and moved, and there was incense coming out of big metal holders that made smells you couldn't find anywhere else. The church didn't have pews; you just stood packed together as the service went on.

I can't say I understood much of what was going on, but that wasn't important to me. It wasn't like here in America, where kids I know complain about having to go to school or go to church. In Sambir, I wanted to be in church with my grandmother, and with my parents when they came. Going to church was important to my Gran, so it meant a lot to me, too. I was brought up that way by her and that's what I believed in.

Natalie liked church a lot, and so did my mother, who went with Gran almost every week. I don't think my father had the same feelings, but he sometimes went, too. When he did, he would drag along behind my mother, stand somewhere else in the church during the service, and make sure he left before we did, as though he didn't want to be seen in public with us.

Sometimes church was fun, even for kids. For example, every Christmas Eve, thirteen kids would get dressed up in costumes, like Halloween here—angel, soldier, ghost, devil, king, other characters. We'd go from house to house, doing a little skit and singing carols, making sure not to go to houses where teachers lived because they punished kids for religious activities. It wasn't that big a town, and you always knew who didn't want you around. Each family would come out and give the caroling kids some rubles.

This went on for the three nights of the Christmas celebration, even though there was school those days and they made us stay late to see movies about Communism, to keep us away from our families and church.

When I was about ten, I got the devil part—a long fur cape, a big mask with horns, a wooden pitchfork. This was fun, even though no girls were allowed to participate. The reason, I think, was that the police sometimes came out to look for the kids. If they caught any, they would throw them into a paddy wagon and hold them for a night in jail or at the police station. They'd throw a scare into the kid, and hassle his parents when they came to get him. I never got caught, but once one of my friends wound up spending the night with the police. Another friend was dressed as a ghost, all in white, with a white mask and carrying a harvest scythe that was wrapped in white, too. When the militia showed up, he ran and accidentally fell into a snowbank. It was the best thing that could have happened to him, because the cops lost sight of him.

But what I remember liking most about church was the sermon, when the priest would compare what happened in the Bible with what happened in real life. Grandmother used to tell us Bible stories, even though she couldn't read and we never had a Bible in our house until my American aunt brought us one.

So I knew a little bit about why Gran wanted to go to church and why her life included this, even though a lot of other people don't have time for church and don't like people who do. As for me, I never wanted to be too near the priest. Instead, I'd stand around the corner from where he led the service, peeking at him.

I didn't want to be close to the priest because the schoolteachers often came to church to spy on us. They always stood near the front of the church and might catch sight of me. If that happened, they would punish me the next day in class.

Christmas and Easter were the most dangerous times for us kids to go. On those holidays, all the teachers from school stood around, and if they spotted you, there was trouble. I don't know who told them to make such a big deal of our going to church, but the next day, they would confront you:

"I saw you in church."

"Yeah, so what?"

"Why were you there?"

"My parents were away and I had to go with my grandmother."

I'd make up any kind of crazy excuse to keep from getting in trouble. No such luck.

"You know you shouldn't go to church. It's harmful. You're going to have to learn that lesson."

Then off to class. They'd keep me after school, writing promises about not going to church anymore, or copying Lenin's Communist rules from a big list of them on a board at the front of the room. That was easy, but sometimes they'd make me scrub the halls. And occasionally they'd deal out the punishment I hated most of all—kneeling in gravel.

Why did they do this to me? We weren't hurting anyone or the Soviet Union by going to church. They didn't mind if the old ladies went to church to pray to God, but they didn't want us kids going, so they punished us. Was it fair? In Ukraine, it didn't matter whether it was fair or not, because there was nothing you could do about it.

When they punished me, I never told my parents, because there wasn't much they could do either—just get mad at me for being in trouble, or go to school and yell at the teachers, who would then be mad at me. Either way, I lost.

I hated the teachers for punishing me just because I wanted to go to church with my grandmother and my family. Our Sunday visits to church were maybe the only time we all did something together as a family, aside from sleeping.

Here in America, I go to church, like my cousin Walter and my sister. The difference is that here, no one watches. That's a big reason why I decided to stay here when my parents wanted to go back to Ukraine. It might have hurt my mother and separated my family. But it was the right choice.

When I landed in the police station in Chicago, I had the memory of my grandmother's words to guide me. She always told me to be strong, be right, and to look out for myself. She told me God would watch out for me. I believed her.

NATALIE POLOVCHAK WILCOXEN

I was about five when Walter was born. I remember when he was brought home—just a little tiny baby. I rocked him sometimes. I'd even change his diapers and when he got a little older, I used to take him to the park. My mother was back at the factory, and I just did my job like any older sister. It was expected of me.

Walter and I were brought up by our grandmother. Our parents always worked—my father was never home, and Mother went five or six days a week, sometimes even seven. It was just a basic candy factory, making soda and candied popcorn, but she had to spend a lot of time there for her pay, about sixty rubles a month, worth about $100.

There are no such things as part-time jobs in the Soviet Union. If you're a woman in a factory, as our mother was, you work eight hours a day. By the end of the day, there are no groceries in the stores but there are almost always shortages in every store—deficits, as they call them. In winter, when there is little to find in the markets, a woman might spend another two or three hours looking for food to cook.

By the time a mother gets home, she's exhausted. She doesn't have much time or energy to spend with her kids. So somebody else raises them. If she is lucky, there is a babushka—a grandmother—to bring up her child. If not, she turns her kid over to a kindergarten teacher: the government.

Walter and I were very lucky. Our *babunia* never worked. She was always at home, so we never had to go to the government kindergarten, the *sadochok*, which begins when a kid is three years old. Babushka taught us our ABCs, addition and subtraction, before we went to the first grade.

She told us the Bible stories she knew. Where there are no Bibles, the only way you can learn to know the Lord, to know what God is about, is to talk.

You spend time with your grandmother because you love her and listen to her and you learn what's true and what isn't. Then you go to school six days of the week, from nine in the morning to three in the afternoon, listening to the teacher and learning to become Young Pioneers, and then you join the League of Young Communists, the Komsomol.

So you become in-between. You just don't know what's right. For a certain period of your life, you go through a stage like being lost.

Finally, you really have to decide what you believe. You either become a person of your own—you learn things within your family and its beliefs, and you believe in them—or you are pulled into the society. Either you become a Christian, a believer in God, or you become the absolute opposite.

In the Soviet Union, everything is against God, against religion, against Christianity. Everything is for Communism. But Communism doesn't work. So this contradiction makes you think, question things. You press for answers and you have to guess for yourself what they are.

But we were lucky. We had our *babunia*. She taught us everything she knew about God, and about believing in Him and in knowing what was right.

Walter was always a kid in his own world. He made up his mind all by himself, and once he did that, forget it. He would not change.

That's what made him decide to come with me when I left my parents in Chicago.

I was scared to death when I saw the police and my father carrying him off that day in Chicago and throwing him in their patrol car. But I also knew that if any kid could take care of himself, it was Walter.

I said a quick prayer. I had one person who would help me in this emergency: my cousin, Big Walter. He was at his job but I telephoned him just the same. I was frantic.

FROM SERGEANT ROJEK'S REPORT, JULY 18, 1980

. . . Upon arriving at Area 5 Youth Division, Walter Polovchak was processed as an unreported runaway under J#733713. During the processing the youth stated that his father is attempting to return to Russia, but he refused to return and wished to remain in this country.

At that point, Special Agent Patrick O'Hanlon, U.S. Department of State, 353-6163, was contacted and informed of the circumstances. He informed the undersigned that he would get in touch with the Office in Washington and request advice on what to do with the case. . . .

---

chapter three
GROWING UP SOVIET

When we got out of the car at the police station, the cops looked like they were ready to handcuff me. I didn't want that. So I just told the Ukrainian speaker, "Don't worry, I won't run."

It wasn't as if I didn't want to take off. I did. But I didn't know where I was. I didn't recognize the neighborhood at all. Even if I could escape, where could I run to? I was on foot, they had cars and guns. I didn't have a clue how to get out of there, and they knew the place like the backs of their hands. Even if I found a way to make a telephone call to Natalie, I couldn't tell her where I was.

They put me in a small, windowless room and stared at me for a while, as if they didn't know what to do with me. And I don't think they *did* know—after all, I hadn't broken any law by living peacefully with my cousin instead of my parents, had I? It wasn't like I had stolen a car.

They didn't offer me anything to eat or drink—sort of like, welcome to the zoo, but you have to wait till feeding time. At that moment, I guess I was too distracted to think about lunch anyway.

My father was nowhere to be seen. I was all by myself, not knowing anybody. I thought that maybe all was lost.

After a while, a woman was brought in. She sat down and the police talked to her for a while. Finally, she began jabbering at me. I couldn't make out what she was saying. Some of the words sounded like Russian, some like Ukrainian, and others something else. The words seemed to slip past my ear, just out of reach.

I wished she would just speak in Polish, because if people talked normally, I could more or less understand things, at least get an idea what they were saying. But as I listened, I began to realize that she was Polish, trying to speak Ukrainian. It didn't work.

A guy was talking to her. He was either a cop or a probation officer, I didn't know which. She translated for him. When I listened carefully, I finally caught on to her single question: *Why did you run away?*

"Because I don't want to go back."

"Why don't you want to go back?"

"Because I like it here."

"Your parents want to go back to Ukraine . . . it's their home."

"Then let them go. I don't want to go with them."

"Why not, Walter?"

"I told you . . . I like it better here in America. I don't want to go back."

She looked puzzled by this answer. So she asked me the same things all over again. I gave her the same answers. She looked a little angry now. Very slowly, as if maybe I hadn't understood her, she repeated everything again. She got the same replies.

But that was just the beginning. She wasn't going to take what I said for an answer. It seemed as if I had just opened the door. She began to treat me like some kind of challenge. Questions and answers went on for a couple of hours, but they all pointed in the same direction: why didn't I want to go back to my parents? She seemed to think that if she asked this enough times, or in enough different ways, I'd somehow change my mind, or maybe make a mistake. Or maybe she thought I'd just give up. The one thing that came to me was that she just didn't want to understand my point of view. In her eyes, I wasn't supposed to be able to tell my parents to go back to Ukraine by themselves.

So we were on opposite sides of the fence. She thought it was a crime for me to stay here; I *knew* it was a crime to go back.

After a while we broke for a rest, then the police gave her some papers, which she shuffled in front of me. "You've got to sign these saying you refuse to go back to the Soviet Union with your parents."

I stuttered at her in part Ukrainian, part Russian, even some Polish: "I'm n-not s-signing anything!"

"You don't understand . . . this has to do with legal custody of you. You're just a child, a minor."

I shook my head. "No. I'm not signing."

She insisted, pushing the papers at me.

"Get lost," I said. "Don't talk to me! I'm not signing!" I turned my back on her, refused to look at her. I stared at the wall. I was shivering in the air conditioning.

Where was Natalie? Where was Big Walter?

I was real frightened. Where I came from, people never signed anything. I had the same feeling about these papers. As I sat there, I recalled my father's warning when I once told him I'd run away if he tried to take me back to the Soviet Union: "I'll pay the cops a hundred bucks and they'll do whatever I want. They'll get you back."

Was that what he had done now? My dad had showed me that in the Soviet Union, if you had the right connections, you could get around almost any law. In Sambir, he did it every day of the year. My father was a master of the black market there, and he never got caught.

From an early age I went to Sambir's black market many times with my father and learned a lot about how he got around the law in the USSR. The first thing was that black marketeers were fearless. They were always sure of themselves, quick and confident in a way that set them off from the rest of the people in the marketplace. With their confidence, they would quickly case the place to see who was looking for things *na livo*, as the Russians say—"on the left."

Once they'd figured out the lay of the land, who was interested and who wasn't, who might deal and who might be an informer, they would carefully get the word out: "Hey, I got American jeans, Levi's."

People didn't care about the price. They'd gather around.

"Levi's?" they would say.

"Yeah, right here in this bag. Want to look?"

"Yeah."

They'd go behind a building and the buyer would take a quick peek, hunting for the name tag, and then buy the jeans real fast.

If you got busted by the police, you got busted. But when that happened, rubles landed in the cop's pocket just as fast as the Levi's got snapped up. Only fools went to jail.

Other things worked that way, too, and my dad knew his way around. If he got busted, the hell with it. He wouldn't take it seriously. He'd pay the guy off and think to himself, Next time I need something, this is the guy I might come see. That's the way life was there, and the way my father lived it.

My father was luckier than most, because he had two sisters in America who sent us gifts of clothing that he used for his black-market dealings. With a source in America like that, he was able to build up regular customers who knew him.

"I want this size Levi jeans," they might say. He could more or less take orders and fill them by writing to my aunts in California and Chicago: "Send me such-and-such a size men's Levi's," and they would send that size next time. It didn't matter if it was denim or corduroy—as long as it was Levi's.

My father could sell a pair of new Levi's for 150 or 180 rubles, about two hundred dollars. He cleared seventy or eighty rubles' profit every time he made a sale—three times as much as the jeans cost in the first place. And that's almost as much as many people make in a month in the Soviet Union. That's why a pair of American jeans was a big deal.

My father would advertise his American connection by walking around in jeans or wearing a leather jacket that said "Made in America." The rest of us advertised the same way. We dressed a little differently from others in Sambir, and this never hurt his business. Natalie would wear Levi's, a leather jacket, or an American scarf. That's noticeable right there. Sometimes packages would come for me. My aunt didn't know how big I was, so she didn't really know what to send, but she knew I wouldn't keep the things anyway. My dad would take them to sell, and they'd be gone.

The police gathered around me again, talking among themselves, as though I couldn't make out what they were saying.

"What's wrong with him?" they asked the Polish lady.

"He doesn't want to sign these papers."

"Why the hell not?"

"He doesn't want to go back."

"Oh. . . ."

That stumped everyone.

Meanwhile, my father began bobbing in and out of the room. "Everything's going to be just fine," he kept saying, somehow sure things would be quickly straightened out. He really wanted to get moving back to Sambir. He had once told me that if he was able to get out of America within six months of first arriving, the Soviet government wouldn't hassle him to get new papers—which could take months, the way they do things.

I was so mad at him and the police. I was ready to punch the hell out of all of them! All I could think was, I don't want to talk to you . . . or you . . . or you. I looked at each of them. *I don't even want to see you*, I shouted at them—to myself.

If they'd had even the slightest idea how we had lived there, they wouldn't have wanted me to go back, either. I know that. That was one of the things that made me so mad at these Americans.

Our home in Sambir was brick. My father had built it and paid for it with his black-market profits. So it was bigger and nicer than my parents could have afforded if they'd had only their salaries.

While it was like houses here, there were some big differences. It had a big ground floor and an unfinished upstairs with low ceilings under a pitched roof. Downstairs were my parents' bedroom, a dining room, a hall, and a room where we kids slept. There was a little porch out front with a storage pantry attached. In the kitchen were a gas stove and refrigerator. We had electricity, but no running water and an outhouse instead of a bathroom.

Behind the house, across a small courtyard, was another building, with a kitchen on one side and a barn on the other. Gran did the laundry there. The washing machine was modern by Sambir standards. You throw the clothes in the top, pour in the water, let it grind away to clean things. You change the water for rinsing and wring out the clothes with a hand mangle. Then you throw the wet clothes on the line and wait until they dry. Some washing machine.

The kitchen where the washing machine was had a hand water pump and a stove for heating water and keeping the place warm. Behind that was the small barn where we kept a cow, some pigs, and chickens. My grandmother usually collected the eggs, milked the cow and looked after the animals. Every spring, we'd buy a small pig, fatten it up, then butcher it in the fall.

We had no telephone, but did have a black-and-white television set and got two state channels. They showed news in the morning, went off the air, then a movie or soccer game at night. Dull compared to what's on television here. But it was what we knew.

The only car in the neighborhood was owned by a man who had a blue Moskvich, a small car you've probably never seen because they don't ship them to America. (Nobody here would want to buy one anyway, they are so badly made.) Our neighbors were Communist Party members and that's how they got the car.

We had a radio, but it wasn't a shortwave set, so we never heard foreign broadcasts like the Voice of America. Who cared about America, anyway? It was so far away, and for years we never even thought about trying to get there. It was enough that my father had sisters there and could get things from them.

Soviet television would show a man in the street in America, and then one in, say, Bangladesh, and there wouldn't be the slightest difference between them. You were shown that American people were lazier, a lot of them had to eat out of garbage cans, and many people lacked food, money, or jobs. You see this and nothing else all the time, and naturally, you think that's the way it is over there. You don't hear too many good things about America in the Soviet Union. I didn't know any better, I didn't see any better, and I thought what I saw on television was the way people lived all over the world.

School was a few blocks up the street, a two-story building where hundreds of kids went. There were pictures of Lenin in every room, and signs over the blackboards that said things like "Lenin lived, Lenin lives, Lenin will live." This was just the beginning of indoctrination about Lenin at school.

I remember one of the early stories we learned about him was that he was a real friendly kid who grew up to be very smart, but nobody would give him an opportunity. So he used to draw pictures that nobody cared for, and other kids picked on him. His parents died when he was young, and so he developed on his own into a world leader. That's the kind of thing they taught us. The teachers tried to portray him as a man who loved kids, loved drawing pictures for them, just a person who wanted the best for his people. They put him on a pedestal, portrayed him bigger than life. They didn't talk about the lines at the stores.

Schools out on the edge of town were taught in Ukrainian when

I started first grade, at the age of seven. When I moved up to the fourth and fifth grades, it was half Ukrainian, half Russian. The kids were mainly Ukrainian, but there were quite a few Polish kids too because Poland was nearby, and the border had been moved during the war, making a lot of Poles into Soviet citizens. In Sambir itself, they taught everything in Russian, and I studied a lot of Russian in school, but never got very good at it. We never spoke that language at home—always Ukrainian. And now, of course, I don't use Russian at all.

Classes began on September 1 each year, and went six days a week. We wore uniforms—brown slacks and jacket, white shirt, white shoes, red tie for the boys; brown dresses for the girls, with black aprons except on holidays, when they wore white aprons.

We walked to school, arriving at nine, and about noon, after four classes, I'd get a twenty-minute lunch break. There was a cafeteria with snacks like tea, coffee, and sweet rolls, but I'd run home, and Gran would have a big lunch ready just for me because Natalie stayed at school. I loved Gran's borscht! She'd cook *varennyky*, little meat pies, and there was fresh milk from the cow, and tea, and something sweet for dessert. My parents were always at work during the week or home resting from the job, so my Gran cooked and looked after me. Her last name was Tzap, which means "goat" in Ukrainian. People used to call me that all the time, like a nickname. But I didn't really mind because it was my Gran's name, and I loved her.

I was an average student. Classwork and homework didn't interest me that much. To tell the truth, I thought a lot of it was boring. While I wasn't a top student, I wasn't the worst, either. I liked sports, but unlike U.S. schools, Soviet schools don't have any real team athletics. For sports you go to a Pioneer palace or a special sports academy where they have good training and equipment and concentrate on athletics. But if you just happen to be a kid who likes sports more than studies and isn't going to be competing as a possible national champion, forget it. Find something else to do with your time. The state isn't interested.

Sophia Mironivna, my first-grade teacher, was the nicest teacher I had, a woman with a pleasant voice who taught me to read and took a real interest in me. In class, we sat two by two at little desks, and there were plenty of ways to get in trouble.

After first grade, I found a lot of them. I was often punished for just goofing around. The teachers could be pretty tough if they wanted, rap your knuckles with a ruler for being late, beat you across the back with a stick for doing something wrong, whip you in front of everybody. Sometimes they'd make you stay after school to clean the blackboards and scrub the floors.

But the worst punishment was the kneeling treatment. A teacher would bring in gravel and spread it on the floor in a little area and make you kneel on it for an hour or two. That hurt a lot. I had to kneel plenty of times because I was seen going to church.

There were lots of kids along our road and we played together almost every day after school. It didn't matter what the weather was—I was a kid who roamed. And since my parents were seldom home, they didn't much care where I was.

Summers in Sambir were as hot as Chicago's, with plenty of storms and wind. In July and August, we played soccer in a nearby field, or went to the Dnister River close to our house and stayed until dark. I taught myself how to swim there. There weren't diving boards or beaches, but where the river curved around a high hill, you could dive in. It was scary, but we all did it. People didn't have boats or water skis, or any of the things you see on a river or lake in the United States where people vacation.

In winter, it got so cold cars wouldn't start. Only the main road to the city was paved, and none of the roads was ever plowed. Buses ran into ditches, cars disappeared into snowdrifts until spring, and nothing on wheels moved very far.

We played hockey all winter. There were no rinks, but we banked up snow or dirt on the road, rain would freeze, and we had our hockey rink. With so few cars and no snowplows, nobody ever bothered us, and the rink lasted all winter.

There wasn't any political training in school in the lower grades, but every kid belonged to the Young Oktobrists from the first to the fourth grade. This was the first of a number of political organizations that were part of life for us kids. You had to join and learn Communist Party songs and poems about Lenin. Then you became a Young Pioneer, with a red cap and a red scarf. It's just like any kid's organization, but you must pledge to help the Communist Party whether you want to or not. It wasn't well organized, just school parades and going to camp in the summers.

I went to Pioneer camp a couple of summers and liked it—peace and quiet in the country, and the adults let us alone. But there was marching and preaching about Communism and this bored me. If I had stayed in Sambir, I would have had to worry about joining the Young Communists League, as many older kids did. That was a serious step, because it lines you up for full Communist Party membership. But I never had to face that.

Each May 1, we paraded from school through the city. Like me, half the kids didn't want to march, but had to anyway. You got to carry a big picture of Lenin, or Marx, or maybe Brezhnev and the other leaders. Sometimes it took four people to carry those big pictures. My mother and father also had to march on May 1. They didn't like marching, but they went because it was safe that way.

We learned at home that you could believe whatever you wanted to believe, just keep your mouth shut. You could tell a friend you didn't like Brezhnev, and they probably agreed. But as long as you didn't carry a big sign announcing it, you were okay. Free expression was dangerous.

Every Soviet kid knows this.

I thought that in America, free expression was all right. But here I was in the Shakespeare Area police station that July day, in deep trouble for trying to be free.

FROM SGT. ROJEK'S REPORT, JULY 18, 1980

. . . [State Department Special Agent] O'Hanlon . . . [then] informed the undersigned that as per orders of Mr. Warren Christopher, Deputy Secretary of State, 202-632-8671, the child is not to be returned to the family, and this was also confirmed with Mr. William Farrand, Department of State, Chief of the Soviet Desk, 202-632-8671.

Assistant Deputy Superintendent McDonaugh was notified and responded to the scene. Lieutenant Wm. Bransfield also responded on the scene. Contact was made with Judge Peter Costa, who recommended the child be detained overnight as a runaway under Y#182901 and be presented in Juvenile Court on 19 July 1980 at 0830 hours for a custody hearing.

Mr. William Farrand, Department of State, called and related that he wished to be notified of the outcome of the hearing and attempt to have the Immigration Department appear in court to represent the juvenile.

Walter Polovchak (son) accompanied by Natalie Polovchak (daughter) F/W 9 Jan 61 were placed with Julian K. Kulas, attorney for the child at his residence, 1334 Monroe, River Forest, Illinois.

On 19 July 1980, the parents of the youth will be transported to Juvenile Court by Y. O. M. Flynn and the undersigned.

Sergeant Leo G. Rojek
Acting Commander,
Area 5 Youth

chapter four
HELP ARRIVES

Confined in the small room at the police station, waiting for something to happen, I was pretty depressed. The whole day was wasted, and as the hours dragged by, it almost seemed I had been forgotten.

At one point, my dad stuck his head in and said, "Don't worry, everything is going to be okay."

"Yeah, everything will be okay if you just leave me alone," I said. I was so angry at him. And no one was helping me.

But I found out later that things were happening fast, bringing the U.S. State Department and the Immigration and Naturalization Service into the case on my side.

There were going to be judges, lawyers, psychologists, police, federal agents, and other strangers in my life for years to come.

COUSIN WALTER POLOWCZAK

About 4:00 P.M., Natalie called me at work. She was crying, "They have taken Walter away!"

"Where did they take him?"

"I'm not sure . . . I have no idea."

I was shocked . . . anger, fear, shock . . . everything.

Once Wally and Natalie had decided to leave their parents and come stay with me, I didn't anticipate that the police would arrest him.

But once the father called the police, it was not hard to find me. I didn't try to hide. I had a phone, a listing in the directory, and everything else.

They hadn't seized Natalie because the father, for his own reasons, hadn't put her name on the All Points Bulletin. I don't know much about juvenile law but I realized fast that because she was just seventeen and legally a minor, they had the power to take her into custody if her father wanted it done.

Natalie told me the police had a Polish-speaking assistant with them and she had been able to convey the idea that Wally didn't want to go back to the Soviet Union.

We hung up, and a few moments later, a police sergeant called to say Wally had been arrested. He didn't threaten me or anything, or accuse me of committing a crime. Just said that Wally was there. He hung up and I realized it was up to me to protect the children. I was shocked, and upset. The policeman was stern and tough, and even though I hadn't done anything wrong, I was apprehensive.

I knew enough about the American way to know that most disputes are settled by lawyers, judges, and courts. I quickly called Julian Kulas, a Ukrainian-American lawyer in Chicago who had once helped my relatives sell a house. His office was on Chicago Avenue, in the middle of what's called the Ukrainian Village.

A few weeks earlier, I had gone to Mr. Kulas to talk about the Polovchaks' situation: after living in America just six months, the father wanted to return to the USSR, and his two older children wanted to stay here. At the time, the whole family was living with me in an apartment I rented.

Michael Polovchak was also blaming me for supposedly influencing them to stay in the United States. Mr. Kulas had told me then that if I thought it wasn't safe to stay in the same apartment with the family, I should get out.

"If you feel tension, it's unwise for you to stay there. Something could happen. It's not that the father's going to kill you, but if he hurts you, what are you going to do? Sue your uncle who's just come here from the Soviet Union? There's a strong Ukrainian community, and it's not going to look right if you do something like that. You're a big man—get out of his way."

He told me that since Natalie was seventeen, just a year less than legal majority, if she wanted to stay, "it probably wouldn't be a problem for her. She's almost of age."

But Wally's situation was much different, he said. "Who knows? He might change his mind. He might not. But what can you do? There's nothing you can do. The parents want to go and the boy doesn't want to go. Currently, nothing is happening. Maybe they won't go. Maybe they'll just stick around and it'll blow over."

He made the point that the parents weren't doing anything illegal, hadn't violated any laws. They didn't abuse the kids, so there was no filing against them on grounds of negligence.

Later, I talked with Walter and Natalie and I told them that if it came to a split between them and their parents, there would be help.

"How there's going to be help or what kind of help, I don't know," I said. "I don't know what's going to happen. But I have to get out myself."

So in early July, I found another apartment a few blocks away, and one afternoon, I told the family I was leaving. Michael was furious—now they'd have to pay the rent and other bills by themselves, without me.

Certain that Natalie had been influencing Walter, they wanted to get her away from him, and didn't care where she went. "Get out! Get out of the house! You don't belong here," they screamed at her.

A few days after I moved out, I came back with a friend, walked into the old apartment, and took out some of my belongings—my clothes, one of the two sofas, and that was it. I left the bed I had bought them and the furniture. I wasn't going to leave them empty-handed.

"Now you're on your own," I said.

At that moment, I was in no position to get further involved with them. I was working full time at a computer firm and had my own life to live.

But when I started moving my belongings, it abruptly brought things to a head. Natalie had already decided she was going to leave her parents' house. Now Walter also quickly decided that he was coming with me, too.

Disbelieving, the mother said to Walter, "You're leaving?"

"Yes," said the little boy. He quickly packed up and came with his sister. They just walked out.

That first week, I played devil's advocate with Natalie and Walter.

"Do you want to meet with your parents?" I asked.

"No way," said Natalie. "It's hopeless. I can't stay with them."

To Walter, I said, "See if you miss your parents, and would like to go back."

But he would not budge.

I made crystal clear to them that if Wally ever changed his mind and said he wanted to go back, I would make sure he went back. There wasn't going to be any joke about it.

Some people have imagined that three or four people sat in a dark room with a bright light shining in Walter's face, telling him, "You're going to stay, you're going to stay . . ."

In fact, many people played devil's advocate and questioned him about whether he really wanted to stay. If he had ever balked, he would have been returned to his parents, because I never wanted to be in the position of his coming to me someday and saying, "Well, you separated me from my parents. You made me do it."

If Walter had ever decided to go back to the Soviet Union, I would have bought him the ticket, brought him to the airport, shaken his hand, and said, "It was nice meeting you, nice knowing you, and I hope you're happy."

There was no motivation to hold him here. None. In some ways, it would have been a lot easier if he had gone back.

My emergency phone call to Mr. Kulas caught him just as he was leaving his office for a weekend in Wisconsin, two hundred miles away. His wife was on the way to pick him up, but he immediately headed for the police station. That's the kind of person he is.

I left work right away, and reached the police station about the same time he did. It was mass confusion there.

The parents had tried to claim Wally, the police had tried to hand him over to the parents, even the Polish translator was in the act. But he wouldn't go anywhere.

The police were trying to dump him, but through the translator Wally had said enough to make the police cautious.

They didn't know what to do. It got all tangled up. In the

confusion, a sergeant called the U.S. Immigration and Naturalization Service, and Immigration said it was not going to turn Walter over to the parents. Then Immigration called Washington to find out what Walter's status was.

I believe that if the police had handed Walter over to the parents, by nightfall they would have been gone for good.

Then somebody called Channel 5, NBC News. A television reporter showed up. Everything changed.

PAUL HOGAN, TELEVISION REPORTER

I'd been working as a reporter at Channel 5 about a year, and I was real anxious. I would run on everything.

About a week or ten days before the Polovchak story broke, I had been out on a very ordinary, run-of-the-mill story, a roundup of illegal Mexicans by INS. The arrests had already occurred, and all Immigration could do was parade these people around for us at the Dirksen Federal Building downtown.

So I went over and my crew shot tape of this scene, even though it was the kind of story you don't want to go on, because you know it's going to be buried in the newscast, it's a dog.

During the shooting an Immigration official whom I've never seen again shook my hand and introduced himself as Bob. I started talking to him, saying there must be a lot of good stories that come through his office.

"Oh yeah, yeah," he said.

I gave him my business card and said, "Well, if you ever hear of something interesting, give me a call."

About a week and a half later, a Friday afternoon about 5:15 P.M., I'd just finished my final news story for the week and was getting ready to leave for the weekend when the phone rang.

"This is Bob, over at Immigration, remember me?"

I don't think I did. I just said, "Oh yeah, yeah, Bob, what's going on?"

"You said if I ever heard of a good story, give you a call. Well, there's a cute little feature you might want to know about."

I was thinking, I'm not going to do it, I'm going home. "And what would that be?"

"Well, we just got word that there's a twelve-year-old boy in a Chicago police station whose parents are immigrants and are going back to Russia—and he's refusing to go."

My mind exploded. "You're kidding!"

"No, no," he said. "I don't know if you're interested in something like that, but I thought it was a cute little story."

"I'm real interested," I said. "And how do you know this?"

He said, "Because the police department, when there is a defection, they have a number to call at the State Department. They have called that number."

"What police station?"

"Shakespeare and California."

I knew where it was, and I said, "Okay, I'll get right over there."

I should have asked a lot more questions, but I thought it was just office poop going around Immigration, nothing serious, as they were getting ready to go home, too, for the weekend.

I put down the phone and ran into the executive producer's office. The assignment manager was there, and I said, "There's this incredible story happening."

"We don't have a crew," he said right away. "All the crews—"

"Wait'll I tell you what it is!" I said. "There's a twelve-year-old Soviet boy defecting to America. His parents are going back to the Soviet Union. I don't know if they're here on vacation or what it is, but he's asking for political asylum."

"Get a crew!" they said.

We spun into all this activity, everybody went crazy, and I said, "Don't say it over the two-way radio—no one else knows about it!"

We sped over there, pulled up with a screech, got the crew out, and walked briskly into the Shakespeare Area station. Nobody was there except an old sergeant behind the desk.

"We're here from Channel Five," I said, "about the defecting boy."

"Oh, they're all upstairs."

"What do you mean, 'all'?"

"Oh, there's a mother, a father, kids, there's a twelve-year-old who wants to defect. Don't bother me."

"Well, can I go up?"

"Absolutely not."

So we sat in the lobby, waiting. It was a classic old Chicago police station, since torn down. Nothing in the lobby except chairs and a candy vending machine near the doorway where the stairs went up to the rooms where the Polovchaks were being kept.

In about an hour or so, a kid came downstairs wearing a long-sleeved striped sweat shirt and cutoffs. I said to the crew, "This has got to be him."

I said, "Walter!" and he turned and looked at me, so I knew his name was Walter. I don't know how I got that name—maybe the sergeant had told me. I asked him some questions and he sort of answered. It wasn't much, but it was enough. He got some candy from the machine and went back upstairs.

I had a portable crew, a minicam just shooting tape. But when a story is going toward deadline and it looks like you can't get the tape to them in time, you've got to get a live crew with a microwave truck that can put a signal right into the newsroom.

So I ordered a live crew in and hyped the story again. "This thing is big, it's really happening, the kid says he's not going back."

I tried talking to the parents. The father was brusque, didn't understand English, and I subsequently learned he believed TV was part of the government. He had come to believe the government was behind his troubles, and viewed us as an instrument of government. In the weeks ahead, I repeatedly tried to convince him that I wasn't necessarily opposed to his point of view, I just wanted to elicit it. But he never let me near him.

The mother eventually came around, let me in the house, and talked to me, and even went live with me once on a broadcast. But father Michael remained very, very negative about the press.

Just before news time that night, about 9:30 P.M., they all came down. Julian Kulas, Walter, Cousin Walter, and Natalie, all went off together in one car, and the mother, father, and little Michael went off in another. No one would tell me what had happened.

But the police let me know it was a hot potato; they were going to fire it into Juvenile Court and put the kid in the custody of the lawyer.

It was a big story for that Friday night, and led *The News at Ten*. It also was the lead for all newscasts for the next three weeks. It helped make my career.

TRANSCRIPT, CHANNEL 5 *NEWS AT TEN* TELECAST,
JULY 18, 1980

PAUL HOGAN: This is the 14th District police station, at the corner of California and Shakespeare. This has been the scene of a daylong drama that went all day and into the evening where a drama that is tearing an immigrant family apart already has had international repercussions and may in the end result in the defection of two Soviet children to the United States.

Forty-two-year-old Michael Polovchak left his home in the Ukraine six months ago. He wanted to make a new start in America, along with his wife, and their seventeen-year-old daughter, Natalie, their twelve-year-old son, Walter, and their other son, six-year-old Michael. But Polovchak and his family have spent the entire day and night here at Area 5 police headquarters.

Polovchak has decided he wants to return to the Soviet Union. The Russian embassy in Washington has agreed to make that possible. Only one hitch: Natalie and her brother Walter do not want to go. . . .

CUT TO—NATALIE: Yeah, I like it in America. . . . That's better than my country, you know?

HOGAN: Natalie has hired Ukrainian lawyer Julian Kulas to fight her father's attempt to return them to the Soviet Union. Kulas thinks because she is seventeen, Natalie will be granted asylum here.

But twelve-year-old Walter is another story. He is a minor. He may not be granted asylum because of that. Even though Walter seems to know what he wants:

CUT TO—WALTER: I like here. . . .

HOGAN: Like it?

WALTER: Yeah. . . .

HOGAN: Now the Soviet desk at the U.S. State Department is working on this case, has worked on it all evening, and would not make any statement for Newscenter 5 this evening other than to say they do believe they will be prepared to comment on this case tomorrow morning. Late tonight, twelve-year-old Walter was placed in the custody of a private party.

He and his sister will appear in Family Court tomorrow, at which time their attorney will attempt to have Walter and the girl placed in the custody of a guardian, someone who will assure the court that the boy and girl's desire to stay in America will be honored.

This is a very unusual case. A U.S. court is going to be asked to separate children from their parents, parents who want to return to the Soviet Union. Children who have stayed here six months and who say they have a love affair not only with Chicago, but ultimately, the United States itself.

ANCHORMAN JIM RUDDLE: Why does he want to return so desperately?

HOGAN: He's given several reasons. Number one, he doesn't like it here. He's concerned that his children may be wooed away from the religion which they were being raised under in the Soviet Union.

Plus, he told me this evening that he had contacted the Soviet embassy and had been given certain promises. But those promises, of a job, and other unspecified things, would not be kept, according to Mr. Polovchak, unless he returned along with his entire family to the Soviet Union.

COUSIN WALTER

When the news was carried on TV, it was a hit.

It was the bear versus the eagle. It was a human-interest story— a little kid who looked absolutely adorable on TV. I think that had a lot to do with it.

He could barely say a few words, but when his picture hit the next day in the newspapers, front page, of course, he looked like a little doll. As his face started playing on TV, everything changed. The situation was no longer in the control of anybody.

I didn't count on that. I couldn't imagine in my wildest dreams that something like that could ever happen.

The media created the bad guy, the good guy. Didn't create it, I should say, but reported it and the public's perception of the bad guy, good guy.

In the long term, the press helped Wally. He would never have been in this position if it wasn't for the press. Although public opinion at times was against us, in the long term, it was for us.

Anybody who saw the TV or the photos, they just couldn't say, "Send him back to the Soviet Union."

JULY 28, 1980, SOCIAL INVESTIGATION REPORT,
COOK COUNTY JUVENILE COURT,
BY PROBATION OFFICER JACK GOGGIN

Name: POLOVCHAK, Walter   Court Date Scheduled: 7/30/80
Address: 3624 W. Fullerton   Age: 12
Sex: Male   Ethnic Group: Caucasian
Date of Birth: 10/3/67   Place of Birth: Ukraine
School: Monroe   Date Dictated: 7/28/80

Walter Polovchak, a 12-year-old Caucasian boy, recently immigrated to the United States from Russia and currently enrolled at the Monroe School, was referred to Juvenile Court on a MINS Petition alleging Runaway.

Walter is a small, 12-year-old boy who has a pleasant appearance and was very candid. He was cooperative and very direct in his statements concerning the recent past. He seems to have an outgoing personality, without any apparent personality problems. The boy seems to be quite mature for his age and does not hesitate to make his opinions known in an agreeable manner.

This is a family that has been dependent, to a large degree, on relatives since arriving in this country, and therefore the relatives feel vitally interested in the problem. . . . all feel they have a vital interest at stake here. . . . This undoubtedly has caused more pressure on Mr. and Mrs. Polovchak. The mother feels that she has been betrayed by little Walter; she also feels that her daughter Natalie unfairly influenced her son in making this decision to stay in the United States. She feels Natalie, at the age of 17, being unmarried, and without a husband to support her, is not qualified to offer such serious advice to her son. She also is resentful of little Walter's change in attitude over the past three months and she stated that he emotionally seemed to remove himself from the family. This three-month time period coincides with the time Walter became aware that his father was going to return to Russia with the family.

chapter five

MY AUNT FROM AMERICA

I was getting real hungry sitting in that room. All at once, a man I had never seen before walked into the police station. It turned out to be Julian Kulas and he turned out to be my attorney. I didn't really know what a lawyer was. "He's going to stick up for you," somebody told me in Ukrainian, and that sounded pretty good.

So I told him some Polish woman was trying to force me to sign some papers.

"Which woman is it?" he asked.

I pointed her out, and he went off to talk with her. Pretty soon, I didn't need to worry about signing papers anymore.

About this time, I was able to get downstairs to the candy machine in the lobby. I remember I had punched a big Toot-sie Roll out of the machine and was just getting the wrapper off when somebody called out my name. I turned around and here was this guy in a beard with a couple of other men carrying equipment.

Just like with Mr. Kulas, I didn't know who the heck this was either. It turned out to be Paul Hogan, who is now a real friend. He asked me why I wanted to stay in America.

"I like here," I said—just about all the English I could manage. It was kind of confusing.

Natalie came downstairs, and Hogan asked her the same questions and she told them she wanted to stay, too.

Leaving Hogan behind, we went back upstairs and after a while, Mr. Kulas convinced the judge and all the other people who were getting in the act to grant him custody of Natalie and me.

Next thing I knew, my parents went off in a car without saying anything, and Natalie and I were with Mr. Kulas, heading out to his house. Big Walter went back to his apartment to pick up some of our clothing, because we had to go to court the next day and had to look okay.

Mr. Kulas's home was real big, with lots of rooms. I had never seen a house that nice.

I was shaken up by what had happened at the police station, but at the same time, I felt safe. Natalie and I sat in the living room and he questioned us: "Why do you want to stay here?" He had come from Ukraine as a kid and spoke good Ukrainian.

"I don't want to go back with my parents because I like this country. I want to stay here. I can go to church without people following me around," I went on.

We talked for about an hour. He tried to reassure us, telling us we were going to court the next day and we'd see what happened. He never promised me I was going to stay in America.

"Nobody can give you a guarantee that you're going to get to stay here," he said. "But I'll try my best."

Mrs. Kulas had taped the Channel 5 news, which we watched. It was interesting seeing myself on TV. To see your face in color like that, and then on the front of a newspaper, is very unusual. After a while, it became like anything else that is annoying, because everybody asks the same questions over and over and over again, until you feel like a tape recorder, answering the same thing.

But this first time, I looked . . . well, I looked kind of cute. I hadn't realized that.

Later, they took us up to a second-floor bedroom. I was kind of uncomfortable. Imagine it: the first time you meet somebody, it's in a police station. The next thing, you've got to spend the night in his house. And you don't even know him.

We went to sleep, but Mr. Kulas stayed up half the night, writing up things for court the next day.

It was kind of a miracle, having him there to help. I could trace the miracle to my Aunt Anastasia, who had sold her house in Chicago a few years earlier and had asked Mr. Kulas to help.

* * *

In 1976, when I was nine, my aunt Anastasia came from Chicago and visited us in Ukraine. She sent us packages for years, helping my father live a better life. But that was impersonal—like mail from the moon. When she actually showed up in person, the idea of America became real to everyone in my family.

For weeks before she came, I was excited, and I had plenty of questions. What was an American like? Did she speak Ukrainian anymore, or would she sound like a foreigner? Would Aunt Anna, as we called her, look like my father? Would I recognize her?

No one in the family could answer my questions. My father had been just a little kid when she left home and didn't remember much about her. The last time he had seen her was in 1941 or 1942, after the Germans invaded, when he was three or four years old.

Years later, out of the blue, she reestablished contact with him. That was long before I was born. He wrote her and she began sending clothing to us. Then she decided to visit us herself.

My father was going to go up to Moscow to meet her plane and show her around the place. Then they would come down to Lviv. That was the plan, anyway, but my father had plans of his own.

He took off for Moscow the day before she came. When Aunt Anastasia arrived at Sheremetyevo Airport, he never showed up. She made her way to her hotel and settled down to wait for him. We didn't know he'd disappeared.

Then the first telegram from Aunt Anna arrived, asking where he was.

I've never seen my mother get so worried. She thought he'd been killed or something. But Natalie, Gran, and I just looked at each other—he was out with some woman. You might think a nine-year-old like me wouldn't know about things like that but I'd seen and heard enough between my parents to reach my own conclusions about where he was. He'd disappeared plenty of times before and it always turned out later he'd been with another woman. So I knew what it was this time.

I think my mother knew what had happened. She just didn't want to admit he had gone to be reunited with a sister he hadn't seen in more than thirty years and wound up two-timing my mother instead.

After about three days, Aunt Anastasia sent word she'd arrived in Lviv. Soviet visitors' visas say exactly where the tourist is supposed to be each day of the tour—no exceptions. Even if Aunt had wanted to wait in Moscow for my father to turn up, they wouldn't allow it.

When my dad finally came home, he had some story about missing her at the airport, then the hotel, and said he'd spent the rest of the time looking for her. I could just see him, walking around Moscow asking strangers if they'd seen his sister.

But now that he'd had his fun, he wanted to see his sister. He and I grabbed a bus to Lviv, a ninety-minute ride. My father knew the schedule and all the drivers, so he just waved down the right guy coming along in a city bus, and off we went.

It was comical how I acted when I finally met Aunt Anastasia. I was afraid to look her in the face. To this day, I can't say why. Just a little kid, I guess.

When some strange relative you've never met shows up, it isn't always love at first sight. And this wasn't some country cousin visiting from the next town. This was an *American*.

When we got to the hotel in Lviv, I would barely say hello or give Aunt Anastasia a hug. I hung back, peeping out at this foreign woman. She was short, about five feet, even shorter than my father. She had a round, nice face, and talked fast, like my dad and Natalie.

She spoke good Ukrainian, no accent. That reassured me a little. After a while, I got close enough to her that she grabbed me and gave me a hug. She seemed okay, but I was wary. Especially when she kept telling me how she wanted to take me away with her to Chicago—wherever that was.

Oh, no you're not, I said to myself. No way. I'm staying right here with my family and friends.

She had bags of clothing, candy, chewing gum, and other American gifts with her. My father's eyes got real bright—here was plenty of stuff for his black-market buyers.

That night we all slept in the same hotel room. I had a trundle bed, but I couldn't sleep. I kept getting up, wanting to run away, then falling asleep again. This went on half the night! That's how scared I was of my American aunt.

Aunt Anastasia had a lot of photos of America—her husband, her car, their home in Chicago. Her stories of life there were pretty interesting, but she was like somebody from another planet. I had no way to imagine how she really lived or what life was like in America, no matter how much she told me. It seemed as far away and strange as Mars.

The next day, she came down to Sambir with us. This side trip wasn't on her visa and she wasn't supposed to make it, but she wanted to see our family and her other brother, Uncle Dmitri, who lived near us.

It was a quick visit, about an hour at our house, and another hour with Dmitri. My mother had asked a priest to come and say a prayer, but this wasn't such a great idea because the priest was Orthodox and my aunt had become a Baptist. He said a blessing anyway and there was no trouble. They had refreshments to celebrate, then drove to Dmitri's in a car my father had rented from a friend.

Uncle Dmitri was scared the police would discover Aunt Anastasia riding around Sambir without permission and throw her in jail. Or worse, throw *him* in.

"You'd better cover up with a scarf," he told her as they rode along past the booths of the traffic police. But she was stubborn and told him off. "I'm not going to hide from anybody! If you get into trouble, that's too bad for you!"

I don't think my father was used to hearing this from a woman. Pretty soon, he and Dmitri quit worrying about the police. Aunt Anna was right: no one ever bothered them.

ANASTASIA JUNKO

My life has been a long journey from Volo where I was born in 1923. There's been a lot of pain along the way. The war forced me far from home, but wherever I was, I thought about the family I had left behind.

Of all the things that can befall a person, the worst fate is not to know what happened to your loved ones. I would rather suffer any pain than live as I did for more than a decade—not knowing what had happened to my family.

Even when I was living in a displaced persons camp in West Germany after the war, my thoughts turned every day to my family. Were my parents alive? Did anyone who might have survived the war know that I also had survived? Where were they living? I'd seen whole villages and cities turned into rubble.

As a child, I survived starvation and sickness in my hometown, lived through Hitler's terror, and the war. Always, there was fear. Stalin, Hitler . . . what difference did it make? Armies, violence, corpses, horror on horror.

In 1943, the German occupiers took me to Germany to work.

At the time, I was living in Sambir, working as a servant in a German household. When the Germans demanded I go, one of my brothers told me, Whatever you do, don't go to Germany—you'll die there. But if I refused, I was sure the Germans would kill my whole family.

My father was crying, but I said, "No, Papa, I'm going. I won't let them come kill us here."

Frightened, I went to the train station. Often there were big lines of Jews being taken off with their children. They would hold hands, and some went crazy.

German soldiers with dogs grabbed mothers, pulled children away.

There was nothing you could do. If you interfered, the Germans would kill your whole family. So I went to Germany. I think now it was God's intention, because I was saved.

I worked for a family in Germany through most of the war. We survived sickness and bombs that destroyed hotels and houses all around us. When the war ended, American soldiers arrived and supervised our village. I helped clear rubble of bombed buildings, and met a man from another camp who was also helping. We started speaking in Polish but soon realized we were Ukrainians. His name was John Junko, and he had been captured in Warsaw and taken back to Germany. The Americans assigned us to the same DP camp, and our friendship turned to love.

The camp was run by UNRA—the United Nations Relief Agency—and we had good food, baths, and quarters. It was like being free. You could go where you wanted and nobody stopped you. Then Russian soldiers arrived nearby and things suddenly changed. The UNRA workers said the Germans didn't want us, and we should go back where we came from. "You're free, go to your own land—Poles to Poland, Ukrainians to Ukraine, Russians to Russia—everybody is free, please go home."

They probably thought they were doing the right thing, but this was terrible news. Many of us feared the Red Army, didn't want to go back, and didn't understand why this was happening. One camp flew a black flag, the people there vowing to die before going back. The Americans found that they'd rather starve than go back. The DPs told them, "You don't want us, and we don't want to go back. We will die here first. Kill us all, just don't turn us over to the Russians."

The Americans were always good. You could do almost anything to them, even hurt them, and they would forgive you. They're the only people in the whole world like this. And now some Americans began doing everything they could to help us, saying, "We'll protect you, take care of you . . . we're not going to give you back."

Somehow, while thousands of other DPs were shipped back to Russia, with the help of the Americans we escaped this fate. So for me, there was just one place in the world to live: America. I prayed to God that I might someday live there. And I also prayed that if any of my family was alive that they join us there.

John worked with American soldiers at their base. They gave him cigarettes, coffee, chocolate, old army uniforms and clothing he sold in the black market. When the authorities began allowing families without children to go to the United States, we were among those chosen.

One day in 1949, a man came to us at the DP camp, told us to bring our documents, whatever papers we had . . . were going to America! In April 1949, John and I arrived in the United States.

We settled in Chicago, and I hoped to find if any of my family had survived. During the war, there had been no word at all. But even now that we were safe in America, Stalin still ruled the USSR and I dared not write—a letter might bring prison or death to whoever received it. However, after Stalin died in 1953, I sent letters to my husband's relatives and friends from Ukraine and Poland asking if they knew whether any of my family had survived. One day, I got a letter saying that most of my family was alive— including my parents, who still lived in Voloshynovo. Imagine my joy!

I learned that Maria, one of my sisters, was living at home with my parents. She had a son, Walter. Our younger brother, Michael, who had been three or four when I last saw him, now was a grown man with a wife and daughter, Natalie. Later, he had a Walter of his own, about ten years younger than Maria's son.

Michael had served in the army, lived in Moscow for a time, and never wanted to return home to the countryside. His wife had connections to the party in Sambir, so they moved there, and he was a city bus driver. Such normal lives!

We began corresponding. I wasn't surprised to hear how hard their life was because I remembered hunger and want when I was a child. I started sending them clothing, the most practical way I could help.

But I never suggested they come to America as I was sure the Soviets would never let them. I was also sure the police read letters from relatives abroad; making such a suggestion might be dangerous for my brother and his family. Years later, I sent them photos of our car, our house, and other things to give them some idea of how good life in America was for us. While I never mentioned coming here, I wanted to send them everything—enough clothes, enough to eat, whatever they could use. I felt sorry they didn't have life as I did in the United States.

My mother died in Ukraine in 1966 and my father was very sick. These losses made Maria very sad. She told me that Father wanted only to join Mother. She asked me, "What am I going to do with myself without them?"

Her son, Walter, was a very bright, intelligent boy, but there was no husband. I began thinking, I wish I could take a plane and go get them. With no children of my own, Maria's boy Walter would be like my own son.

Other people were bringing in relatives caught inside the Soviet Union, so I went to a Ukrainian-affairs office on Chicago Avenue and asked about affidavits to bring people here.

"How much does it cost?" I asked.

"Fifty dollars," said a man at the office.

Fifty dollars, I thought. How little! "How long would it take?"

"I don't know," he said. "That's not always clear."

"Okay." I'd heard enough. "We're going to try it."

People were willing to help after all. But it was now 1968, the Soviets had just invaded Czechoslovakia, and it might take months to get Maria and her son out. Was all this hope in vain?

John and I were sitting at home one night in Chicago when a Western Union telegram arrived, telling us that "Maria Polowczak and Wolodymyr Polowczak" would fly into O'Hare in a few days. A dream come true!

Within weeks I heard from Michael in Sambir, saying how happy he was that Maria had been able to leave and find a better life in the United States. He always wrote how poor he was. Send me this, send me that, he asked. He told how hard he worked and how difficult it was to feed five people on his salary of a hundred rubles a month.

He told me about their old house with its leaky roof, and how his children were always sick with pneumonia or other serious illnesses. I believed everything he told me. Why shouldn't I? He was my brother.

So I sent him packages to help out. Please help, he would write, and I would answer with a pair of jeans or corduroy pants and jackets for his family. He sent me the sizes and I sent him the items. Over the years, it came to thousands of dollars.

Then I decided I wanted to go see them. I found that my little brother had grown into a man with dark hair, a sly smile, and a constant stream of talk. He ran the family his way, and they let him. I didn't see too much of Natalie and Walter, but I liked them a lot. Natalie took after her father, dark hair and stubborn. Little Walter looked like his mother, smaller, light hair and soft eyes. He was a quiet little boy who kept to himself but was very curious about everything. He watched me very suspiciously at first, like a little cat. When I asked him if he wanted to come to America with me, he shook his head and laughed.

I brought them Bibles and talked with Michael about coming to America. I was sure he could do fine and there would be plenty of people to help out. Imagine, I told him, the children could live in freedom. Any parent would want that for his kids.

When I left, I was pretty sure he was ready to come, and since I had been able to bring over Maria and big Walter, I was sure my brother and his family could make the journey, too. I was ready to send them official invitations, because I was certain that they'd love America the same way we all did.

NATALIE

Aunt Anastasia had sent us pictures of the John Hancock Tower, one of the tallest buildings in Chicago. We puzzled over it, trying to figure out how a building could be so tall. I just couldn't imagine it, because in the Soviet Union, the highest buildings are seldom more than twenty stories.

What I remember most about her visit is how she kept asking if I would like to come to the United States. She told me that when I was eighteen, I could come on my own and see how America lives. What a thought!

I began asking her what people were like there, what they did, how they lived. I was so curious and, in fact, I had always been sure, deep down, that I wouldn't live my entire life in the Soviet Union. I think I knew that from when I was a very small girl.

It was hard for her to explain how different it was in America. Here's one thing she said that I remember: she said the dogs in America eat better than people in the Soviet Union. I thought to myself, What can she possibly mean? She told me you could go to the grocery store and get a whole cart and fill it up with soda if you want it. You could have everything you wanted and there were no lines to wait in.

Walter and I didn't talk much to each other about her. We just said we didn't believe her and left it at that.

From Jack Goggin's report

At this time, Walter appears to be in good physical health, however, according to mother he has had physical problems in the past. At the age of 6, he hit his head on a curb and damaged his skull. The mother said that after that, he suffered dizzy spells and had trouble keeping food and water down for several months. Mrs. Polovchak added that from birth to about the age of 10, her son was in poor health. She stated that he was a small child who had pneumonia twice, mumps, and chicken pox. Nonetheless, he progressed at an acceptable rate during his early years, in that he walked at 11 months and talked by the age of 2. The mother stated that she did not recall any unusual nightmares over prolonged periods of time, or any unusual aspects in Walter's emotional growth during this period. . . .

The Polovchak family is, of course, in a state of great stress. They are a family that is currently divided over a critical issue and this has caused a great deal of pain and mental anguish to all members of the family. The parents appear to be confused and bewildered by the recent turn of events. The sister, Natalie, and the minor respondent, Walter, appear to be more controlled, during the times of the interviews, and seemed to be very determined in their course of action.

The father, for his part, is extremely angry and is very resentful towards both his son and his nephew, Walter. He feels that many people have taken advantage of him and that he was not given what he was promised if he came to the United States. Mr. Polovchak appeared to be under the impression that when he arrived in the U.S., he would receive a significant sum of money from his sisters, and also a new home. While he did receive some money, he did not receive a home. According to his sisters, they offered to help him financially and to help him with the down payment if and when he wanted a home.

---

chapter six

THE MAN WHO DEFENDED ME

JULIAN KULAS, ATTORNEY

1

I was about to go to Wisconsin for the weekend that Friday afternoon when out of the blue a police sergeant, Leo Rojek, called me at my law office.

"Counsellor, you'd better get down here real fast," he said. "I've got your client."

I was surprised. "Who's my client?"

"Walter Polovchak."

I'd never met the child, but for several weeks before Rojek's surprise phone call, I had talked on a number of occasions with Cousin Walter. We had talked in general terms about the family's problems and the father's demands that they go back to Ukraine. But I hadn't even known the two kids had left the parents and gone to stay with the cousin. This was very serious. I headed to the police station, all thoughts of a weekend in Wisconsin gone for good.

I arrived to find the police station in confusion, with people milling around everywhere. It was shift change, so the police were trooping in and out, everyone talking at once, a real hubbub. The Polovchaks were in different parts of the station. The Polish woman who had tried to serve as a translator had brought some of her family, perhaps to help out, and they were mixed into the scene as well.

The media also were already there—camera crews and some reporters. Several of them knew me, because I have been active for many years in world human rights matters, and a spokesman on affairs of concern to my Ukrainian community of Chicago, one of the most important concentrations of my countrymen anywhere outside the USSR.

A TV reporter tried to grab me. This turned out to be Paul Hogan of NBC. I didn't know him, but later he followed the case closer than anyone else, and became a real friend of Walter's. But that was later.

Our first meeting wasn't very promising. Hogan, making the kind of common American mistake that instantly drives us Ukrainians up a wall, alluded to the fact that Walter was Russian.

"If you're going to call this kid a Russian," I said, hurt to the quick and angry as well, "he's not going to talk to you!"

Hogan was taken aback, but quickly recovered. "I apologize," he said. "I'll wipe that off the tape. But can I talk to him?"

"As soon as we get things untangled. I've got to find out a little more what's involved."

The police took me into a room and I met Anna and Michael Polovchak for the first time. I'd never seen or spoken with them before, but in my law practice, I deal with many of my countrymen and feel familiar with a lot of the problems that newly arrived families can have.

I must say I was extremely curious about them. In all my years of practicing law in Chicago, I had never met a family from western Ukraine who actually wanted to go back to the Soviet Union. So this made the Polovchaks quite unusual, whatever reasons he might espouse.

They looked very typical of recent émigrés from that part of the world: wearing workaday clothing, somewhat tense, perhaps confused because of the way things were unfolding. Events were already taking shape in a pattern unknown and unfamiliar to them.

As soon as they saw me, Michael approached. We introduced ourselves, and he quickly said, *"Pane, Procuror"*—Ukrainian for "Hello, honored Mr. Procurator."

His form of address bordered on the obsequious, and was quite typical for people from over there are used to thinking of anyone who has any kind of authority as being part of the government—prosecutors, bureaucrats, and so on. Ordinary folk there learn very early to fear such officials as devious, untrustworthy, and power hungry. And truly, if Americans encountered "public servants" of the Soviet model, we, too, would be very much on our guard.

I corrected him immediately. "I'm not the procurator, I'm a private attorney, an *advokat*." I wanted him to know from the first moment exactly how things worked here. "I have been asked by Natalie to come in here. We will see what's involved in this situation and see if we can resolve it."

He was a short man, powerfully built, thinning dark hair, and thick, dark eyebrows over dark, intense eyes. The eyebrows were his most distinctive feature. They conveyed power . . . and anger. He was uneasy, but polite. He was full of bottled-up energy, the kind of man who gestures a lot, paces, uses his voice, doesn't fear to interrupt a conversation if he disagrees or wants to get his own point across. He behaved this way throughout the legal case that unfolded in the months that came. He spoke no English.

His wife was seated quietly in a chair nearby. I went over and introduced myself. She didn't say much. I could see she had been crying and was very subdued. I felt sorry for her, but could get little clue as to what her intentions were. She had a bland, unremarkable face, careworn and with a kind of exhausted aura about it. She seemed a bit dazed and deferred completely to her husband. I had the very strong initial impression that he completely ran the show.

"Can you give me a piece of paper showing that you're taking Walter away?" Polovchak asked after the introductions. "So that I can show something to the people in Washington? And they will give me a visa back to the Soyuz in return." He called it "Soyuz," short for Soyuz Sovietskikh Sotsialisticheskikh Respublik, the USSR's official name in Russian.

"Why do you need a piece of paper?" I asked. This was more than a casual question. After all, here was a man who had gotten the Chicago police to arrest his own son as an accused runaway, had spent most of the afternoon trying to take custody of him, and now was asking for a piece of paper instead of his son. Did he want custody or not? Or was the child nothing more than a pawn to the father, a possession Polovchak needed to get himself readmitted to the Soviet Union?

"They keep telling me that since Walter is on my passport, they won't let me back in the country without him," Polovchak said. "But if I had a piece of paper from authorities here saying Walter was being taken away, then I'm sure the Soviets would let me back, even though he's still on the passport."

"Well," I replied, saying exactly what was on my mind, "we'll see what we can do about removing Walter from your passport."

He didn't take offense or alarm at this at all. On the contrary, my statement seemed to partially satisfy him. To my mind, there was something faintly disturbing if not sad about him—he seemed so distant from his own son.

Later, even though Michael Polovchak became a stubborn foe who fought bitterly to take the boy back to the USSR, where reprisal against the child was virtually guaranteed, I came to think of him as a man being used by his own government for propaganda purposes. He was himself a pawn.

During an earlier conversation, Cousin Walter had related to me that when they all lived together, he himself paid the rent and telephone bills as a gift to help the family get on its financial feet. So he saw all the phone bills. He told me he recently had noticed long-distance calls to Washington, did a little checking, and had found out the Washington phone numbers were listed to the Soviet consulate. This had increased Cousin Walter's alarm about the situation of the children and in part had caused him to move out. Now this brief talk with the father raised my own worries as well. How closely were the Soviets advising Polovchak about the children?

There surely was no law against a Ukrainian immigrant—or anyone else—talking over innocuous subjects with Soviet diplomats. This smacked of something entirely different. The father appeared to be consulting with Soviet authorities, who always put their own propaganda interests ahead of anything else. It seemed to me likely they had told Michael that once he got the child under his control, they would take care of the rest of it. They would force Polovchak to do what they wanted. The fate and freedom of a child were at stake.

The Polovchaks faced no legal bar to leaving the country immediately. Unlike Soviet citizens in the USSR, these former Soviet citizens in our country were virtually free to come and go as they pleased across America's open borders. If Soviet diplomats once got the family together, I knew the visas would materialize instantly, and the child would be gone for sure.

It also seemed to me that in some part of his soul, Polovchak half wanted his son to stay here. Thus his request for a piece of paper. In his mind, this would give Polovchak what he wanted— a return to the USSR—while allowing his son to stay here. Let the Americans take the blame. Polovchak thought he could get off the hook, but I had to protect the children. I now had to see for myself what Natalie and Walter actually wanted.

Leaving Polovchak, I got a police officer to find a small room where the children and I could talk privately.

We talked for about five minutes or so before the cousin joined us and explained that they had left the parents' apartment the previous Sunday to go to church, how the father had chased his daughter down the street, screaming "whore!" at her, and that the children had spent Sunday night at Cousin Walter's and then had moved out of the family apartment permanently on Monday. When they finished, I asked Natalie what she wanted to do.

"As I told you over the phone a few weeks ago, not only do I want to stay . . . but Walter does, too." Her face was untroubled by any doubt; her voice was firm and certain.

I looked at Walter closely for the first time and was somewhat shocked. Standing before me was a puny little kid, very small for his age. A good-looking boy . . . big eyes, pleasant expression, hair parted down the middle, freckles across the bridge of his nose. He was wearing cutoff jeans. He looked like a little angel.

My very first thought was, Here is a boy of twelve and a half who looks like he's eight or nine. I had sons of my own, so I was very aware that an average American boy of that age would already have started looking like a teenager. But this kid certainly didn't. Instinctively, I knew it wasn't simply a matter of America's more sophisticated way of life bringing on early maturity, or even of a poor diet that could slow down growth in Ukraine. Walter Polovchak's small size and solemn expression told me other things about his family's life. When you see a child like that, you often find it to be traceable to nutritional or emotional deprivation.

It struck me very strongly: *My God, this is not going to be easy.*

Since he looked so small, so cute, I realized it might be extremely difficult to convince anyone unfamiliar with Soviet life that twelve-year-old Walter Polovchak was able to make up his own mind just like an adult and to know exactly what he was doing by running away from home. I also realized that on strictly emotional grounds, which can have great impact in legal deliberations, it would be extremely difficult to make a case for keeping this winsome little boy from his mama and papa—if they truly wanted him.

Yet here he was. So I said to him in Ukrainian, "Walter, why did you run away?"

"Because he wants to take me back to the Soyuz," he replied at once, his voice light but steady. He did not call his father Daddy or Papa or any other name. Just the distant pronoun: he.

"You don't want to go back?" I asked. "Why not?"

"Because I like it here," he said. "We waited so long to get out. He promised life would be different here, and it *is*. I definitely don't want to go back." There wasn't the slightest hesitation in his answer.

So here were two clear-headed young people who had thought things through and were determined not to go back to the Soviet Union. At that moment, I was very afraid for them because courts have seldom granted minor children the right to leave home permanently if they don't want to move somewhere with their parents.

Years earlier, I had done some work with the Juvenile Court, and I knew that in a normal runaway situation, the police captain will talk to parents and child and send them all home to work it out among themselves. This sort of reconciliation, called a station adjustment, usually works.

But if they gave Walter back to his parents, I was certain we would never see him again.

Even so, I had to reassure the kids. "This is not the Soviet Union," I told them. "This is not the same kind of police station. You've got certain rights. You're not going to be locked up or anything like that. You have rights, too."

This calmed them. Cousin Walter, a bundle of nervous energy, quit pacing. Natalie managed a smile and Walter looked a little happier. I asked the sergeant if I could call the State Department in Washington. He said, "Go ahead."

Holding my breath, I called. It was Friday evening in Washington, an hour ahead of Chicago, and it seemed unlikely I would find someone able to respond to this crisis. However, I was in luck. A veteran diplomat, Bill Farrand, was available.

I had to quickly make the point that this was a real emergency. So with hardly a preliminary, I said to him, "If you don't want another Kudirka case on your hands, you'd better do something."

"What do you mean?"

"You remember Simas Kudirka, the Lithuanian seaman who tried to defect, and how we sent him back to the Soviets without giving him his day in court?"

Farrand remembered.

"I've got a twelve-year-old Ukrainian boy out here whose family came to the States a few months ago. Now the family wants to go back to the Soviet Union, but the boy and his older sister want to stay here. I feel he ought to be given his day in court. Presidential guidelines that were put in place after the Kudirka case apply in this situation."

Farrand didn't hesitate. "Give me your number out there and I'll have someone get back to you."

I hung up, wondering what would come of my call. Things had to move fast in my direction, and bureaucracies don't usually work that way—especially on a Friday night and the problem is eight hundred miles away.

Farrand, I learned later, had served in the U.S. embassy in Moscow and was very experienced in Soviet ways.

As I waited, I thought back to the first phone call Aunt Anna Junko had made to me some weeks before.

"You have to help me," she said. "My crazy brother wants to go back to the Soyuz, and after all the trouble I went to getting him here."

She said she thought her brother was involved with another woman and had come to the United States solely to dump his wife and family so he could return to his mistress free of them. It had sounded to me like a domestic crisis, not a political fight, but the call had started me thinking about the situation. As a human rights activist, I already knew of a lot of asylum cases.

The very next day, Cousin Walter had called me. He had asked if a minor child aged twelve could be compelled legally to go back to the USSR with his parents. I told him that under Illinois law, a boy of such a tender age obviously would have to go with his parents.

However, I knew of a California juvenile case involving two Czech brothers aged about seven and eight, who had been brought to the United States by their father while the mother had stayed behind. Then the father died, an elderly couple took the boys in, and the mother arrived to take the brothers back to Czechoslovakia. They didn't want to go, but as the mother of minor children, she obviously had such a right. The California court had decided the children could not be forced to go back, that it would not be in the boys' best interests.

"What the law is is one thing," I had told Cousin Walter. "Sometimes, there are exceptions. Your little cousin's situation is unusual. We're dealing with a society in which there is systematic repression, and even though parents have substantial rights over their minor children, courts *do* look at what is in the best interest of the child. So there might be a chance."

Some days after that, the cousin and I talked more about the situation. He told me the father slept with a knife under his pillow and that he had become increasingly abusive, accusing Cousin Walter of influencing the children against their own father.

"So why do you stay?" I had asked him.

"I'm helping them out economically because I want them to get on their feet. The children don't speak the language, and they need guidance. That's why I'm there."

I admired what he was trying to do, but I told him that if the situation got worse, he must think seriously about moving out.

Natalie's call came a few days after that. Through her tears, she said she and Walter didn't want to go back to Ukraine with her parents. She added that she didn't think her mother wanted to, either.

I told Natalie that since she was seventeen and very close to the legal majority of eighteen recognized under the laws of both the United States and the USSR, I didn't think they would force her to go back. I told her this was especially true if the mother refused to go back.

Natalie said her father was threatening the mother, saying he'd kill her if she didn't return, and that if she stayed behind, he'd get someone here to take care of her.

"They've got long arms," Natalie said Polovchak told his wife—meaning the KGB secret police.

Natalie explained that she had her own Soviet passport, and that she wasn't concerned so much about herself, as about Walter, little brother Michael, and her mother. "How can we protect them?"

I told her again that I didn't think she would have a problem. I added, "It isn't up to American Immigration authorities; it's the Soviets who refuse to give him a visa without his whole family."

Since that call I had had no contact with the family. Now my mind was searching for legal hurdles to put in Polovchak's path.

As I waited at the police station, I got a call from a State Department official right in Chicago, Patrick O'Hanlon. He said the case had already gone up to Warren Christopher, Assistant Secretary of State, who needed time to consult before getting back to me via O'Hanlon.

The wheels seemed to be moving—faster than I could have hoped. But in our direction? Meanwhile, I'd just have to wait.

The unusual situation and the unusual presence of the media worked in my favor. The local police commander didn't want to tell the juvenile sergeant, Leo Rojek, to make a station adjustment on the spot and send the boy home with the parents. At the same time, the commander had no instruction *not* to allow the parents to take Walter and leave.

After a while, an assistant police department superintendent named McDonaugh arrived and got filled in. I told him I'd called State and we were waiting for instructions. He didn't seem greatly impressed with this. "Can't bypass normal procedures," he said. "I'm going to call the duty Juvenile Court judge."

He put through the call and after a while, I was talking with Cook County Juvenile Court Judge Peter Costa, whom I knew. I told him exactly how things stood, mentioned the Kudirka case, and asked for as much help as he could provide.

"I know the sensitivity of this kind of case," he said.

"Judge, this is not a normal juvenile runaway case," I said for emphasis. "I would appreciate it if you could schedule us for an emergency hearing as soon as possible—tonight or tomorrow. Please, whatever you decide to do, let's not give custody of Walter to the parents immediately. The father's been in touch with the Soviet embassy, and if the parents regain control of this boy, we may never see him again."

Costa asked to speak to the deputy superintendent. I waited while they talked. This might have been the worst moment of the entire day.

After a few moments, the police commander hung up. "I've been instructed to place the brother and sister in your custody for the night," he said. "You will bring them to the Saturday session of Juvenile Court tomorrow for a full hearing."

Here was a small but vital victory!

I huddled with the parents. "This is a police station, not a place to settle disputes," I said. "I'm going to take the children with me for the night. We're all going to meet in court tomorrow when a judge will listen to what we all have to say and will make some decision about what should happen to the children. The police will pick you up at your apartment and bring you to court. Just because you're going to be picked up in a police car doesn't mean you're going to be arrested. It's only transportation, because you don't know the city."

The mother was a little unhappy she couldn't take Walter home, but Polovchak didn't seem too surprised. They went home with a police officer, and I took the children home with me.

A police car tailed us out to the house and came by occasionally that night. They were taking the situation as seriously as I.

2

My wife prepared something to eat, and I questioned Walter and Natalie.

They described the relationships in the family, and quickly sketched in everything else. After a while I understood that this wasn't just a question of Walter's returning to the family. I realized something more profound: he'd never be able to live a normal life within that family. For many reasons, there had been very little bonding between the father and Walter; because the mother worked all the time, her relations with the children were not the best, either.

Walter said his one true parent had been his grandmother. From his birth until just before they left, she had taken almost total care of him: "She cooked for me, washed for me, took me to church, took me to school." Her death had left him to fend for himself with little help from his parents. It was a very unpleasant picture, relieved only by the family's emigration to the United States.

I began to think that if we could bring some of these seemingly simple yet important family details out in court, we'd have a chance to win Walter's freedom.

Then Natalie told me a painful story about the gift of a dress sent her in Sambir by her aunt Anastasia.

"I loved that dress, Mr. Kulas, but one day, it just disappeared. I never knew what happened to it. I thought someone had come into the house and stolen it. No one in the family, including my father, had any idea what had become of it.

"Then when we got to Chicago, we were unpacking, and I saw a photograph of a strange woman—she had my dress on!

"We knew people were saying unpleasant things about how my father was seeing other women, but when I saw that picture of the woman in my dress . . . he brought that photo with him to the States! I can't ever forgive him for any of it."

I was amazed Natalie would speak so openly of this in Walter's presence, but the little boy was roaming around the living room, staring at the stereo, the TV, and the other appliances. Walter became so absorbed in trying everything out that he didn't pay much attention to Natalie.

For Juvenile Court authorities accustomed to dealing with domestic problems, this case had unique political dimensions. Since the state would be asked to take legal custody of Walter in any Juvenile Court proceeding, I hoped the issues would be clearly visible to the state's lawyers.

As we sat watching the ten-o'clock TV news shows, it was clear the issues were going to be writ large. Every station reported how a twelve-year-old boy would rather leave his parents forever than return with them to the Soviet Union.

Seeing this, I knew the Soviet Union would be completely embarrassed by what the situation made clear: *even a twelve-year-old knows the difference.*

After my wife tucked the children away upstairs for the night, I began considering the legal matters.

First, it was clear that whether the parents loved him or not, their act of taking Walter back to the Soviet Union would be reckless, guaranteeing punishment against him. The USSR has no use for citizens who embarrass it before the world, and Walter was certainly doing that! If the parents had even elementary regard for their son, they would not insist that he return, since they knew how the USSR deals with its own people.

I decided I must turn to American immigration authorities for help in saving Walter, asking them to grant him political asylum so I could build a legal base outside the framework of any proceedings in Juvenile Court.

I also believed we could show in court that Walter had run away not because he disliked his parents, but was acting rationally and must not be punished for it by being forced to do the one thing that would harm him—going back to Ukraine.

I also wanted to argue that the intense publicity around the case guaranteed a reprisal from the Soviets, and since the parents knew the disastrous consequences facing Walter if he went home, they were guilty of neglect. To my mind, this was as tangible an example of neglect as if the Polovchaks failed to feed or clothe their children.

The first testing ground would be Cook County Juvenile Court. As in many other states, Illinois juvenile law gives the state a form of legal guardianship over any child found by the court to be beyond the control of his parents or legal family—a Minor in Need of Supervision. MINS cases were the bread and butter of juvenile courts. Arguing for a MINS finding on behalf of Walter made sense because it would legally bar the parents from any move against the child without state approval.

A MINS finding would also enable the state to physically remove Walter from the parents' custody and put him in foster care since his parents could not keep him from running away. The judge must conclude that the twelve-year-old was beyond the control of his parents, behaving in a way that endangered him. There were major pitfalls to opening a legal battle centered solely on the narrow question of Walter-as-runaway.

This was because courts generally treat runaway cases the way old English common law treated dogs—most dogs are entitled to one bite before you can call them vicious. In Illinois, in fact, first runaway cases seldom wind up in court. It takes repetition by the runaway and a pattern of self-endangerment to justify a MINS petition.

Indeed, Walter's case was actually weakened in the eyes of juvenile law by his rational, careful behavior. If he had run away from a reasonably peaceable household to consort with drug addicts, perhaps a MINS finding would have been appropriate. Although he had fled an unruly, threatening environment to find political safety and emotional stability, the court couldn't concern itself with such things. The ironies of this legal situation were ludicrous—or outrageous.

3

I was very emotional, very worked up, and sleep was impossible that night. My thoughts were agitated, moving in many directions. After a while, I got up and went downstairs where I got myself a glass of milk and sat at the kitchen table, thinking. The night closed in around me.

This boy sleeping upstairs was about the same age as I had been when I came to the United States in 1950. I began thinking about my first days in America, remembering how things looked, how neon lights impressed me, and everything else—an ice cream cone, the food, all of it.

Initially when you come here, American life is confusing and alluring at the same time, draws you like a magnet because you want to understand what is going on here and to belong to it.

I thought, Let me put myself in Walter's shoes and see where I would be if my father had wanted to go back. Would I have stayed? Would I have run away, too?

My parents, my three brothers, my sister, and I were from a village in western Ukraine called Boratyn, now on the Polish side by two kilometers. I was born there in 1935. During the war, my father was a slave laborer in Germany, as Walter's aunt Anastasia had been.

Toward the end of the war, when the Soviets attacked from the east, we fled west. Eventually, we were reunited with my father in Germany, and spent five years in a DP camp there. We considered ourselves lucky because after the war the border was moved, and where we had lived wound up on the Soviet side of the line.

We were brought to the United States by a Catholic relief organization, first to New York, and then to Sylvania, Georgia, a small town about eighty miles north of Savannah. The Catholic Church was not very strong in that part of the country, so they tried to settle some Catholics in the South. We turned out to be doubly exotic to Georgians: not only were we Catholics in a land of Protestants; we were *foreigners*, too. This had some amusing sides, which entertained us amid the strangeness of our new lives.

For example, some people in Sylvania had never heard anyone speak a foreign language. The biggest thrill for some schoolkids was asking us to speak Ukrainian. I'd answer, and they'd burst out laughing!

That first year, my father, brothers, and I picked cotton, making two dollars a day apiece. My father was an accomplished cabinet-maker and carpenter, and by our second year he quit the fields and went to work for the parish for much better money, building pews for a new church in Statesboro.

I had taken some English in DP camp and could speak the language a little when we got here. I continued studying and got good enough that a priest from the Catholic relief organization asked me to be his interpreter. For five dollars a day I translated while he met Ukrainian immigrant refugees from European DP camps who were getting off ships in New Orleans.

I made many trips with Father Smith, meeting people at the docks, putting them on trains or buses, and traveling with them to their new homes. Most of them stayed with Southern farm families. The priest and I would go back months later to see how they were getting along.

On one trip I met a big Byelorussian family, five daughters and a son, who all moved to Chicago, where thousands of Ukrainians lived. Soon I journeyed to Chicago and lived with the Ukrainian farm family I had helped Father Smith resettle. After a while, my parents and the rest of the family joined me. We've been here ever since.

I began practicing law in the 1960s, concentrating on the Ukrainian community. But nothing I had ever handled would come to mean more to me—or to my special Ukrainian-American countrymen—than the case of Walter Polovchak.

I never imagined the struggle would consume years. In the beginning, I didn't think twice about such things as getting a special telephone line installed at home to handle the calls about Walter. The line is still in place, and we still receive inquiries on it. The interest of people all over the world tells me about the importance of making that fight.

Symbolically, we drew a line in the dust, and for all the world to see, we defended that line, telling the world that a police state cannot reach beyond that line.

When all the legal arguments and all the verdicts and learned opinions had been written and discussed and appealed, what remained was the fact of what we said. This child would be freedom's child.

FROM JACK GOGGIN'S REPORT

CHILD'S STATEMENT:

Walter agreed with the Police Report, in that he did run away from his home, on the 14th of July, without the permission of his parents and stayed in the home of his cousin Walter until he was picked [up] by the Police on the 18th of July. The minor respondent stated that he and his sister Natalie, and cousin Walter, packed up their belongings and Walter and Natalie left the apartment. However just prior to their leaving, the mother came home from work and asked what was happening. They said they did not wish to return to Russia and that they were leaving the home. The mother stated to cousin Walter that he was not the father and had no right to take the children. Cousin Walter said that they were leaving of their own free will and he was not coercing them or forcing them in any way. As they were all packed, they then proceeded to leave. [Cousin] Walter and Natalie left, followed by the minor respondent. The minor respondent stated that he then rode his bike from his parents' home to his cousin's home.

PREVIOUS POLICE AND COURT CONTACTS:

The minor respondent has only been in this country for six months. This is his first Referral to Juvenile Court and there have been no previous Station Adjustments.

---

chapter seven
THE FIRST HEARING

JULIAN KULAS

1

I'll never forget the ride to Juvenile Court the morning of July 19. Here was a routine step that happens thousands of times of day in the United States—a trip to court. I'd been making them for almost twenty years myself.

The circumstances this time made it a very important, unusual occasion to me. We were about to put before an American judge—and perhaps one day an American jury— the case of two immigrant children who wanted to escape the Soviet Union.

Plenty of people have found fault with our system of justice but no nation's is better. For this reason alone, the world watches closely what happens in American courts. Natalie and Walter had given me their trust. It was up to me to make certain they won their case.

Whatever my thoughts, Walter brought everything straight down to earth, the way a twelve-year-old should. I had a new Mark V Continental automobile, with lots of equipment in it. As soon as Walter jumped in, he was all over it. This was heaven for him!

"What's this? What's that?" He twisted the knobs, pushed buttons, watched with delight as things went up and down. He got so absorbed that he seemed to forget we were headed to a court hearing. His delight was infectious and lifted all our spirits.

I told them how the Illinois Juvenile Court system works. I wanted them to know that whatever rights parents had, children in America also had certain rights. Above all, I wanted them to understand that the state would be interested in their overall welfare.

"First, the judge is friendly, and he runs things. You've got bailiffs in different uniforms, a little like police. There's a clerk sitting there, and a court reporter, who will take down every word you say. It's important to say things clearly and loud, because if you don't, the judge will ask you to speak up . . . and who needs that?"

I tried to point the children beyond the brief hearing ahead. I'd seen many cases drag on for years, beyond anyone's wildest nightmares, and I wanted to explain what might be in store.

"This case will not be over today. This is an emergency court. The judge who will be handling our case only makes temporary decisions. It is more than likely we will be back in court in a few days."

As we pulled into the Juvenile Court parking lot, a huge crowd of reporters and TV crews came chasing after us. Walter and Natalie were dressed in fresh clothing that Cousin Walter had retrieved from the apartment. Considering the cameras, I was very happy about this! But I truly wasn't prepared for this amount of press attention. Although the previous night I had realized the dramatic impact of the confrontation, especially on the Soviets, I was still coming to grips with the strength of the story in the eyes of the media, as well as the sheer power of the press.

I had sometimes served as a spokesman for Chicago's Ukrainian community, so I had a familiarity with the press and felt comfortable around reporters. While there are always some obnoxious people in any profession, I believed that for the most part, I could trust reporters not to twist my words.

Now they were barraging us with questions as we headed toward the building. Even under the best of circumstances, it was the kind of attention that can rattle anyone. I was not in a position to refuse their questions, nor did I want to. I needed the press to get the story out. But it was not going to be a circus.

"Walter doesn't speak the language, and we're not going to make any comment before the hearing," I said. "If there's anything to be said, we'll talk after the hearing."

Natalie was astonished. "Does the whole country know about this?"

"Natalie, in this country, when there's news, everybody wants to know about it."

"Well, in the Soyuz, they only report the good news . . . who is the champion farm milker or which collective farm has the most pigs," she said. "That's big news over there. People aren't big news. Accomplishments, not people. Like, you get a blue ribbon for giving birth to quintuplets. That's big news, but it's sort of an accomplishment, not actually *about people*."

"I used to like to watch soccer on TV over there," Walter offered hopefully, his voice barely audible in the din.

I loved soccer myself and took Walter to pro games and occasionally kicked the ball around for fun. He even got to play on a local Ukrainian schoolboy team for several seasons, and used to go to a summer camp in Wisconsin where soccer was a specialty. He's more interested in girls these days, but when he was smaller, soccer was king in his life.

Demonstrators arrived from the Reverand Olexa Harbuziuk's Ukrainian Baptist Church, where Cousin Walter, and his aunt worshiped. Neatly dressed and polite, they held up signs demanding that the children remain free: "These Kids Love America." When I watched the TV news that night, I was pleased to see the signs were easily readable behind Walter and Natalie. It was a message worth reading.

The demonstrators fell in quiet, orderly step around us. This was the first public display of the fierce wave of emotion that swept from the Ukrainians in my community, and from Ukrainians everywhere in the Free World, in support of the children.

Ukrainians have extremely bitter feelings about the Soviet Union and the massed power of Moscow and the Russians that has always been directed against Ukraine. Suffering at the hands of Moscow and the Russians is deep in the history of our people. Russian pressure that could efface our separate, distinctive culture has been a constant part of reality for Ukrainians for decades. This has made resistance to Russia fundamental to the survival of the Ukrainian nation.

From the moment the Bolsheviks took power in 1917, right down to today, Ukrainians have suffered at the hands of Russians and the Communist Party. So the case of Natalie and Walter instantly touched the deepest, strongest, most enduring part of the Ukrainian soul. From the moment that word of their plight flashed out over television, radio, and newspapers, the brother and sister would never be far from the thoughts of hundreds of thousands of Ukrainians who had never met them, nor ever would. That is part of being Ukrainian—an unquenchable national kinship.

Any of us so-called hyphenated Americans—those who came here from another country, and who remember, respect, and seek to preserve their national roots amid our larger culture—will know exactly what I mean when I say this. Even Americans whose ancestors came long ago—perhaps on the *Mayflower* itself—recognize what America promises the world: freedom to preserve your own heritage even as you become an American.

Ukrainians didn't need to know Walter and Natalie personally to join in common cause with them. Binding all of us was a strong sense of shared danger, pride, and destiny.

Nothing made our worries plainer than those quiet demonstrators and their signs, all bearing witness to our history and our hopes. The children's case was becoming a cause. For me and my countrymen, it still is.

Within a few days, Walter began receiving letters, telegrams, and telephone calls from Americans, and from people in other countries. People offered him shelter. Mothers wanted to care for him, fathers to provide for him. Church groups prayed for Walter. The fervor of the concern was startling.

I remember a man in Idaho who even wrote to say he could hide Walter in the mountains so the police would never find him. Other families offered themselves as foster parents. They were outraged and saddened by the apparent lack of feeling the Polovchaks had for their own son. This outpouring came from every part of the country, even from Americans who had no Ukrainian connection or any firsthand experience with the USSR. Most people just wanted to express support, good wishes, and admiration for what Walter had done. That made their interest all the more special. The power of a determined twelve-year-old!

I took the children to the courthouse cafeteria to wait for the judge to arrive and court to begin. A few minutes later, Anna and Michael Polovchak arrived.

We greeted each other, and Polovchak quickly asked, "Can you give me the piece of paper I asked for yesterday?"

"Depending on what happens in court, I can probably get you something."

"Well, Walter's on my passport," he said, repeating his complaint from the previous day. "That's the problem."

"If your wife is going to stay, there would be no problem," I said, looking for a simple resolution of the matter. "Then Natalie could stay . . . Walter could stay."

"Oh, no," Polovchak said, glancing at his wife. "They told me that she goes with me." He looked around for Natalie. "Now, Natalka's another story. She can stay. But this with Walter is a condition set by *them* . . . they said, Everybody goes, or you don't go back."

So nothing had changed. I knew that he wanted a court order, but he wasn't going to commit himself and say openly to Walter, "You can stay." Once *they*, the Soviets, found that out, he would be in deep trouble.

At first he publicly said, "I want my kids," while in private telephone conversations and correspondence with his sister Anastasia, he wasn't so strong. He was much more concerned about getting his own visa than about Natalie and Walter returning with him.

There were two different worlds for Michael Polovchak: the public role he had to play and the hidden role of his own feelings. As the contradictions of his situation increased, he became more frustrated and antagonistic.

"We're also going to the Immigration Office later today to separate Walter from your passport," I told him.

"Well, can you give me a piece of paper specifying it?"

"I don't know, but it will be known that legally he is no longer on your passport, because he will have separate status."

"Can you give me a letter or something?" he asked again.

"Yes, if we get the request approved, I will give you a letter showing he has been given *prytulok*." I used the Ukrainian term for asylum, so they would have no confusion or doubts about what I intended.

Polovchak was pleased. He said with satisfaction, "*Dobre, dobre*"— Good, good.

"Who will pay for Walter's support?" his wife, Anna, asked, speaking to me for the first time.

"If the children don't live with you, then you won't be required to pay for them," I said.

She was surprised by that. "I thought we had to pay for their food, their clothing."

We began exchanging personal information. I told her we had three children, just as they did. She asked their names, ages, and the rest of it. She was curious to know when I had come to the United States and what my wife did for work.

My village of Boratyn was about eighty kilometers from Sambir, which also gave us a point of reference. As we talked, the sense of confrontation faded.

"Nobody's going to get hurt by this court," I told them. "We'll try to get the family together." She liked hearing that, and I really felt that reconciliation might be possible.

But Polovchak's reaction was different. When I told him the family might be able to get together, he said, "Fine, she can take care of them. If only they let me go, I have no problems."

His single-minded attitude seemed to confirm what Natalie had told me—that hardly had they landed here before Polovchak told them he wanted to go back.

During our Friday night conversation Natalie told me Soviet authorities at first had denied them exit permission on the grounds that the family's domestic life was troubled. But then, she said, her father had been able to make a connection with a senior KGB official named Yuri. After Michael had bribed him, the exit visa had been issued.

Although I didn't think it impossible that Polovchak could bribe a top KGB agent, it seemed far more likely to me that the secret police had easily learned his real motive for wanting an exit visa and issued it willingly, knowing he soon would be applying for a return visa.

What Polovchak didn't realize was that they had plans of their own—setting as a condition of his return that he bring his entire family as well. It would be a big Soviet propaganda victory. They would greet the Polovchaks at the airport, give them roses, and tell them how smart they had been to come to their senses after a few months in the decadent West.

This may sound farfetched to the average American, but the average American doesn't realize how much fuss Soviet authorities make when an émigré rejects the West and comes back to the Motherland. It's one way to deal with the fact that over there, millions talk or silently dream of leaving.

If the Soviets anticipated a big propaganda victory, they had overlooked one detail: the children. They had never imagined the children would take matters into their own hands.

Under Illinois law at that time, in a runaway case, lawyers from the Cook County State's Attorney's Office separately represented the Illinois Department of Children and Family Services (DCFS) and the child. Since I also was representing Walter, I talked before the hearing with a young assistant prosecutor who initially worked on Walter's behalf.

I wanted to raise with this woman my concerns about confining Walter's defense to a simple runaway case. I knew that no matter how effective our work, the judge likely would send runaway Walter home, and I had no doubt Walter would be in trouble if that happened.

"I think we ought to file a neglect petition against the parents," I said. "It's ironic, but the law that won't let you abuse your children here apparently will allow you to take them back to the USSR. After all this negative publicity, the children are certain to be abused if they go back."

"Well, that's anticipatory neglect," she said. "For example, it applies to small children where a mother has been neglectful and now she's pregnant again. In cases like that, we take the child away in anticipation. We've never had a case like this. We can probably handle it with a MINS based on a runaway."

"It's not such a simple runaway," I said. "He didn't just run away from home—he ran away for a reason. Not because he didn't like his parents, but because he didn't want to be shipped back."

"You've got nothing to worry about," she replied. "He ran away, and stayed away for four days, and we will obviously have supervision of the case."

I felt uneasy about these answers. She didn't want to grapple with the political implications of the case. If she treated it as a normal case, Walter would be in serious difficulty.

We were ushered into the quiet courtroom of Juvenile Judge Joseph Mooney, who had a relaxed but businesslike manner. It was a very brief hearing, with Walter, Natalie, Cousin Walter, and parishioners from the Baptist church taking up most seats. The Polovchaks had no attorney, and since the proceedings were in English, they couldn't understand them.

The young assistant prosecutor representing Walter, Mary Ellen Nash, noted that both we and the lawyers representing DCFS "have agreed to the appointment of a temporary custodian for this minor on a temporary basis."

But, she noted, the Polovchaks "do not have an attorney, nor are they conversant very well in the English language, and I believe it will be necessary to give them some time to hire an attorney, if they wish to do so."

"Okay, well, do we have a legal issue here?" Mooney asked.

"It is my understanding that the parents are not in agreement with the [temporary custodian] order . . . and that being the case, I believe that they are entitled to be represented by counsel."

"Of course, under the law they are," Mooney said dryly. "After all, this is their son." He said that in his mind, the question was whether the child should be returned to the parents or temporarily placed outside the home.

I didn't waste a moment. "Our concerns are . . . the safety of the child. . . . Of course, if the parents wish to be represented by counsel, they have every right to do so."

"Do you have anything to say to the court?" the judge asked the Polovchaks.

They couldn't answer. "Do you understand English?"

Again, silence.

An impromptu search of the courtroom turned up a young woman who said she could serve as volunteer interpreter. She was sworn in to help the parents.

"For volunteering, you won't be better paid than thank you," said the judge.

"That is the best pay," she replied.

"Do you understand English, Walter?" asked the judge.

"A little bit."

The judge then briefly laid out the positions: the state's attorneys and I wanted Walter put in temporary custody of the state of Illinois, while the parents "want to take the boy home with them."

This was translated for the parents; then Mooney said, "I will set this for trial . . . but I will give temporary custody to the State of Illinois, the Department of Children and Family Services."

Walter was put in the care of Cousin Walter. "I can assure this court that the child will be cared for properly," I told the judge. ". . . proper supervision . . . proper support, shelter, clothing . . ."

"All right, you are co-counsel," said the judge. "I will accept your representation." He turned to the interpreter. "Would you tell the parents that I have set this case for trial on my calendar for July the thirtieth . . ."

"I already explained it to them."

"At which time they should have their lawyer here," the judge said, and adjourned the hearing.

We filed out. We had just passed the first, if lowest, hurdle. I now had eleven days to prepare a full legal case for Walter. I had no idea whether Michael and Anna Polovchak really cared enough to get a lawyer and build their own case.

But I was certain the Soviets would not remain idle after this little boy had humiliated them.

Polovchak wasn't too disappointed with what had happened, but his wife was very unhappy. As a social worker began explaining that they would bring Walter over for regular family visits, Mrs. Polovchak became increasingly unhappy.

In a way, I sympathized with her. I was always close to my mother, and I felt that some of the same kind of special closeness existed between Anna Polovchak and her son. In another way, I had to look at it as it was: if not for the father, whom I suspected of wanting to go back to another woman, everything would have been all right for the family.

So I felt mixed emotions. With three children of my own, I know how close a family can be. It would have been tragic for me to see my kids taken away. But then I kept reassuring myself that this was the best way, because if Michael took them back, that was it for Walter. By thinking this way, I was defeating the emotional feeling I had for the mother.

She was dissolving into tears. Little Mikey came over and grabbed Walter by the legs. How can you separate two brothers like that?

As this scene unfolded, I felt we could have a reconciliation somewhere down the way. It was an optimistic idea, but I thought that with social workers helping them, calming them down away from the media, parents and children could mend their differences. Maybe it was just a groundless hope of mine that the parents could pull themselves away from Soviet influence and the father would come to his senses.

Outside the courtroom, I told the press it would be to Walter's detriment to return to the USSR. "They might take action against him now that he has shown he doesn't want to go," I said. "Certainly, they would not treat him favorably."

The reporters clustered around Walter. Why are you doing this? they asked.

"Here is free country," he answered in English, with a shy smile. The quote went around the world.

Meanwhile, Polovchak got increasingly irritated. When reporters reached him, he said something he was never to say again in public.

"This is a free country. It is a good country. But I want to go home. . . . Children should stay with their parents." He became more agitated. As he and his wife left, he angrily shouted, *"They've kidnapped my children!"*

That quote also went around the world.

2

We left Juvenile Court for the Chicago district office of the Immigation Service. I intended to seek political asylum for Walter.

At the INS office, criminal investigator Phil Leadroot and a supervisor, Thomas Schiltgen, took charge. With help from a translator, Walter began filling out an asylum application consisting of numerous questions about the applicant's life and beliefs. I did not participate in this; it was a matter between INS and Walter. But here are some of the questions and Walter's answers:

Question: Have you taken any action which you believe would result in persecution in your home country?

Answer: Yes. This filing.

Q: Has the request for asylum become known to the authorities of your home country?

A: Yes.

Q: How has this become known?

A: Media.

Q: What do you think would happen to you if you return?

A: Prevented from receiving higher education.

Q: Can you provide any documentation or evidence, letters, newspapers, court orders, in support of your request?

A: Yes, newspaper.

Q: Would you return to your home country? If not, why not?

A: No, I would be persecuted.

Q: Explain specifically what are the racial, religious, ethnic or political grounds which you feel would result in your persecution.

A: Prevented from higher education; considered suspect; restricted in mobility.

Q: What is your religion?

A: Baptist.

This answer in fact was wrong—Walter was a Ukrainian Catholic. But he had gone with his aunt to Baptist services after the family arrived in Chicago, and he mistakenly thought that was what the Immigration officer had asked him. It took months of effort later to make sure that the record of Walter's religious affiliation was accurate.

Meanwhile, INS officials on orders from Farrand in Washington gathered a special group of federal agents, with walkie-talkies and pistols, to guard Walter around the clock.

Some time passed, and we were ready to leave. Besides the work awaiting me, the children needed to resume something like a normal life. They were eager to return with Cousin Walter to his apartment and have some peace and quiet.

Accompanied by INS official Ted Georgetti at the head of the new security detail, the children left the Immigration office with Cousin Walter.

For the first time since the frantic phone call of the previous day, I felt secure. I had fought for time and won.

FROM JACK GOGGIN'S REPORT

Michael Polovchak, born 6/13/38 in Ukraine. The father is a very short man, approximately 5'3" tall, medium build, currently employed at the Henry Valve Company, 3215 W. North Avenue in Melrose Park, as a machine operator, where he receives $202.00 per week net. He got this job through intervention of his brother-in-law, Dmitri Gusiev, from whom this information was obtained. He works from 3 P.M. to midnight and has had this job since his first month in the United States. The father did not wish to co-operate initially, however, P.O. wound up having an approximately 30-minute interview with him, during which time he expressed great anger and dismay about what was going on. During the entire course of the interview, the father was extremely angry.

Anna Polovchak, born 2/17/41 in Ukraine. Mrs. Polovchak is employed as a housekeeper at St. Elizabeth's Hospital. She works from 7 A.M. to 3 P.M. She is of average height, somewhat taller than her husband, was cooperative and friendly and, during the course of her interview, became quite emotional at one point. The hospital public relations man, Mr. Woods, referred to Mrs. Polovchak as the best worker they had in housekeeping and [said] they will hate to lose her. During the entire course of the interview, she continuously looked at her watch as she was afraid she would not be able to finish her work if we detained her too much longer. She was panicky despite assurances that any work she could not finish, she would receive help with. She did not want help.

Mr. and Mrs. Polovchak were married on March 6, 1962, in Sambir, in the Ukraine, where they also raised their family. There was no information obtained from father or mother as to the quality of their marriage during this time, however, daughter Natalie stated that she did not feel her parents get along that well, as her father was only home about three days a week and never seemed to be around the house. She did state that when he was home, he was not abusive to them but she did not feel he really interacted with the family as a father should. Natalie also stated that she no longer trusts her father and does not believe him in many areas. She feels that he just cannot be trusted. She stated he has lied to her in the past, but did not give details. The girl is sure her mother loves her but she does not feel her father does. In a way, she feels that both mother and father wanted to get rid of her in the sense that they told her, when they got to America, that the family would stay in Chicago, however she would go to California and live with the aunt. Natalie feels that she is the unwanted child in the family.

As of this time, the father has a great deal of resentment towards his nephew, Walter, who he feels influenced his son and daughter to stay in the U.S., and has some antagonism toward his two sisters. However, [he] did state that he knows his son left home voluntarily and was not coerced. Mrs. Polovchak also stated the same thing. Cousin Walter, for his part, stated that the boy's decision was his own, as was Natalie's, and that he had nothing to do with it. All he did, he said, was to provide them with a home when they wished to leave their parents. At the time they left, Walter stated, the atmosphere in the Polovchak home was tense and in his opinion, dangerous. He certainly felt threatened. During the last two weeks, when Cousin Walter lived in the home on Fullerton, he stated that Mr. Polovchak threatened him and Natalie and stated they were responsible for influencing his son's decision to remain in the U.S. During this time, Mr. Polovchak would slam windows, bang doors, and otherwise try to harass and intimidate Cousin Walter in order to add to a threatening atmosphere in the home.

At one point, according to Natalie, he said he would kill someone, without naming any particular person, and did not care if he had to go to the electric chair for it. It was during this same period of time that Natalie and the minor respondent, Walter, found a knife under the father's pillow . . . and when they told Cousin Walter about this, he made the determination at that time to leave the home. He then rented an apartment on Byron Street, and he, Natalie, and young Walter subsequently left the Fullerton Street home and went to live on Byron Street, where they still reside. . . .

chapter eight
AFTER THE HEARING

JULIAN KULAS

Walter and Natalie were safe with their new security guards at Cousin Walter's apartment and I was back in my law office when the telephone rang. I picked it up and got a nasty surprise.

"This is Pyotr Prilepski of the embassy of the Union of Soviet Socialist Republics," said a tense voice. "I'm calling from Washington."

Before I could even answer, he demanded, "What right do you have to slander the Soviet Union?"

"Every American has the right to say what he pleases," I replied. "We're fortunate to live under a system where we can speak freely."

This didn't slow him a bit. "Under what law are you taking the Polovchak boy away from his parents?"

"I didn't take the boy away from his parents. The boy ran away from his parents on his own."

"Well, we shall see . . . we shall see," Prilepski said. "This is considered a kidnapping. You are doing this for political reasons."

"What political reasons? I never saw Walter Polovchak

before I met him in the police station yesterday. I was called in as a lawyer, not a politician."

"I will see you in court!" he declared and abruptly slammed down the phone.

If I had ever doubted doing the right thing in asking for asylum and twenty-four-hour security for Walter, Prilepski dispelled it for good.

Just a few hours earlier I had told Art Anderson, an Immigration official, that I was genuinely worried about Walter's safety.

"After the enormous exposure of the case by the media Friday night, Walter's life could be in danger," I had told Anderson.

"What do you mean?" he had asked. I don't think he'd ever heard anyone say such a thing before.

"Well, if the father's been in contact with the Soviet embassy, as we know he has—"

"What's your evidence?"

"The children told me they heard him on the phone with Soviet diplomats. And the cousin's phone bill lists calls to the Russians in Washington. There are all kinds of agents who could be in Chicago right now. They could put him in a car and take him off and that's the last we see of Walter."

"You may have a point. Let me see what we can do."

They had set up the security team after that, and barely an hour later, Prilepski was telling me, "We shall see . . . we shall see." It didn't take much imagination to interpret his words as a threat.

His calling it a "kidnapping" made clear how seriously the Soviets were taking this public relations crisis around a twelve-year-old child.

This was 1980, years before President Reagan demanded a reduction in the number of Soviet diplomats at their missions in Washington and the United Nations in New York.

I knew that travel for Soviet diplomats in the United States was restricted, but how do you really monitor that? I was very glad I had asked for the safety precautions that the State Department ordered.

COUSIN WALTER

That evening, there was full protection at my apartment. Two agents staked out the backyard, right where Wally had been snatched the day before by the Chicago police. How fast everything had changed! Now the police were on our side.

In fact, as night fell, the local police commander at the Shakespeare station house came over to chat with the INS agents and check out the arrangements for the children's safety.

The agents were all in a good mood: these were American lawmen out to stick it to the Russians.

There were unmarked cars up and down the block and television crews in vans also were staked out along the curb. The agents wouldn't let them near my apartment, so the reporters clustered down the street, and neighbors came out to see what was going on.

The agents knew the go-ahead had come from Washington, and at headquarters there had been a buzzing about Ted Giorgetti, how the word had come all the way from Washington, and so there was a feeling of "go, go, go get 'em."

Some of the agents had reported for duty in jeans and sneakers, right out of their backyard barbecues or off their garden tractors. One even came in a tuxedo—he had been in a wedding. A few weren't very happy to be working on a weekend but to them, it was serious. When we got to the apartment, there were six agents there. They were very friendly, but it was all business.

I think they realized that Judge Mooney had concluded he was not going to put Walter and Natalie in the custody of the parents, so that on Monday morning, the press and everybody else in the country would think Judge Mooney put the little boy on the plane back to the Soviet Union. There was no question the judge was not going to be a goat. No way.

Immigration also realized that if Wally did end up on a plane, it would be seen as their fault. So they were afraid, too. They were aware that he was a Soviet citizen and had no protection beyond what they could give him.

Adding to their worry, I think, was the fact that the law was not really clear as to who had custody in this kind of case. So while they joked around, they were taking it seriously—they were not going to screw it up. I felt very secure, thinking to myself something like, Let's go for it. The tide seemed to be turning.

So while it was a little tense, there were good feelings. These were adults for sure. Big guys, very competent, looking around the neighborhood, checking out the doors, the angles of vision, and the location of alleys, garages, and streets all around my little apartment on Byron out west of the Loop.

They started talking to Wally, and I did the interpreting. "We don't want you getting out of our sight, understand? We're real serious about this."

Wally nodded and agreed, but he seemed amazed, as excited as if he had been in Disneyland. To me, it was almost as if he didn't fully understand why any of this was happening, so I laid it out for him. "The reason they're here is because you could end up on a plane. You understand?"

He nodded and his eyes got bigger.

"These agents are going to guard us until they're sure you're safe."

"Aw, I want to ride my bike around and go play."

"They don't want you doing it. They don't want you going off in some plane."

He never said anything about changing his mind, or wanting to go back to his parents. Unless they decided to change their minds and stay here, Wally wanted it the way it was—separated from them.

At this point, the very beginning of the struggle over Wally, everyone I knew, from Aunt Anna to Mr. Kulas, to my mother, even to Natalie and Walter himself, all thought deep down that after a few weeks, the situation would cool off and everyone would be able to talk to each other.

Mr. Kulas told us, "The best way to succeed is to talk to the parents at every opportunity, keep the process going in some positive direction. The best, friendly, polite, and nicest way of ending this is to cool the parents," he told me. "And either the parents agree and say, 'Okay, we'll go back and let him alone,' or they say, 'Well, we'll stay here for a while to settle it.' "

And while I felt my heart and adrenaline pump-pumping that night from the excitement of the situation, I also was hopeful and positive, with the agents making sure it would be a peaceful night.

The next morning, when I saw articles about Wally on the front pages of both the *Chicago Tribune* and the *Chicago Sun-Times*, I knew it was even more serious than I had imagined.

A strange incident happened that Sunday to reinforce the point. There were agents sitting out front and back. The shift had changed earlier that morning, and nothing much was happening. A quiet Sunday morning in a quiet neighborhood of little duplex apartment houses and bungalows. An old dump truck rattled and roared down the street. The agents were sitting relaxed, just watching things. The same truck rolled down the street again. There was a little stir among the guards but nothing more than that.

Suddenly, there was the dump truck again, an old junker, coming down the block a third time. They jumped up and were on the walkie-talkies in an instant, yelling instructions to us to stay in the house and stay low. In a second, they had their guns ready, and two agents suddenly were in the street.

I was stunned. From peace to threat in a split second. It almost took my breath away: these guys were real serious.

Maybe it was curiosity seekers or hell raisers in the truck. No matter. The agents were not taking chances. It hits you: these people mean business. They are prepared to shoot to protect that little boy.

As the weeks went by, they would take Wally to the go-carts, to the store, to get ice cream, even to the movies. Anything to break up the boredom, get him out of the house. They didn't want to sit there every day with nothing to do. But they would never allow him to go beyond the end of the block, even riding his bicycle. When he did ride up and down the block, one agent would go out and station himself watching the back alley. Another agent would sit out front with a clear line of sight up and down the street.

WALTER

For the first few days after the hearing, I had six guys sitting around the apartment, twenty-four hours a day. Nothing happened. Nothing at all. So after a few days, they cut it back to two agents a shift, round the clock.

They were real nice guys, but that much security is annoying. They follow you everywhere you go, practically to the bathroom.

Since I spoke little English and didn't have any friends, I went around with these guys all the time. They took me out to the movies, we'd go for pizza, or bowling, or they'd just drive around with me. One of the guys was a weight-lifting fan. He had a super, super build. He took me to his health club where he worked out. This was something different, all right.

All the agents carried guns. They never fooled around with them, but sometimes they'd take out the bullets and show the weapons to me. These things aren't toys, I learned that.

There were reporters outside Cousin Walter's apartment everywhere. They didn't know it, but they were a help in guarding me, because my father hated reporters. Whenever they spotted him, they would run up to ask questions: "Why do you want to go back? Do you like it here? When did you decide to go?"

He knew a few words of English, and would start screaming, "Get the hell out of here! Get lost!" So when they were around, he would be sure not to come around.

The reporters were spending eighteen hours a day in front of the apartment, but there wasn't any work for them, because the agents kept them away from the entrance. This drove everyone crazy. There was one female reporter who used to try to break right through the bodyguards. She was determined to get in but she never did.

Sun-Times and *Tribune* photographers sat behind trees down the block, with telescopic lenses, trying to take a shot of me riding my bike. I couldn't talk to the reporters anyway, by order of the judge. So even if I had been able to speak good English, I couldn't have gone out there and said anything.

It was interesting seeing myself in the papers almost every day, even though I couldn't talk to the reporters. Some of them were stubborn, and although there was nothing I could do about the gag order stopping me from talking, they hung around for days. They never got any words out of me.

HOWARD TYNER,
CHICAGO TRIBUNE FOREIGN EDITOR

I was sent out on a quiet Sunday afternoon to see if I could find Michael Polovchak, the father. The *Tribune* had run a brief story the day before, but it wasn't very good. Nobody understood what was going on.

It was early afternoon, warm, sunny, a typical midwestern July afternoon. I found the house tucked away off Fullerton Avenue. I walked around behind into this courtyard and here's a guy sitting on the wooden steps up to the second floor of the little two-flat they lived in.

I walked up and asked in English for Michael. He said something like "That's me," or pointed to himself. I spoke to him in sort of half Polish, half Russian, and he spoke Ukrainian, which I mostly was able to understand. We both understood what was going on, and we stood and talked for about half an hour.

He was a bit wary at first, and I had the impression he wasn't even sure who I was, but he was still so angry and upset at what had happened the day before that he wanted to talk. I suspect that I was the first person even halfway sympathetic to him, and that helped him along.

I had spent a number of years reporting from the East bloc and felt I knew something about where he was coming from in his head. I had been stationed in Poland for United Press International in 1972–74. In 1974, my wife, Jane, and I went to London, and in the autumn of '75, we went to Moscow for UPI. I came to the *Trib* to be a general assignment reporter some months after that.

As it happened, I had spent part of the summer of 1980 in Poland on a reporting trip and had just returned to Chicago a little while before the Polovchak story began.

At the time, I was trying to convince the paper to cover ethnic things in a serious way, as a full-time beat. I wanted to link Chicago ethnic matters to the old country, to cover Poland and also cover serious Polish things in the city. I wanted to include immigration things. I wrote about that. Anything that was foreign in Chicago basically came to me. That's why I was sent out on the Polovchak story.

We sat and talked for a while, while Mikey played in the yard near us. Polovchak was pleasant, but as he talked about what he thought had happened in court the previous day, he got very agitated. He suddenly said he wanted to show me the house, that it was all nice and clean, it wasn't a place run by a drunkard, but that it was a very pleasant home.

I think he probably said, "Well, you want to come and look?"

Now very angry, he went upstairs and started stomping around. I followed him inside.

Their flat was very sparsely furnished; it looked like they had not acquired anything since they had arrived. There was a folding couch and little else. It was very simple, not much there, but it was well kept and very clean. One of the things I remember very clearly is that there were no toys around.

He started complaining, "Look at this, is this the house of a child beater? I'm not a drunk. I don't deserve this. I'm not a drunkard! Why are they taking this kid away from me? What are they doing?"

He went on like this, frustrated and angry, but he never asked me if could I help, or what I would do if I was in his situation. His wife wasn't there; she was working.

The longer I talked to him, the more I realized he didn't really know what was going on. He knew that Walter had been taken away, but he didn't really understand the whole court aspect, what had happened and why anybody could have done this. That was when he started saying, "There is no reason for you to have done this to me, because I haven't mistreated my kid."

I spent about an hour or an hour and a half and then I went back to the paper to write a story for the next day's editions about his situation and what he had to say.

FROM *CHICAGO TRIBUNE* INTERVIEW
WITH MICHAEL POLOVCHAK, JULY 21, 1980

"Am I drunkard? I am not. Do I starve my children? I do not. Have I broken any laws? I have not.

"So who is the government to take away my child? It is against the law and against the Constitution.

"It does not matter why I want to go. Who is to say why someone comes or someone goes? What I know is that this is my son.

"Does a 12-year-old boy tell his 42-year-old father what to do or does a 42-year-old father tell a 12-year-old son what to do?

"They will never give [me] papers because they know what they are doing is illegal."

HOWARD TYNER

To Polovchak, it was as if his kids really had been kidnapped. The whole legal part of it, he just didn't know what the hell had happened.

I recall asking him if he had a lawyer, and he said, no, he didn't know where he could get one. He didn't ask me where he could find one and showed no sign he had the faintest idea even where to get one.

He only said he had been in court, saw the judge, and the judge issued this order and his son was taken away, and he didn't know anything else. Period. There had been no interpreter that first day, and Polovchak himself didn't speak any English, so it was all foreign.

He specifically said he didn't know what was happening because there was no interpreter. Now whether there was no interpreter by design, or what else, I don't know.

In any event, I became rather concerned because it was clear he didn't know what was going on. I had had dealings with some of the Ukrainians in Chicago, especially Kulas. I first met Julian when I was covering a dispute along Chicago Avenue, when the Mexican and Puerto Rican neighborhoods were pushing in on the Ukrainians. Some Hispanics complained that the Ukrainians were causing trouble with them. I went out and did an interview and wrote a story about the two faces of the neighborhood out there. We met then, and have been friends since.

I don't go along with Julian's attitude on Eastern Europe and the Soviet Union, but on a number of occasions, I've spoken at Ukrainian-American functions.

Anyway, when I learned he was going to be involved, I had visions of super-anti-Communist Ukrainian émigrés collaring the kid to get him away.

At the time, there was a lot of speculation Julian was going to run for public office. I'm not sure about political motives, whether he saw this as a chance to use this for his own political purposes—which is not to say he didn't also do it out of genuine concern.

Those concerns were just part of what I was thinking. I was mostly aware that Polovchak didn't have any legal representation.

So I called the American Civil Liberties Union (ACLU), which I suppose was a breach of journalistic ethics. I thought, What the hell, whether Michael Polovchak's a good guy or a bad guy, he certainly ought to have some legal counsel. I called Jay Miller, the ACLU executive director, at home that night and said, "I don't know if you know about this case, but you might be interested."

I said I felt that I didn't know any great detail about the case, but the father didn't know what was happening, and he clearly was not going to get himself any sort of legal assistance because he didn't have the faintest idea where to go.

"You ought to call him up and see," I said.

It was probably a two-minute conversation and that was all.

Miller said, "Thank you, we'll look into it," or something like that.

Then Lois Lipton, an ACLU attorney, called me the next morning. I told her basically the same story and that was the end of it. That's how they got into it.

As a human being, I'd do it again, although probably as a manager of a newspaper, if somebody came to me and said, "Should I do this?" I probably would have said no.

I wasn't advocating a position, I was simply saying somebody ought to allow the father to argue his case as effectively as the other side was arguing for Walter. So I guess that was running through my head at the time.

The irony is, I don't think the ACLU argued it very effectively for the father. I think that the forces behind Walter on the other side were so strong, and that Michael was such an unappealing character, they couldn't win it.

As for Walter, while covering the story, I had the impression that someone had turned him. The kid had been with the cousin, and he liked driving around in the cousin's car, and that was the one real attraction.

Between going out for a McDonald's burger in Chicago or waiting in line for pirogi on Lenin Allee in Lviv, he liked it better here.

FROM JACK GOGGIN'S REPORT

Walter, the minor respondent, has a relationship with his sister, Natalie, for obvious reasons at this time, that is very close. It is however difficult to assess his relationship with his parents. His mother stated that she feels betrayed by Walter's attitude over the past three months. The mother added that during that time, Walter grew distant from both her and her husband. He did not talk to her very much, did not eat in the home very much, and in general started to part, emotionally, from his family. The time sequence of three months is interesting since that appears to be the time when Walter found out his father was planning on returning to Russia. . . .

chapter nine
GOODBYE, SOYUZ . . .

My father first mentioned the idea of emigrating to the United States a few months after Aunt Anna had gone back to America in 1976. My father said we all ought to go to America ourselves. We'd have a better life there, he said, with more opportunities. This was a real change of heart for him.

I never thought he'd want to leave—what with doing exactly as he pleased, he had as good a time as he could ever expect for himself. Although he once had spent some time in Czechoslovakia visiting relatives, he was never interested in foreign countries—much less the capitalist West where, as people said, you really had to work for a living.

However, my father wasn't in the habit of explaining himself to anyone, least of all his family. Nor were we in the habit of demanding answers from him. We went along as best we could, and that was that. We didn't know how to ask the questions.

It turned out that Natalie had thought about possibly visiting Aunt Anna when she turned eighteen, and my mother at least was interested in seeing what America looked like.

NATALIE

My aunt used to write me a lot, telling me I was her adopted daughter. Relatives always said she and I had the same kind of temperaments, so I thought that perhaps she would send me the papers, and I'd go visit her.

From the moment we got her official invitation, I was certain we would be able to leave. I just felt it, and I prepared myself for it. I had always felt different from the other kids in school anyway, and this was just one more part of that feeling. I always went my own way in school, questioning teachers and stubbornly refusing to accept their propaganda as an answer. Sometimes the teacher would get hysterical, storm out of the room. Then they'd call me down to the office to talk to me.

They would hassle me, but they couldn't convince me that Communism was right. They didn't give any basis for it and, therefore, I didn't believe it and wasn't going to go along with it. They would send me back to class, sometimes lower my grade. Even so, I joined the Young Oktobrists and even the Komsomol. You needed to be a member of these party organizations for kids or you wouldn't get a good job later on. They kept track of all this, and so there wasn't much choice. That's another reason I wanted to leave if the opportunity came.

Walter was just as headstrong. He was always a wild kid. He had his own mind and his own world. If he wanted to do something, he did it. He was real stubborn—just like me. There's no one who could stop us from anything. You could beat us, you could do anything, but if we didn't want to do it, that was it.

Walter always learned everything by himself. Ride a bike: go out by the tree, push yourself away, and pedal until you stop or hit something. He loved to ski, skate, ride a bike. He fell so many times learning these sports, he would be bruised all over. Black and blue from elbows to ankles. But until he knew how to do it, he never stopped trying.

Maybe we got some of this from my father. He was a pretty tough guy who went his own way. When the documents had to be filled out, the authorities would ask our neighbors whether they

thought we were a good family to go to the United States. We were
afraid some of them might say my father was away all the time,
never around to be a good father.

"I'll go see that guy and get him to sign the paper for us," my
dad said. "And if he doesn't, he'll get his fingers slammed in the
door!"

That's the way he talked, and he meant it. He knew how to
threaten and get his way.

WALTER

As for me, once Aunt Anastasia went back to the States, I didn't
spend a whole lot of time thinking about moving to America. I'd
gotten pretty good at looking out for myself so I wasn't in a big
hurry to head anywhere far away. In fact, it seemed about as likely
as moving to the moon. At least that's what I thought for a long
time.

But after my father began talking about it, I started thinking
about it myself and got real excited. What an adventure! It was the
kind of thing they did in storybooks—setting out for another land!
When I thought about it like that, it seemed like a terrific thing to do.

We began gathering documents for emigration. The state required forms, statements, questionnaires, releases—papers of every
description: school grades, health, graduation, debts, marriage, work
record, and so on. Much of this applied only to my parents. They
had a stack of stuff to worry about if they wanted to receive permission from the authorities.

There even had to be a form from *their* parents, saying they
allowed their children, my parents, to go, and a form from the
trade union saying they didn't owe any money. Since three of my
grandparents were dead, my parents had to come up with some
sort of document proving that. The polyclinic and the local party
committee had their own forms as well. It was all rigmarole to make
getting out twice as hard as anyone thought and a lot of people
didn't even try to apply.

We had to show the authorities we had close relatives in America,
since that was the only reason we would be allowed to leave the

Motherland. So Aunt Anastasia sent us an official invitation to come to Chicago.

We had heard scary stories about what happened to people who wanted to emigrate. After they put in their documents, they were fired from their jobs or their kids were tossed out of schools or college. The KGB made a mess of their lives. It wasn't a simple thing to try to leave the USSR.

Some people spent years waiting to leave, and there were stories that some people had ended up in jail instead. Most of them were Jews, and they were called refuseniks. But that didn't mean it couldn't happen to us if the authorities got good and mad.

My parents told us to keep our mouths shut about what we were doing for fear our teachers or someone else would catch wind of it and get mad. Then there would be nothing but trouble for us. Most people in Sambir were already afraid that some neighbor would settle scores right in the town by lying to the cops or the party. They didn't need any new excuses to make a complaint.

Plenty of people would resent it when they found out we were going to America. So even though the teachers knew as soon as my parents started collecting documents, I didn't tell any friends, just kept the thing locked inside. That wasn't hard to do.

My parents and Gran worried that we might just get into big trouble for applying to leave at all, because if Soviet officials didn't agree, we were out of luck.

Several times my parents got all the papers together, took them to the right offices in town, and were refused. Then they had to fill the forms out all over again. Each time my father was refused, he got more angry and more determined to beat them. After a while it was hard to know which he wanted more—to get to America or simply to prove to the Soviets he could get his way. That's the kind of man he is.

This went on for more than two years. With every passing month, the interest Natalie and I had in America grew. We didn't go out and find a shortwave radio to suddenly start listening to Voice of America or anything like that. It was more that the thought of leaving the USSR for good became part of our lives. We somehow *knew* it was going to happen.

My father started hunting for an angle he could work to get permission. That's when a big secret police guy named Yuri whom my father had known for some time nosed his way into the case, and the bribes to the KGB began. Yuri was supposed to be the top KGB official in Sambir, with a lot of power and influence to help out his favorites.

I don't know how my dad got connected with him but Yuri was just as greedy as anyone else my father dealt with on the black market—jeans, jackets, you name it, the KGB man wanted it. So my father got Aunt Anastasia to send American clothing, and he passed it on to Yuri, free of charge. We all figured Yuri was reselling the stuff.

Yuri got to be a privileged member of the family: he always had first pick of anything my aunt sent and he didn't even know it. Aunt Anna didn't know it, either, but my father paid big KGB bribes to get us out of Ukraine.

There was one major problem: if we got permission to leave, my grandmother would not be able to come with us. The authorities told my parents that since Aunt Anastasia was my dad's sister, and Gran was my mother's mother, they were not blood relations. That meant Gran had no right to leave the country, no matter how many times Aunt Anastasia invited her to come to Chicago.

My mother was very upset to hear this, but that's the way things are there. Since the borders are closed, there's no way you're going to take matters into your own hands and leave on your own. My mother reconciled herself to leaving Gran behind. The same thing had happened to other families that left, and we weren't any different. My parents told her they'd write and send her things, keep in touch, and that maybe someday she'd be able to come, too.

But my grandmother was hit real hard by this news. She didn't want to be left behind. As the months dragged by and she kept thinking about the separation that was coming, she got more and more upset.

She cried a lot and went to church looking for help. It wasn't up to anyone but Soviet officials, however, and they had said no.

She got real depressed and lost interest in what was going on. As I watched, she seemed to get a lot older a lot quicker. Her dark hair went gray, then white.

On Christmas 1978, Gran took to her bed. She went to the clinic for tests and they gave her a lot of medicine, but nothing helped. She got sicker and sicker, and soon she was just a bag of bones. I didn't know what was wrong with her. Natalie told me later she had cancer of the liver and could never have lived.

I got depressed myself. My grandmother was my very best friend. She had looked after me better than my own mother and father did.

After school I'd spend time at her bedside, fearing what life was going to be without her. I wanted to tell her something nice, but I felt as though there was no hope.

Gran died in February 1979. In her last words, she called for me. It was one of the saddest moments of my life. With all the confusion over whether we were going to America or not, it seemed like things were going off the tracks. When Gran was buried, my father cried like the rest of us. It was the only time I ever saw him cry.

They'd exchanged plenty of angry words over the years, but in his own way, he liked her a lot. I knew he was going to miss her. There was a lot of sadness in the family that day, but now there was even less reason for us to stay in Sambir.

About that time we got word we'd be allowed to leave. The exact departure date remained unknown, but the feeling in the family changed. Now that they had approval, my parents suddenly began to worry a lot about how they'd get along in another country, where they didn't know a word of the language or anything else.

I remember trying to imagine flying in a plane and the kind of place we'd live in. I wanted to tell my friends and the teachers at school, but we still kept quiet. We weren't out of there—*yet*.

My father was really hustling the black market and making payoffs to Yuri. One of my last trips in Sambir was a visit with my father and Uncle Dmitri to Yuri. We stopped outside a big apartment building about two blocks from the central police station.

"I've got to go see this guy Yuri about something," my father said. "You two wait outside. I don't want you in there. I don't want to make it look like there's something going on here."

We stood around for a while, and when my father came back, everything was set for us to leave. That's how much power this KGB man had.

Even after we reached America, my father continued sending clothing to Yuri. "I got to keep sending this guy the stuff he wants because I owe him a lot of money," my father said. "If I don't pay him back, he's going to come over here and get me!"

Back then, I also believed that the KGB had as much power as my father thought it did. I was sure somebody like Yuri could come after us in America.

It was usual for someone departing the Soyuz for good to leave his house to a relative. Otherwise, the government would take the place and nobody in the family would get the benefit. My father made an agreement leaving our house to Uncle Dmitri after one year. Later, when all the troubles broke out, my aunt and others in the family asked why he had set a one-year limit if he expected to stay with his family in Chicago for good. If we actually were successful in getting to America, we would never be welcomed back by Soviet authorities.

People who came back were treated by neighbors as though they were traitors—to America. I think only my father actually hung on to the idea that we would ever live again in our house once we left. A trip like ours was a one-way deal.

The funny thing is this: after my parents took little Mikey and returned to Ukraine, they never lived in that house again anyway. They might have feared the neighbors, because if those people could find an excuse, they'd probably try to poke his eyes out for what he did—leave America, and leave two kids behind, too.

When school opened on September 1, 1979, I went, even though we were close to leaving for good. I studied less than usual, which wasn't much to begin with. I kept thinking that we'd be gone soon and there'd be no school at all for me for a while.

Then one day that fall, our exit visas arrived. They set a November deadline for leaving the USSR. If we failed to go by then, the visas would expire and we'd have to start all over again. We certainly weren't going to miss *that* date.

Suddenly my parents were rushing here and there trying to get rid of the last valuable stuff in the house. The excitement picked up. There were nights when so many things were on my mind it seemed I'd never sleep.

We knew we'd go to Moscow in October to get approvals from Americans at their embassy, as well as special international Soviet passports. I didn't want to have to say goodbye to anyone at school, so I told them nothing—even the last day I was there. I was pretty sure we could slip out of town quietly, with no one knowing we had gone.

But the morning we departed, I was surprised to see a big crowd of kids gathered outside the house. Neighbors had figured out this was the day, and it seemed like three hundred kids were waving goodbye. I didn't know we had that many friends!

It got to me then—for the first time I realized I had a lot of buddies in Sambir, knew the language, and had a lot of other advantages, like packages from my American aunt . . . and I was about to go to some country I didn't know anything about and that I'd heard a lot of bad things about, too, thanks to Soviet TV! I knew I would feel lost, like I was on another planet.

Thinking all this, I suddenly didn't want to go outside. The kids were sure to ask why I hadn't told them we were leaving, and I didn't want to answer. I just waved at them out the window. Pretty soon the kids went off to school, and we got a taxi to the main train station.

It was an overnight train trip to Moscow and when we got there, we had to find a hotel, which turned out to be harder than you might think. The first clue about how tough this was going to be was right in the station. The place was jammed with people who looked like they had been living there for weeks. Boxes, bags, and suitcases were piled everywhere, kids slept on benches and adults sprawled in the aisles and corners. Crowds shuffled everywhere and waited in long lines at ticket windows.

It was no better on the streets. What crowds! Moscow is always jammed with people like us, in from the provinces, buying clothing, fresh meat, things they can't find in the countryside. They had all gotten there ahead of us.

We lugged our bags to three different hotels and were turned away at every one, supposedly because they were full. At the last place, after a woman clerk told us to get lost, my father took her aside and gave her some money. Then she said, "You've got a room now."

There were six of us: my parents, the three children, and a neighbor my father had brought along for help. If customs inspectors refused to allow us to take some valuables, like jewelry, with us, the neighbor would take the stuff back to our relatives in Sambir.

At the hotel we met another Soviet family who were heading to the States, too. The mother was a Ukrainian and the father a Greek who had got stuck in the Soyuz during the war. His wife spoke Russian and English as well as Ukrainian. We struck up a friendship with their son and daughter, who were close in age to us. We used to play cards together in our rooms, or the son and I went around the hotel fighting with Armenians we found in other rooms.

These new friends left before we did, and now live in Morton Grove, a Chicago suburb. Small world!

We spent almost three weeks in Moscow while my parents got the various additional papers they needed. Natalie and I roamed around with Mikey or went sightseeing with our parents.

It was our first time in Moscow, and since we didn't plan on coming back, we toured its famous places, like Lenin's Tomb in Red Square and the Kremlin. It seemed like every other person in Red Square was a cop.

There were long lines for Lenin's Tomb, no way to get in there, so we went into GUM, the department store across the square from it. Long lines there, too. They had a lot more variety in Moscow shops but a lot more people were trying to buy the stuff. My father found a shoe sale going on and got himself a new pair for America.

One day we all went by taxi to the American embassy. I got real scared because when we got out in front of the building, Soviet guards in gray uniforms ran up to us like big watchdogs, shouting, "*Dokumenti! Dokumenti!*"

My father pulled out the special papers we'd been given and shoved them at these guys. They kept yelling, "What are you doing here?"

My father yelled back while we huddled around him. My mother was as scared as we were.

They checked everything for about ten minutes, then waved us in: "Okay, okay, go! Go!"

We hustled through an archway in the building and then there were some American security guards there. They barely looked at us. I guess they figured that if the Soviet guards had let us through, there was no reason to check us out. We went up into the consulate rooms on the first floor. First thing I saw was a big American flag. I liked the colors and the stripes.

There were magazines in English that I couldn't read, but some had a lot of pictures, and I spent most of the time staring at them, trying to figure out what America must be like. I saw that America didn't look like Mars. In fact, it looked like a place I could live with.

When we left, the Soviet guards just kind of scowled as we walked out. Now that I'd seen the Stars and Stripes, did I feel like an American? Not yet.

After three weeks we headed for the airport. No more waiting around. This was the real thing.

At the ticket counter, my father handed over all his documents and the officials went through them with angry faces. Then we went to customs, where agents opened all the bags and dumped everything out. They even took my father and mother off to separate little rooms and strip-searched them, to see if they were trying to smuggle anything out of the country. The agents set aside a bunch of things they wouldn't let us take.

For example, we all were wearing gold rings, and Natalie and my mother had women's gold watches and gold earrings as well. The idea was to try to get as much gold to America as we could, to make things a little easier for us there, and also to have some presents for Aunt Anna and Aunt Maria. Nice idea. But the customs agents wouldn't let any of the gold through. Here's where the neighbor came in. He took the jewelry back to Uncle Dmitri in Sambir.

Next stop: Passport Control, where KGB border guards, the "Green Hats," gave our passports a real going-over. This was scary. Standing in little booths, they took our passports and just stared for ten minutes apiece at them. They finally stamped a lot of papers and shoved it all back at us.

We spent some time in a waiting room, and then boarded a bus to go to the plane. There were guards all around, like we were criminals headed for prison, or they expected spies to attack the airport. But they just looked at us as we were driven out to a big white jet with red and green stripes and got aboard. It was an Alitalia plane, not Aeroflot. It turned out we were going to Rome before America.

Since I'd never flown before it didn't make any difference to me what airline it was or where we were going. When we took off, I felt so strange I thought I would throw up.

I looked out as the land fell away; then we were in thick clouds. After a long time, we were up above them and the sun shone brightly. I felt bewilderment, fright, and joy all at the same time.

It was November 25, 1979. I was with my family and it was goodbye, Soyuz!

FROM JACK GOGGIN'S REPORT

The relationship in the home appeared to deteriorate between the parents and the children, after they became knowledgeable of the fact that their father did plan on returning with the family to Russia. At that time, living in the home was mother and father; minor respondent, Walter; his sister, Natalie; and Cousin Walter. It should be noted that the apartment on Fullerton Avenue was rented by Cousin Walter, who then invited the Polovchak family to live with him. Previously, they were, all of them, resident with Cousin Walter's parents, Mr. and Mrs. Gusiev, however the accommodations were too small. That was why Cousin Walter rented the apartment on Fullerton Avenue for himself and the Polovchak family.

In any case, after the children and Cousin Walter found out that they were to return to Russia with the parents, the situation grew tense. Both children strongly opposed returning to the Ukraine, and this upset the father. According to Natalie, he at first tried to persuade them but when they would not be persuaded, he became angry and threatening. The father later became convinced that Cousin Walter and Natalie were using their influence to convince the minor respondent, Walter, not to return to Russia with the family. At this time, he threatened both Cousin Walter and Natalie. This statement was given to this officer by Walter and Natalie, and it was at this point that Cousin Walter felt he better leave. He then rented a different apartment on the Northwest side, and it was this event that led up to him, Natalie, and young Walter moving from the home on the 14th of July.

chapter ten
HELLO, AMERICA!

Italy was real interesting but real dirty: garbage in the streets, papers and trash flying all over. I thought it was a lot dirtier than Moscow. But everyone had a car, the clothing was a lot nicer, the stores were crammed with things. The restaurants didn't mind having customers. Despite the dirt, people were living better. Explain that one, I said to myself.

We stayed in a hotel in Rome for a couple of weeks while my parents got their papers processed. They went over to the American embassy three blocks away. I remember walking into the building and this time no beefy guards in gray uniforms hassled us.

Most of the time, Natalie and I went sightseeing, just like in Moscow. We'd take a bus here, there, get off, get lost. We went to the Vatican and walked around. It was crowded but peaceful. We didn't see the pope, but there were plenty of priests around.

We got sick of eating spaghetti all the time at the hotel, so we'd find markets to buy vegetables and fruit we had seldom seen, like bananas. We ate a lot of bananas those first few weeks! We also tried out pizza. Pretty good food. Something different from Sambir.

The hotel room was very small and we were crammed in with hardly space to turn around. The bathroom and shower were down the hall, shared with others on the floor. Just like a communal apartment in the Soyuz, where you might have six families living in six rooms, with just one bathroom for everybody at the end of the apartment hall.

The weeks in Italy were the longest continuous time we were ever together as a family. It turned out this was as close as we'd ever be. My parents didn't have jobs and we spent a lot of time with each other. You could get on each other's nerves pretty easily, but it was a foreign country, and that drew us closer, regardless of who was annoyed or upset at someone else.

Toward the end, everyone seemed to be getting angry with everyone else, sometimes for no reason at all. We'd just argue and fight because we weren't used to being together that much. It was something you had to work at, and we had never done it before. The way life went for us, we never found enough time together to learn, either.

My father said he was expecting that America would be better than Italy. "Wait till you see it there," he said, but he was quiet a lot of the time in Italy, almost as though the foreign language and foreign ways scared him.

NATALIE

Leaving the Soviet Union was scary and sad. You think to yourself, I'm not going to be able to come back to see my friends ever again and my relatives are left behind for good. But you go along with it.

When we got to Rome, our first feeling was—*nothing can happen to us here!* This was such a different world. In Moscow, it had been cold and snowing—the usual weather for late November there—everybody bundled up in heavy coats, scarves, fur hats. Here, close to December, it was warm, people wore sweaters. It almost seemed as though the orange trees were blossoming!

We were given about ninety dollars apiece in Italian lire by a Catholic group that was handling our refugee case. We ran to a store and our eyes bulged. All the apples, bananas, oranges, grapefruits! We bought bunches of oranges and bananas, brought them back to the hotel and ate and ate until we all broke up laughing. How good!

It was like we had never seen oranges and bananas before, because in Ukraine it's a dollar for an orange on the black market, and even then, hard to find. Italy was like heaven: forty-five cents for a whole bag of oranges. Come and get it!

But my father was not happy. In fact, he was miserable: "Oh, I hope America is different," he'd say. He couldn't make clear what was bugging him.

Maybe my dad couldn't bring himself to talk about what was bothering him, but I think the basic reason was that it was a shock to him to be with his family twenty-four hours a day, every day of the week. In the Soyuz, he was always free to come and go as he liked. He never spent that much time with the family in Sambir.

His situation in the Soviet Union had been this: you do what you want, live on your own, never once spend an entire week with the family. Suddenly, after twenty years of marriage, you have to learn how to live with the family, no more just going your own way. That was a real shock to him.

WALTER

After three weeks in Rome, we got our papers for America. The Catholic group dropped us off at the airport and that was it for Italy.

The plane was a Pan Am 747, a giant filled with hundreds of people. Scared, we were shown to our seats. They made announcements in English and Italian. Everyone was laughing and talking and seemed to know what was going on, except the Polovchaks.

We quickly discovered we could get Pepsi for the seven-hour flight ahead. We kept going up to the galley area or drink carts and drinking Pepsi, 7-Up, whatever there was—drinking and drinking.

I had a little pair of Russian binoculars and kept looking out the window to see what we were flying over. But we were up so high, and there were so many clouds, I didn't see much. Some of the time I watched a movie, which I didn't understand, and the rest of the time I just slept.

When we landed in New York, we called Aunt Maria in Chicago

to tell her when we'd be arriving there. I was getting real excited. The journey was almost over.

And like a miracle, a few hours later we were in Chicago, surrounded at last by all our family!

Cousin Walter was there, and Aunt Anastasia from California, Aunt Maria and her husband, a cousin named Emily, the daughter of the brother of my California aunt, a friend of Cousin Walter's named George . . . it seemed like the whole place was filled with real relatives. We hugged each other, sitting and talking, waiting for the baggage to come through.

My father hadn't seen Anastasia, who now lived out in California, since 1976, nor his other sister, Maria, since 1968. We'd never met their husbands, and my cousin Walter was another person I never knew about. They all spoke good Ukrainian, including my cousin. I was surprised at this because I thought they were Americans. I watched them all and the family resemblance was there—they were all short and dark-haired, talking fast, very excitable.

We piled into cars and headed for the city. Before I knew it, we were stopping at a booth of some sort. I thought, damn! I need a passport! That's where I got my first lesson in what America was all about.

It was a toll booth for the parking lot. No passports needed. Just money! Somebody paid the toll and off we went. I thought, You can go anywhere you want here, nobody cares.

Driving into the city, there were solid streams of cars and trucks whizzing all around us, thousands of streetlights everywhere. I could see row after row of small houses sitting on quiet streets beside this big road.

My aunt asked, "Can you read the signs?"

I stared out at the big signs hanging over the road, trying to put two or three letters of the English alphabet together. "I can," I said in Ukrainian, "but you're going too fast!" We all laughed.

I couldn't really read any of the signs, but I could recognize Coca-Cola and Pepsi signs. It was only common sense, since I'd seen them in Italy and on the plane to America.

When we got off the main highway, the city seemed to stretch everywhere, and cars were parked all over the place. My father was silent during the ride into Chicago. He never said a word that I can remember.

When we got to my aunt's apartment, everyone crowded in.

They had four mattresses on the floor for us. Not much, but a good start. I crawled in. We were all so tired, it didn't make any difference what kind of beds there were.

Then I heard something that chilled me. I lay very still in the darkness. My father was talking to my mother. Through my sleep, I could hear some of it. "I'm bored . . . I'm depressed here . . . I want to go back. I can't handle it here. I just can't."

I was stunned.

"How can you say that?" my mother asked. She sounded tired and confused. "You haven't even seen anything. We only drove from the airport to the house. We haven't been anywhere. You haven't been anywhere. It's dark out there. You haven't seen anything, maybe two or three roads around here."

This was the strangest conversation I'd ever heard, and a strange way to begin our new life in the United States. I never thought my father would back out of anything. Maybe he was tired, or just doing a number on my mother. I fell asleep. I was looking forward to tomorrow.

The next day, my aunt took my father to a bank and gave him two thousand dollars to open an account. Aunt Maria gave him almost the same amount, so before he even began work, he was already up in the world.

In a few days, he got a job with relatives of Cousin Walter's stepfather, Mr. Gusiev. The men, all Ukrainians, worked in a factory, the Henry Valve Company, out in the suburbs. The relatives worked in the machine shop with lathes and drill presses, making ship's valves and other equipment.

My father couldn't speak a word of English and was earning six dollars an hour right off the bat, cleaning up factory waste and debris and oiling and cleaning the machines. The Polish and Ukrainian guys in the plant wanted to groom him as a skilled worker. One relative was a foreman and he backed the idea. Even though he had never been a machinist, my father said he had been trained in high school as a specialist.

He was surprised at how few people worked—and how hard they worked. "In the Soyuz, there would have been ten men doing the same work I do," he said. "Over here, money doesn't grow on trees!"

The other men lived in the neighborhood and took him to work in the morning and brought him home at night. They looked after him and tried to show him the ropes. Even though they knew English, they spoke Ukrainian or Polish with him to help him feel more at home.

My mother started working at St. Elizabeth's Hospital as a night janitor, at about four-fifty an hour. So from the start, they weren't doing as badly as a lot of immigrants.

While this was going on, Natalie, Mikey, and I were going to school. Natalie was in high school, but Cousin Walter took us boys to the Monroe Elementary School, where we were put into classes where no one spoke Ukrainian. This was hard, but it got me started trying to understand English. In a few days, I had some words, and my father didn't.

I loved television and everything looked good at first, but the Three Stooges were my favorites. I'd even turn the radio on, sit there, and listen to some kind of hot music—drums, guitars, trumpets. It sounded fine to me. Then my cousin would come by. "What the heck are you listening to? That's Mexican! Find something American!"

My first favorite food in America was Jell-O. I had never seen anything like it—bright colors in the bowl, and so many different kinds! That's what I survived on in the first few months in Chicago. I wouldn't eat anything else. I ate it morning, noon, night.

Then came bananas. Bananas are a real rarity in Sambir. You might see a line five blocks long waiting to get bananas in Sambir, and here they were everywhere. I ate *them* morning, noon, and night, too. Delicious!

Then came hot dogs, McDonald's, Wendy's, everything. In Ukraine, we had sausage, but we never had a bun for it. There, you eat them with bread. We had mustard and we had catsup, but without the hot-dog bun, it's not a hot dog.

I was anxious to get out and around, even though I was just like a lost kid in space. I needed something to get around the neighborhood, so Walter said, "Well, there's a bike down there—if you clean it up." That was the Bozo Circus bike. He bought cleaning stuff to remove the rust, and I scrubbed for about a month until it looked as shiny as new. It even had a little speedometer to tell how many miles you put on it. I started taking it around the home block, then another one, and every ride kept extending a block or two at a time.

I wanted to go farther, so my cousin drew me a map, down Fullerton, Diversey, Belmont, Addison, Irving Park, Milwaukee, and showed me how they all run. I followed this map all over. I learned more about how America works by just riding and watching.

One place I knew was a factory over on Pulaski and Fullerton. One day, I saw a lot of the workers parading around with signs. I thought they were doing some advertising, like a commercial. I didn't understand what was going on, so I asked my cousin about it. He explained that this was a strike—they wanted more pay, or didn't like how they were being treated by the owners. I'd never seen anything like this in the Soyuz, and neither had my father. That was one way I caught on to how people had freedom to do this, do that, speak out against the employer, or the government.

There were a lot of Mexican and Puerto Rican kids in my neighborhood. Half of them didn't speak English, either, so I fit in there. Monroe Elementary School was just a normal Chicago public school: black, white, Hispanic, Vietnamese. You name it, they were there. This was something new for me. In the Soviet Union, the only black I'd ever seen was a guy who showed up one day in the illegal market, speaking Russian. Everybody was staring at him, and I joined right in. It was interesting to see a person so different, just sitting there talking to somebody in Russian. But the Monroe kids thought I was Polish, not Ukrainian.

"Polack! Polack! Polack! Commie Polack!"

If you don't know how to speak English, you're a Polack. Life was real simple at Monroe.

You want to say, "Hey, I ain't no Polack." Something. Anything. But you don't know how. It was just aggravating. You feel like, turn around, and I'll say something real good. With my fists.

They were calling me Polack for a while, until the teacher said I was Russian or something. They handled that with no trouble: "Russian Commie!" Kids are kids, I guess.

Later, when the family split apart and I got out, people who didn't know a damn thing would call out, "Go back to Russia, you Commie!" Boy, did *they* have the wrong guy.

Mikey and I got into a few fights here and there in school. He was in first grade and one day a couple of older Puerto Rican kids took his hat and threw it in the mud. I chased them, caught one, and beat hell out of him, and motioned the rest of them to get the hell out of here.

Next thing I knew, a whole gang of Puerto Ricans landed on top of me. Where'd all these dudes come from?

I got my butt whipped, that's all. My cousin Walter went to the school and told the principal, who turned out to be a Ukrainian who helped his countrymen. They found the Puerto Rican kid, called him into the office, and he got into trouble. No one ever bothered me or Mikey from then on.

We lived on Drake Street in a crowded apartment for the first month or so. My cousin was there, his mother and stepfather, even Aunt Anna. That was four, plus five of us—nine people crammed into a two-bedroom apartment. We had mattresses spread all over the floors, and there wasn't much privacy. It wasn't so bad for the start of an adventure. Then Aunt Anastasia found an apartment for us two blocks away. We moved over there and my cousin came along. He paid the rent for my parents.

My cousin was more than a friend. He was more like a friend, a cousin, a father, guardian, and everything else together. He showed us around, bought us food, clothes, and even let us stay at his place. He did a lot more than usual cousins do.

COUSIN WALTER

We went to the airport to pick them up—January 4, 1980. To be perfectly honest, they looked awful. Like space cadets. Like immigrants coming from anyplace. Walter: wearing oversized shoes and pants, looking bewildered. Probably not any better than when I came more than a decade earlier.

Natalie opens her mouth and there are two gold teeth in front. A sixteen-year-old girl and it turns out she's got six teeth missing. Well, the mother worked in a candy factory, so that explained it.

In a sense, looking at them was like looking back in time. They were sort of like throwbacks to the Stone Age, an earlier life, the old days when there was no indoor plumbing, no cars, no dentistry . . . no freedom.

Coming here from a foreign country, you face an immediate

struggle. You don't speak any known language. You point at things. You don't know what's going on. You just try to pick up enough English to survive.

They had that far to go. They were going to live the same tough story as millions of other foreigners. There was no way to escape it. I knew this, I had faced the same journey myself, just like Walter. I didn't speak the language, I had to get going with my new life. My aunt had helped my mother and me, the same way she helped Michael Polovchak and his family. With her help, I went to grammar school and junior high, and then to Lane Tech, one of Chicago's best public high schools, and I studied English.

When I graduated in 1975, I went to IIT—Illinois Institute of Technology—and worked part time to pay the tuition. I had a job at Soldier Field for a while, and one summer I worked in the CBS newsroom collecting papers and garbage as a janitor. I was just like hundreds of other kids who go to college and work odd jobs.

I graduated in 1979 with a B.S. in computer science. Nothing extraordinary but I got a good job as a computer programmer and when Walter and his family arrived, I was in a position to help them a little. I could give them a hand with the bills. More than that, I was eager to help them understand freedom.

Freedom is a weird thing. People who come from the Soviet Union have trouble understanding freedom. In the Soviet Union, people are told, "We will take care of you. Job is provided, insurance is provided, basic necessities come from the state. We won't let you perish."

When people come from there, they don't recognize there is a difference here. They sort of stand here naked because they have to provide those things for themselves. Immigrants such as my aunt and uncle didn't have professions or anything. They worked as cleaning aides, or at best, worked in factories. Those were good jobs. If it was a skilled job, like a machine shop, that was a big deal, but most of them worked unskilled labor.

Even so, they could live ten times better than they ever had, a lot better than millions of normal people just like them who lived in the Soviet Union. They didn't have to rob, steal, cheat, lie, or do anything else illegal to have a decent material life in America. On another level, they could get together at church, they could talk at the table, say whatever they wanted. There was no fear at all.

There would be a sense of general bewilderment—they had a lot to learn. They couldn't understand what the newspapers and TV said, but even so, they soon would begin to see the wealth of information that's available here. People here weren't afraid to say something critical. It was a different type of circumstance.

It kind of comes over you—"Hey, wait a minute—I was stuck, I was limited by many, many things back there in the Soyuz and I didn't even realize it." When I look back, I see that at a certain point my eyes were opened up. I wanted that to happen for the Polovchaks, too. That's what freedom really is.

But where to begin?

From my own experience, I knew the kids would be fascinated by the gadgets, the packaging, the outsides of things. If we could get past that, I knew I could show them what lay beneath, the real life of the country.

I would come home from work, the kids had watched TV for hours, and they had questions. For example, they couldn't understand why there are commercials on TV. "Why is there an interruption?"

"If they didn't do it this way, you wouldn't know the product existed, so it's a kind of announcement. There are only so many hours in a day, and thousands and thousands of products. The company that makes the product pays the television company to get its announcement on the air. That pays for the program you've been watching for free. The more people watch a program, the more it costs the company to put out its announcement." They weren't accustomed to that.

How do you explain the whole system? How do you explain private ownership, when they don't have a conception of it? They start by thinking all the cars are made by a factory owned by one big, rich guy who sits on a hill and owns everything. Henry Ford. You explain there are shareholders—there's no one, big man who owns everything. Big men, sure . . . lots of them. But not a tiny handful, the way they were taught in the Soyuz.

Questions about everything. Why do they pick up the garbage the way they do? Why is there a landlord, and you pay him rent? Who can afford a house? Why do you pay forty cents at the highway toll booth? Who owns the road? Why is the road there? Why is there a traffic jam?

We go to Goldblatt's or Woolworth's. Why don't people steal

stuff? They would in Moscow, they'd devour this place! Why are there so many different brands of the same thing? Which one is better? Which is worse? How do you distinguish between them? Why do you buy gas from this station and not that one across the street? Why do you like this car?

Can I go west? Or south? Why is one neighborhood different from another? Should I take my bike? Or the bus? Thousands of questions, starting from scratch. They weren't stupid—they were ignorant.

In the Soviet Union, they were told that in the United States there are rich and poor and nothing in between, that the rich have everything and the poor nothing. If you hear something repeated long enough, often enough, after a while, you tend to buy into it, even if it's just a rumor. In school, in the papers, on TV, on the streets, they were told these things over and over and over again. There is wide lying in the Soviet Union.

They knew this, but there was something else that confused things in a different direction. Because of their upbringing, they didn't believe everything they had been told in the Soviet Union. In fact, to some extent, they thought that whatever they had been told by teachers, books, or propaganda about their own country was 100 percent false. But a lot of what they had heard was not 100 percent false. It had truth in it. How do you separate the scattered truths from the huge lies?

They'd been misled. Some of the misconceptions they had to deal with were misconceptions about the Soviet Union itself, not just about who invented the telephone or the airplane, but the truth about their own country. They portrayed it to themselves as ten times worse than it really was. So they had misconceptions not only about outsiders, but about themselves. They had to sort this out, to know who they themselves were.

At times they didn't know how to ask the questions but they were curious and I would explain. Hardly an evening went by that I didn't come back and we talked about whatever was on their minds, what they had seen that day. Even that was a new experience for them. The parents hardly ever talked to them at all. We learned about America on our own.

The kids liked what they saw and were eager to know more.

FROM JACK GOGGIN'S REPORT

The father's relationship with his children, at the time of this Social Investigation, has of course deteriorated from where it once may have been. During the course of our interview with the father, he was so very angry that it is difficult, if not impossible, to give a true assessment of his feelings towards his children. Periodically during the interview, his anger would boil over in an explosion of words and gestures that show a high degree of bitterness and resentment. He feels that he has been taken advantage of and that many people have made money off him, while he has received nothing and was a poor man. He feels he has been [the fall guy] in this tragedy and he resents what he feels people are saying about him. His wife, however, did state that she would return to Russia with him, that after all, she has been married to him for 18 years and will go where he goes.

Mr. Polovchak's relationship with the immediate family and with his sisters and their families appears to have deteriorated rapidly when he stated that he was going to return home to Russia with his family. None of the other members, with the possible exception of his wife, can understand why he wishes to return home after such a short period of time. It seems he was trying for over two years to leave Russia . . . and then after such a short time wishes to return and this has confused his family and their friends. Mr. Polovchak repeatedly stated that the food didn't agree with him and bothers his stomach and therefore he wanted to return. However, other family members believe his decision was made almost immediately following his arrival and they do not understand why.

---

chapter eleven
THINGS FALL APART

NATALIE

Now that Wally and I were safe at my cousin Walter's, with U.S. agents keeping guard, I had time to think over what had happened. My feelings were mixed. I was furious and sad at the same time. Everything had come unraveled. Now I saw that from the moment my family arrived in America trouble was brewing for us.

Right from the first night, my father was unhappy here and made no bones about it. While we were celebrating our arrival, he was moody and brooding, closed away from the rest of the family. He complained like a five-year-old.

I remember clearly what happened that first night. We all were tired beyond belief and lay down on the mattresses spread around the apartment floor and tried to sleep. About four in the morning, I was awakened by somebody talking loudly.

"Oh, God, it's so hard for me in this country. I can't get used to it, I don't know the language, what am I going to do?" It was my father, angry.

The next morning, we were getting ready to go out to look at the stores, maybe do some shopping. "I'm sick of shopping," he said.

"How can it be hard for you? We haven't done any!"

"I don't understand what's going on, I don't like it here where we're staying, it's all a mess."

I think he expected to vacation for a while after we reached America, then get a home and have his wife work while he explored the new situation, but it didn't work out that way. In America you need money to live and he would have to work to earn some. He didn't like that part; he had expected to have everything geared right to him.

Unlike the Soyuz, there is no black market here. This was hard for him, because he couldn't get money the easy way—manipulating people, selling clothing from America that people would pay a lot for.

Basically, it turned out that life had been easier for him there than here. He soon realized he would have to live honestly in this country, which is not what he was used to doing. He'd been corrupted by the Soviets and was too used to working around things to ever get used to life here.

My mother started out loving it here, however. She'd always worked hard in Ukraine, so it was nothing new for her to work hard here, too. She enjoyed the job at St. Elizabeth's, got to know a lot of people at the hospital, learned how to take city buses and get around. She even went to Goldblatt's and bought earrings and clothing for herself. That was easy to do, and fun. She started to change her approach to life, and I think that may have been another reason my father began pushing to return. Even though he had no use for her a lot of the time, it drove him wild that she would ever be out of his control. While she was changing, Walter and I also were changing in a different way.

When Walter and I were younger, we used to fight a lot because we were stubborn and because that was the way the family did things. He would want his way, I would want mine, and I would beat up on him, he would beat on me.

I would usually win because I was older and bigger. He would go cry in the corner, I would feel sorry for him and go over to try to make it up to him. It was our way of life in Ukraine—argue, fight, make up.

After we came to America, Wally and I calmed down a little, quit fighting so much. Maybe if you moved between Canada and the United States, you wouldn't change. But if you moved as far as we did, you'd grow up in unexpected ways.

We learned how to trust each other more. We felt like there was no one to tell on us to our teachers or anyone else, no one to come after us with threats or punishment. For the first time in our lives, we could say whatever we wanted to. This was completely new, something our parents could not understand or really share. The tension of keeping things inside began to relax. Plus, Cousin Walter had a lot of influence on us. My parents were cool and standoffish toward him, but we listened to him.

"You can talk about people openly," he said. After a while, we came to believe this. We saw that he was not afraid to say what was on his mind, so why should we be?

"I can't stand having a wimp like Carter for president," he would say.

That shocked us. In the Soyuz, you don't say those things openly about Soviet leaders. "How can you talk like that?"

"Hey, this is America," Cousin Walter said. "This isn't the Soyuz. You vote for your president in this country, and you have the right to go out there and say you don't like him. Newspapers have the same rights, too. Free speech."

The idea was so strange we resisted it. So Cousin Walter said we should read the Constitution, and we did. We read it and tried to understand it. We began to feel that we didn't have to be afraid.

For people coming from a country where the KGB is everywhere, it takes some time to get used to the fact that there are no secret police anywhere. At first we didn't believe it, but then we realized there were so many people speaking out all the time in this country, saying so many critical things that no American KGB could keep track of it—*they can't do anything to anybody.* This is freedom.

Later, my parents said Cousin Walter was brainwashing us. He wasn't. He was telling us true things about this country, and that isn't brainwashing. We learned we could be more open and talk about things among ourselves. Life began to change for us.

Cousin Walter was very generous, very giving, and more than anything, he always wanted us to learn things—how to speak English, how to get around, how to understand everything about this country. He would take us places and explain whatever we asked about. My father was jealous of him.

WALTER

I was just freaked out, asking my cousin, "Who in hell owns all those cars?" You go down the street and it's cars all over, traffic everywhere, without a break ever. Even late at night cars whiz all over the place. This was like another planet.

"Where the heck do people get all this money? Are those government cars?"

"No, people buy their own," he said, "and sometimes they have two or three cars."

I was like . . . wow. America was an amazing place. Everything was so spectacular. It's like, oh, Lord . . . there's action and stuff going on everywhere, different things to see, different places to go. I was only twelve then, and I didn't know one car from the other, but they all fascinated me.

Sometimes we went to toy stores. I saw all kinds of different toys, remote-controlled cars, that was something I never had seen in the Soyuz. And I was thinking, How do these things work?

I was at an in-between age: I wasn't into cars a lot, and I wasn't into toys. I wouldn't sit there and play with a little bundle of toys. I was too old for that. I was into soccer, repairing bikes, riding them. I was checking things out.

Natalie met some people from the Ukrainian Baptist Church, where my cousin and aunt went, and they helped us quite a bit— had a party for us, gave us some furniture to start with. Even though we were all Ukrainian Catholic, everyone in the family was going to the Baptists for a while.

My dad, who wasn't all that religious, started getting frustrated that we were going to the Baptists and began complaining about it, even though now we were free to go where we wanted because, for one thing, there were all kinds of different churches to choose from.

School that first year was hard, but I didn't feel bad about it; I was just lost. Since I couldn't understand a word, I didn't have anything to do in class. I just sat there like a dummy, looking at the kids, looking at the board, watching the teacher write stuff that made no sense to me. After a while, the teacher started telling me I must copy down what he wrote. So I looked at the board, at the pen, at the board, at the paper, made lines and curves . . . just like drawing a picture.

I was at Monroe for about half a year, then went to Gray Junior High, where I flunked one class, so they put me back a whole year. I did the seventh grade twice. It kind of bothered me because I had gotten to know the kids pretty well. They were a little more friendly than the Monroe kids. I was slowly beginning to feel in place, and then I got demoted. That's all right. I survived.

My parents didn't ever begin to speak English, which frustrated me. My mother worked with a lot of Polish people, and they spoke Polish together. My father and uncle had their good factory jobs, and the Ukrainians and Poles there never bothered with English. So he never tried to learn English. Even my mother knew a little bit more than he did, while little Mikey caught on fast, and spoke pretty good English, with hardly any accent at all. Natalie, going to high school, also was catching on.

We were way ahead of our parents in speaking the language and getting around, seeing things. When Natalie and I were talking and my parents came by and tried to listen, we'd say a word in Ukrainian, a word in English, and they would get lost. That angered my father a lot, but there wasn't much he could do about it.

Then things started to go sour. My parents started to get real mad at Cousin Walter for taking us places in his car. They wouldn't take us anywhere themselves, but they didn't want us to go anywhere with him. They started ignoring us completely. This sounds strange, but they started stockpiling food and clothing in their room in the apartment. They put a lot of money into leather jackets, jeans, scarves. I think they took most of this back to Ukraine when they left.

The food situation was the strangest. It began when my mother started cooking just enough food for my father, Mikey and herself, and none for us. She wouldn't ask us to meals. Or they would go out by themselves, take Mikey but not Natalie and me. Meanwhile, they were buying canned stuff and hiding it in the closet of their room.

I felt like maybe I was going crazy—or they were. My parents are actually hiding food from me—what the hell! How do they expect us to survive?

Some weekends my parents would take off Friday or Saturday after work, head to a campground out in western Illinois, leaving

Natalie and me behind. They would never even tell us where they were going, or leave us any money to buy food or a meal.

On the one hand, my father would leave us behind with no money or food, and on the other, he would scream at Cousin Walter for helping us. What did he want us to do, I asked myself, go off somewhere and starve to death?

After a while, the whole thing about returning to the Soyuz began. My father said straight out, "I'm going back," and for a while, no one really paid much attention to him. We were too busy learning about the new life around us. For him it was talk, talk, talk. When we started listening, everybody, from my aunts to my cousin, said, "Oh, he's not used to it here, it's the change from over there that has him down. But he'll come around after a while and be all right."

But he kept talking and talking about it. We didn't know what the heck was going on with him. Then the calls to Washington began. After a while, I think Cousin Walter asked him, "Who do you know in Washington?"

"I'm going back. Natalie can stay here or do whatever she wants, but you're coming with us," he told me.

"No way," I said. "I'm not going anywhere with you."

"Well, I don't care what you want to do or what you don't want to do!" he yelled. "You come with me and that's the end of it. I'll get the cops to tie you up, put you on the plane, and you're gone and you haven't got one damn thing to say about it!"

He was still mentally in the Soviet system. He thought that's how it works here. I was scared to death, to tell the truth. I didn't know if the police would really do what he threatened.

As for my mother, I think she had started liking America. She would say, "Oh, we'll buy a house," and really was looking forward to doing it. But when my father said he was going back, she got suckered in, followed him along the way she always did.

"Why don't you stay?" I asked her. "If he wants to go back, let him go back by himself. He'll get used to it."

"If he's unhappy, then I'm unhappy," she said. "I'm not going to live with you for the rest of my life. I'm going to live with him for the rest of my life."

She was too loyal to him. Over here, any woman would have said, "Get lost, leave, I don't care what you do."

I don't know if she ever seriously thought about telling him off.

If she had, he would have been sunk, because the Soviets wouldn't have taken him back without his family.

But she wasn't strong enough, she just gave in. She didn't care about her two older kids—us. She cared about him more than anything. She'd chase him no matter where he went.

I feel closer to her than to my father, quite a bit closer. But we're still not close. That's how people are.

Natalie wasn't getting along with them either. She was arguing and arguing and the place became a no-man's-land. My parents had one bedroom on one side, and my sister had the other bedroom. My cousin and I slept in the living-dining room. After a while, things got so bad we didn't even say hi to each other.

Poor little Mikey was in between. He could cross the border zone between my parents' part of the place and ours, run back and forth and play while my parents kept a close eye on him. If we wanted to take him somewhere, they automatically said no.

Mikey would beg or just tell them he wanted to come. It didn't matter; they never said yes. They were afraid they were going to lose him, too.

Finally, one day I turned to my cousin, real quiet, and had a talk with him. I told him I wanted to stay here. He said, "If you really want to stay, I'll help you as best I can. But I don't want you to stay here and then a week later start crying that you want to go back."

I knew I would never change my mind but I was scared to death that they might send me back by law. I tried to look forward, the way I always do. I told myself, I'm going to stay here no matter what—if I have to sleep in the sewers, hide somewhere, I'm going to stay. I was positive. I had a positive attitude, but so what? I was still scared to death. Then my father started to get really furious with my cousin. He threatened to beat him up, or said things like "Maybe something's going to happen when you're asleep." He'd carry knives around the apartment, tear through the place, slamming doors. After enough of this, my cousin got out.

COUSIN WALTER

I signed Walter up at a YMCA for swimming, and got him enrolled in school. The first apartment was so crowded, what with my mother, stepfather, and the Polovchak family, that we found another apartment a few blocks away. The Polovchaks moved there and I went with them to help out.

I slept on the couch and figured, Okay, I'll pay the rent, the electricity, the basics for three months, so they can get going. Then I'll turn it over to them. But for now, get them headed in the right direction until the kids speak a little English. Then they can help out the parents, and little by little, they all will be getting their bearings.

My mother was four blocks away and she brought things over to help. Other people in the neighborhood tried to help them feel welcome.

I talked to them, said, Look, it's going to be hard for you at first. For me, I told them, it doesn't matter if I break stones in the street, as long as the kids have some future. That's what you came here for and I want to help. They accepted the idea of it, but it got under Michael's skin pretty quick.

Meanwhile, Wally was changing fast. The bike, the language, the independence. In Ukraine, he was sort of in the mud. Now, it was amazing to watch what was happening. He was very curious. If he saw something in the store, he'd have to paw it. He was getting into everything, going absolutely wild with what he found around him. It was strange to him, but he began to get used to the strangeness, even like it, while the parents never made much of an adjustment. I think that was probably because the father wasn't going to open his mind to the possibility. He wanted to get back home.

I started taking them to my church, the Baptist church, and the parents came a few times, but it was not to their liking. When the kids continued to come with me, the parents got upset but they couldn't really interfere.

Some of my friends came over to the apartment and would show Natalie things she didn't know—about how women here take care of themselves, things like that. The children weren't completely isolated; this was not like the Soyuz anymore.

Natalie and Walter's relationship was changing, too. When they first arrived, they were like cats and dogs, beating up on each other. The whole family was sort of messed up. Half the time I spent with them in the evening was to sit quietly and explain: "You can't throw things at each other and beat up on each other anymore." Then he'd make a face at her, she'd punch him, and they'd be back at it. At times, I had to sit between them. "If I catch you fighting, I'm going to break both your necks!"

She was older and still stronger then. "You don't hit him!" I'd tell her. Fine. Progress. Then he would take advantage, start pummeling her, and she'd beat heck out of him. If I was in the house, they were fine. As soon as I walked out, they were scrapping.

Then the parents took off by themselves a few weekends, just left the kids without saying a word. They had to look out for each other; they couldn't go their separate ways, as they had done in Sambir. As time passed, the fisticuffs came to an end. I felt they'd really changed. Other things were happening. The situation in the whole family deteriorated. The parents almost drew a line down the apartment floor. They didn't want anything to do with me or their own daughter and son. They only wanted Mikey.

About June, Michael started indirectly threatening me. He wasn't going to challenge me directly, but behind my back, he began complaining that I was exerting too much influence over his children. He said derogatory things about me to my mother, and she called me, upset.

His resentment rose against the box he had gotten himself into and he directed his anger at me. He got braver. It was a big mess. "Things could happen," he would say and scowl at me. The atmosphere got heavier and heavier between us.

He made a bad error along the way, however. One day he simply removed Natalie's Soviet passport from her things in the apartment. When she discovered it was gone, she went wild. I told her that since it was a Soviet passport and she had no intention of ever using it again, it was worthless and foolish of him to take it—it didn't change his situation at all.

That wasn't the point. She was infuriated because he had taken a possession of hers, and she was determined to get it back. There

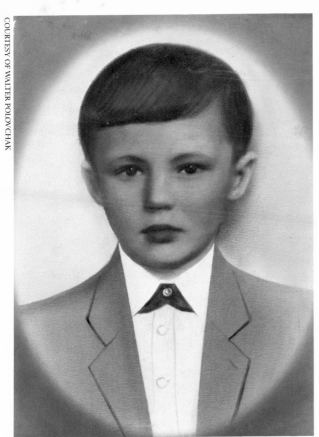

Ukrainian youngster: Walter at age seven in a drawing commissioned by his parents.

The Polovchak family: father Michael, mother Anna, sister Natalie, and Walter in the mid-seventies.

Media star: Walter's appearances on television helped sway public opinion his way.

Safe haven: Walter peeks out of Cousin Walter's northwest side home after his defection.

Federal protection: Surrounded by government security agents, Walter arrives at court.

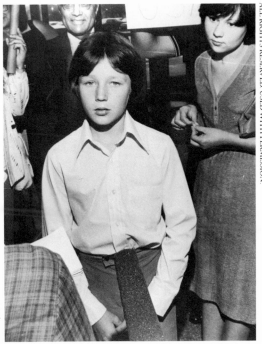

News friend: WMAQ-TV's Paul Hogan, who first interviewed Walter and covered his case.

The first hearing: Walter and Natalie (*right*) enter juvenile court for the first of endless court sessions over their right to stay in America.

Tearful parents: Michael, Anna, Michael Jr., and their lawyer, Richard Mandell (*right*), after appellate hearing on Walter's status as a ward of the State of Illinois.

On the bench: Judge Joseph C. Mooney, the Juvenile Court of Cook County judge who ruled on Walter's case. (*Left*)   The new family: sister Natalie, Aunt Anastasia, and Cousin Walter. (*Right*)

New kid on the block: As legal proceedings dragged on, Walter managed to become one of the boys with his new neighbors.

Back in the USSR: Walter's parents startled lawyers from all sides when they abruptly postponed their fight by returning to the Soviet Union. They walk Michael Jr. through a field near Moscow's airport. By 1983, Anna had given birth to a fourth child, Julia.

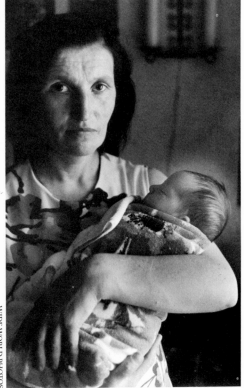

Congressional witness: Walter confers with his lawyer, Julian Kulas, at a 1982 House hearing held to examine the reasons he stayed in the United States.

At last, freedom: On October 8, 1985, Walter turned eighteen and was promptly sworn in as a U.S. citizen in a ceremony at the Capitol.

The celebration: After the swearing-in, Walter cuts the cake with, from left, Senator Dixon, Senator D'Amato, and Julian Kulas.

America's party: His new status was a national event as Walter made numerous television appearances, including this one with Sarah Purcell and McLean Stevenson in Los Angeles.

More milestones: Walter and Natalie celebrating his swearing-in as a registered voter by Illinois governor Jim Thompson.

was hell to pay in the family and there was no hope of a reconciliation between daughter and father.

By mid-June, I had no doubt that Polovchak was going back.
There were letters from the Soviet Embassy, he was filling out
papers, I could see the phone bill, and I believed that by the end
of the summer, he would be gone—with Walter and as much of
the family as he could control. At that point, what do you do?

If they had been a close family, it probably never would have
happened. But they never had been close. There was a problem
long before I got dragged into it. At the point at which he wanted
to go back and the kids didn't, they couldn't do anything to help
themselves out of the deadlock. They had no experience dealing
with such deep differences of opinion.

It all started to get super-serious. I knew enough to predict what
would happen: one day, they'd just vanish. One day, I said to
myself, there'll be plane tickets, an escort, and they'll be gone.
Period.

It was a time of real tension anyway. The United States was
going to boycott the 1980 Summer Olympics in Moscow, and the
Soviets were furious. America and half the world had condemned
the invasion of Afghanistan, and the Soviets were applauding the
Iranian revolutionaries who had taken American diplomats hostage
in Tehran. With all that going on, this situation just didn't feel
comfortable to me.

Around this time, I talked to Natalie about her intentions. She
declared, "I'm not going back." If there had ever been any lingering
doubt in her mind, the passport incident fixed that for good.

Walter was a different problem. "You understand what's going
on," I said to him. "Your father wants to take you back because
he says he can't go back without you." He nodded. He understood
everything very clearly.

When his parents tried to talk him into going, he became more
hostile. He would withdraw and say nothing.

One day, I remember, Walter, Natalie, and I were sitting quietly
when I turned to him and said, "At a certain point, you have to
make a decision. You might be only twelve years old, but you've
got to do some serious thinking.

"I can't tell you to go or not to go. You've got to decide for
yourself. Your father is going. That's a fact. He has started making

out the papers. Your question is: do you want to go or stay here?

"Don't decide now. Think about it a day or two, and when you've decided, you'd better tell me or your sister what you're going to do.

"If you decide you're going back, you're going back. There's nothing wrong with that. They're your parents and they want you to go back. But if you decide you don't want to go back, if I'm going to try to help you and see what we can do, you can't change your mind back and forth. Either one way or the other, you have to decide what *you* want to do."

At this point, Natalie said, "Well, I'm not going back, even if I have to die."

"Walter," I said, "you have to decide."

About two days later, Walter came to me. "I'm staying here with my sister. Here in America, and I'm not going back."

That settled it and made things very dangerous, because I knew I now had to find a way to save him from being forced to go back.

A few days later, I had my first conversation with Mr. Kulas. I took his advice and moved out as soon as I could find an apartment and the kids joined me.

I think that by rushing to the Soviet embassy, Michael Polovchak simply underestimated the shrewdness of the diplomats. He wanted to leave the United States by himself, leave the millstones of his family behind, but the diplomats had power over him because he needed their approval to get back to Ukraine. He was not dealing with a bunch of *kolhospnyky*, collective-farm workers. They really sort of wrapped him in a blanket, and he didn't know what was happening. The more he talked to them, the more they humored him. I think it got further and further along, and he fell in deeper and deeper. They wanted the whole thing—not just some lovesick two-timer, but a big propaganda coup by getting the whole family back.

Then it backfired on them and they wound up in worse shape than if they had just let him come back without the kids and wife.

In the father's case, I think the kids were an accident of nature. I don't think he had any great love for the family. He was not a family man, period.

As for the mother, I think she tried in the circumstances to do the best, but she was working and she was always worried, in a chronic depression. She was more in love with her husband than her kids.

When the grandmother died, the kids didn't really know what to do or where they belonged. They saw the father about once every week or so, and they already had figured him out as a wheeler-dealer who was going to take advantage of them if the opportunity arose. He did it with the packages sent from the sisters in America and he would do it whenever he could score. They had him scouted out.

There was a basic mistrust. If they had had time after the grand-mother died, they might have figured out a way to live in the situation. But then, for whatever reasons, he brought them to Amer-ica. They were going to give him some credit for it, and see what would happen. When he reneged and tried to change direction, they just weren't going to buy it.

When the children fled the apartment and came to stay with me, I was certain they'd done it on their own. I could not have lived with myself if I'd felt I had coerced them.

WALTER

The television crews, reporters, and federal agents might have scared off my father, but they attracted lots of other people who were curious at what was going on, including a kid who became my closest friend.

During the first or second day of the bodyguards, this kid emerged from a crowd of spectators. I was feeling like an exhibit or something when he started talking to me. We began throwing a ball around and next thing I knew, Mike Marian was my best friend. I wasn't stuck by myself anymore. We'd pick a time and he'd come around every day.

The guards wouldn't let me go anywhere far, but Mike was like one of them. He would tell me, "Don't stay out too late at night. You don't know where those KGB guys are."

He's English and Hungarian. He and his sister, Tracy, came by and played Speak and Spell with me. It taught English words and was the first game my cousin bought for us after we moved in with him. Mike and Tracy wouldn't talk, just point to things. It was weird, like dummies communicating, but it worked.

People used to pick on me because I couldn't speak English well. He would tell them, "Why don't you get off the kid's back?" He helped me pronounce words. Like I couldn't say "gloves." I'd say "glubs," or "blubs." Stuff like that.

I felt pretty sure that with friends like Cousin Walter and Mike around, I could get by okay in America without my parents. As far as I was concerrned, they were free to go back to Ukraine anytime they wanted.

FROM JACK GOGGIN'S REPORT

EMOTIONAL HEALTH and INTELLIGENCE:
Walter recently was promoted from the sixth to the seventh grade
at the Monroe School and while it is impossible to make an accurate
assessment, he does appear to be of at least normal intelligence.
Emotionally, although again the time was too brief to make any
kind of an accurate assessment, the boy does appear to be emotionally mature and does not appear to have any difficulties with
his emotional health.

PEER and SOCIAL RELATIONSHIPS and ACTIVITIES:
For the most part, Walter has been associating with his relatives
and their friends in the Ukrainian community. However, according
to his mother and sister, he did make a few friends from the school
and they would stop by periodically to visit and play with the
minor respondent. However, due to the language difficulties, most
of Walter's social time was spent with his family and their friends.

RECOMMENDATION and PLAN:
At this time, the living conditions in the Polovchak home are unsta-
ble, therefore, in the best interest of the minor, it is recommended
that he temporarily stay with relatives, while under the custody of
DCFS, until the tension and anger that is present in the home can
be reduced. It is further recommended that supervised visits be
arranged between parents and children in the expectation that family love will assert itself and overcome the gulf that currently exists
between parents and children.

P.O. Goggin,
North Division
July 28, 1980

chapter twelve
OUTSIDERS ENTER

JAY MILLER,
EXECUTIVE DIRECTOR, ILLINOIS ACLU

I saw a story in the *Tribune* that Sunday, July 20, indicating the Polovchaks hadn't been represented by any legal counsel at the emergency Family Court hearing. They had nobody to interpret for them, and after the hearing, they were saying, "You're taking our kids away . . . what's going on?"

After reading the story, I got calls from ACLU people who had read accounts of the hearing. They were concerned about the obvious denial of due process to the parents and asked if we were doing anything, for it sounded outrageous.

I talked with Howie Tyner at the *Trib*. He related he had been out to see the parents, and said he thought the parents had been treated very badly.

At the time, the ACLU office in Chicago had a vacancy in its top law post, that of legal director. We were waiting for the arrival of Harvey Grossman, who would soon come up from East St. Louis, Illinois, to fill it, but he had not started yet. However, the next day I met with Lois Lipton, a staff attorney, and after talking to Tyner, we decided we ought to try to reach the family. It wasn't easy.

They spoke no English, and the first thing we needed was

an interpreter. I said to myself, They'll never understand what the
ACLU is. They'll think we are part of the CIA.

Getting an interpreter proved difficult, because the Ukrainian
community in Chicago was hostile to the parents because they were
considering returning to the Soviet Union. It was difficult, but
through an ACLU board member's son, who was married to a
Ukrainian, we got somebody who could speak Ukrainian to call
the parents.

We reached the father by telephone and told him we had read
what had happened, and suggested that maybe we could help. They
were very suspicious. Later, the parents got very impatient with
us, but in the beginning, it took some time for him to get back to
us. It might have been a week or so, and we had the feeling he
sought advice from others before he decided to have us represent
him.

Even at that preliminary point, it was clear that the U.S. government and local authorities were acting in a very discriminatory
way against the family—strictly for political reasons. It was because
Kulas had clout with the Immigration and Naturalization Service.
Beyond that, it wasn't just the Immigration Service making that
kind of decision—these decisions were made at a fairly high level
in the federal government.

So for us, it was an easy case to consider taking. We had no
problem with the policy on this. The policy was clear: the family's
lost a right, lost custody of their children without a proper hearing,
without real legal representation, without them understanding the
process.

Press accounts made clear that the twelve-year-old, Walter, had
run away just once, so there was no danger to himself or the community. Yet Kulas and the state used a MINS petition to get him
away from the parents' custody. But the kid didn't fit the MINS
profile, which is that of a constant runaway who is a danger to the
community and/or himself. For a twelve-year-old to make that kind
of decision and be backed up by our government, which normally
would never permit a child of that age to do such a thing—it was
no good.

And that can be distinguished from a decision of a kid who wants
to have an abortion and the parents object. Depending on the age
of the child, custody is a state that lasts many years and covers
many elements of life and decisions, such as residence, schooling,

discipline, character building, religion, and so on. In contrast, I consider abortion a relatively minor surgical procedure, an act that, depending on circumstances, is likely to involve a very short period of time—a matter of days—in the life of a child. The decision to carry a baby has far greater future implications and is rarely done without parental consent. But in custody cases, we've never argued that way because it's something a family works out for itself. The government really should not become involved unless it becomes an impossible situation. The Polovchak case certainly had not shown itself to be that yet. Perhaps somewhere down the line, but at the early stage, it was not that intractable a problem.

Instead, there had been a total breakdown of due process for political reasons, and the family had lost custody of the children without a hearing. The only mitigating circumstance was that one of the kids was a seventeen-year-old, close to eighteen, the year for legal majority and legally independent from parents.

Then for Immigration to throw an order on this kid and put bodyguards on him like he was a young Kennedy about to be kidnapped—incredible! It was such a phony. We really felt outraged by the action the government took.

Even if the judge had ordered counseling, something like "Walter, you belong with your parents, but you've got problems, so let's have a counselor come in, let's work it out in this family," it would have been unusual under the circumstances, but acceptable to anyone concerned about questions of due process. If the judge and the state had done almost anything other than what they did, it would have been something we could have lived with.

The issue of where the parents sought to take the kid—to Ukraine— was irrelevant to us. You could say that this kind of government intervention wasn't going to happen to a Swede, and so to that degree, it was relevant. But not to us.

It's like saying in Skokie, Illinois, where in a famous case we represented the right of Nazis to have a parade if they wanted one, the government was going to stop the Jewish War Veterans from marching. Nobody's politically hostile to the Jewish War Veterans. Under our system, everyone is equal under the law, so the basic issue is the same—if we had a responsibility to represent the Nazis' parade in Skokie, to ensure that everyone remains equal under the law, then we had the same responsibility for the Polovchaks—if they wanted us.

Here you had two federal agencies, State and Immigration, participating for political reasons in a conspiracy to deprive people of their rights. The political reasons were that the parents were Soviet citizens and they weren't happy here.

Now, it's true that as Walter grew older, and the separation continued, it was a more difficult case for us. But by that time, we were all pretty much convinced, certainly by the last year of the case, that whatever worked out with the family, there really would be no coercion. It just wasn't going to be possible.

As it developed, this case took up a lot of our effort legally, and much of this turned into a public relations fight as well. We were doing it with one hand tied behind our backs, because there were a lot of things we could not say about the case, about why the parents felt the way they did, why Walter might be acting the way he was, and the fact that the Ukrainian community basically used it as a propaganda thing. We knew it was just PR and that the legal issues never caught up with the propaganda. People's memories of this case always will be that this is Cold War, East vs. West, Soviet Union vs. America, freedom vs. totalitarianism. Nothing will remain that this was about the American system of due process and political discrimination, or the intervention of high-level government, working with local government, to deprive people of their rights. Very little, if any, of this will remain.

Nobody's ever going to think of the Polovchak case in that way. It will be characterized instead as this little Soviet boy who loves the American way of life, and who wants to stay free against his stupid or misguided parents who don't understand a good thing when they see it and who want to go back to the terrible Soviet Union. That this little boy's choice is for America. And, finally, he was such a traitor to his country—although that's good for *our* country—that if he went back he would have to suffer terribly.

Yet here is our government forcing Salvadorans to go back home who come to ask for political asylum, who claim that they might be killed if they are sent back. Originally, when folks said Walter would be hurt if he returned, that was pretty silly. It's true that after it went on for some months, it was not likely the Soviets would give him favored citizen status. His application to join the Communist Party, if he wanted to join, would not have been looked on with great favor and he would not have gone to Moscow State University, but Walter couldn't have gotten into Moscow State

University anyway, no matter what, just as he would not have the scores to get into a top American university.

I don't know what else might have happened, but certainly nothing compared to what could happen to a Salvadoran returning to El Salvador. And yet we deny political asylum to these people and give it to Walter Polovchak.

EXCERPTS, INTAKE SUMMARY,
DEPARTMENT OF CHILDREN AND FAMILY SERVICES

CASEWORKER:	Virginia Egem
CHILDREN:	Natalie Polovchak B.D. 1/9/63 Walter Polovchak, B.D. 10/3/67
PARENTS:	Anna & Michael Polovchak
SIBLING:	Michael Polovchak B.D. 10/26/74
ID#S:	Parents XO67-81-00 Natalie XO67-81-02 Walter XO67-81-01

IMMEDIATE ACTION TAKEN BY DCFS:

Date, Time & Receipt of Case: July 22, 1980

This case came to the attention of DCFS on a referral from State's Attorney Terry Maganzini. Walter Polovchak was in court on a MINS petition. Request was being made for DCFS to have custody and Walter to be placed with his cousin Walter Polowczak who resides at 5025 W. Byron.

At this point, the case was continued until July 30 because the parents could not speak English and they had no counsel. T.C. [temporary custody] was awarded and after a day with INS officials Walter was placed with his cousin.

July 22, 10:00—On Tuesday, July 22, case was assigned to me as parents' address was in our geographic boundaries. A conference was called. Present were Ellyce Roitman W.A. Intake Sup.; Lilly Vensen, Public Information; and myself. The first visit was arranged through the Immigration Office (Ted Georgetti). He radioed to his investigators that we were coming out to the home to interview Walter, Natalie, and Cousin Walter. Joe Turlow, N.A. Intake, came along (as an interpreter). (Russian-speaking, not Ukrainian.)

July 22, 11:00—Home visit to 5025 W. Byron. Present at interview—Lilly Vensen, John Valtiera, Joe Turlow, Walter and Natalie Polovchak, cousin Walter Polowczak and myself.

Since the children do not speak very good English, we used Mr. Turlow and Mr. Polowczak as interpreters. The children were hesitant to answer any questions without their attorney, Mr. Julian Kulas, being present. I asked them if they had run away from their parents and they said yes. At this point Walter stated that he did not have to say why he did not want to return to the Ukraine or to his parents, only that he wished to stay here in America. They were under the impression that we were reporters and after this was explained they appeared more relaxed, but still evasive.

I explained DCFS procedures re court, custody, placement, possible reuniting with parents, support services, and explained that I would be their caseworker. I left name and number with Cousin Walter and told him that I would contact Mr. Kulas.

July 22, 3:00—Called Mr. Kulas, who informed me that the Soviet embassy would be sending a representative to meet with the parents but at this point, he did not think that the representative would be contacting the children. Mr. Kulas requested that Walter be allowed to appear on *Good Morning America*, which I denied until I could speak to Mary Ellen Nash, G.A.L., at court and Ellyce Roitman. (Denied permission.)

July 23, 4:30—Phone Mr. Kulas to explain that the children should have as little contact as possible with the media and before granting interviews he would contact Lilly Vensen and Mary Ellen Nash.

July 25, 1:00—Attempted to visit Mr. & Mrs. Polovchak at 3624 W. Fullerton with Joe Turlow to act as interpreter. They were home, but would not speak to us. . . .

JAY MILLER

On July 28, after much discussion among ourselves and with the Polovchaks, the ACLU of Illinois announced we would represent the parents because their rights were violated in the temporary custody proceeding of July 19, and because they were subjected to disparate treatment because of their Soviet citizenship and their wish to return to their homeland.

At a press conference, we announced that we would ask that the MINS delinquency petition be dismissed in Juvenile Court, and the boy be returned immediately to his parents.

My guess, and it's only a guess, is that the Soviets wanted us to lose. They weren't very cooperative, didn't make things very easy, but we also discovered things I hadn't known before. For instance, a large number of people come here from the East bloc and the Soviet Union, turn around, and go back. They're not all that enamored of the United States, some for the same reasons that Walter's father talked about.

Regardless, if I'm right that the Soviets were not so interested in an ACLU victory, it would be to their advantage to say something like, "See what happens in the United States? You think that's a great democracy over there, but see what can happen to your kids?"

One of the things that outraged me was that our government could act so stupidly. Then the right wing got in it on Walter's side. This is the same right wing that generally defends the rights of parents and hates the ACLU because we defend the rights of children. In the beginning, in fact, we got a lot of right-wing support. It was amazing. Until they realized they were making a political mistake, a lot of them wrote to support us, and even some right-wing columnists were in support: "Look at the ACLU supporting parents."

On the other hand, we had some ACLU people nationally who only saw what the media were characterizing as this kid who was making an independent decision to leave his parents. They didn't learn anything of what had happened at the court hearing, none of the denial of due process, or that the government was making strictly political decisions. They saw this strictly as a kid who wanted freedom. So there were some ACLU people who initially were very upset with us, until they learned more.

It was always so much easier to characterize Walter the way the media characterized him. It's more dramatic that way, and you don't need to talk about the niceties or complexities of due process.

Finally, the parents never had the capability of snatching Walter. From everything we could figure out, the Soviet embassy was never that interested in the case. These were just insignificant people to the Soviet embassy until this happened.

When all was said and done, the result for us was that we won every major legal decision—win, win, win for the ACLU. Yet Walter won, too. The only people who lost were the parents.

STATEMENT, SOVIET EMBASSY,
WASHINGTON, D.C., JULY 22, 1980

[U.S. authorities' actions in the Polovchak case] may lead to far-reaching consequences with respect to Soviet-American relations, but also with respect to international rule of law as a whole. It appears that no foreign family with minor children present in the U.S. is guaranteed against the possibility that the same thing will happen to it. The indignity visited on the Polovchak family constitutes a flagrant violation of all principles of morality and humanism.

It appears that any minor foreign child can, with the knowledge and encouragement of American authorities, be subjected to corrupting influence by gifts and promises so as to use him for exerting pressure and harassment on his parents. It should be clear to every educated and unbiased person that a 12-year-old child doesn't understand what political asylum is.

The Embassy totally shares Michael Polovchak's belief that the 12-year-old has been kidnapped and put in the custody of strangers.

JULIAN KULAS

When the ACLU learned of the case, they simply entered. The *Tribune*, reporting their press conference, quoted Jay Miller as saying that the parents had "gone into court proceedings without an attorney, without an interpreter, and as we found out, without even understanding the proceedings [in] which they were involved."

This was a distortion of what had happened. While the parents hadn't had a lawyer specifically representing them, the judge fully understood what was at issue and had taken no actions that infringed on the parents' rights. He had judicially recognized the need for time to sort things out, and balancing the children's request with the parents' rights, had simply separated the two camps temporarily in hopes that reconciliation could occur.

We'll never know, but when the ACLU leaped in, that act alone could have ruined for good any possibility the children and the parents had of negotiating a settlement of their dispute, which was what I had hoped for from the very beginning. No one will ever know what the ACLU attorneys told their new clients about the prospects of a total victory—custody of the children and unimpeded departure from the United States. They certainly proclaimed the rightness of their position in a way that would have encouraged many clients to believe they could not lose.

Beyond that, Michael Polovchak knew very well what the hearing was all about. The only thing that had bothered him was that he hadn't gotten anything out of it—either the child or a piece of paper. For a man used to getting his own way the shock must have been enormous.

As for Walter's asylum request, Michael not only was informed of that ahead of time, but he completely agreed with it because he was sure it would enable him to sever Walter from his Soviet passport.

(Later, the ACLU would say that the parents' destination—the Soviet Union—was not important to the ACLU. If that really was true, why did the ACLU lawyers take such strong exception to the U.S. grant of asylum to the child?)

The *Tribune* quoted ACLU lawyer Lois Lipton as saying, "I don't think we can presume that a twelve-year-old knows what is best for him, and then summarily withdraw his parents' rights. It's one thing to say a child has rights and another to say that he can act like an adult."

I found these sanctimonious remarks hard to accept. The ACLU is notorious for taking the side of minor children against their parents in abortion and other kinds of cases.

Mrs. Lipton also expressed concern for Michael Polovchak, telling the reporters that he was "terribly distraught. He wants his son. He loves his son. He thinks they should be together. He would be devastated if he lost his son."

That was patently untrue, as the father had made clear to me the first afternoon we talked in the Shakespeare District police station. Besides, Sarah Snyder of the *Chicago Sun-Times*, who covered the story in the opening weeks, reported three days before Mrs. Lipton's remarks that the Soviet embassy thought Michael Polovchak might go home alone.

She quoted Prilepski, the Soviet diplomat, as telling her, "He is considering going back by himself—just him—and hoping the family comes later. But he has not decided yet. . . . We have no objection. I said it was up to him how to come back. . . . All [family] members are free to choose—to go alone or alternately. . . ."

Reading Lipton's remarks, I couldn't help thinking, What about the distraught children? They had been forced to flee their own house out of fear of their father and his plan to go back to the USSR. The ACLU, supposedly so solicitous of children, ignored the children's feelings in this case.

This was not my first confrontation with the ACLU. I had been the leader of an ethnic coalition when the Nazis were going to march in Skokie years before Polovchak ever came up. The ACLU was siding with the Nazis' right to a parade. I disagreed with their position, and the non-Jewish ethnic communities also found abhorrent the idea of Nazis walking around with swastikas on their arms and on banners, trying to stir up memories that we'd like to forget.

In the Polovchak case, how do you justify that in most situations, the ACLU said, Well, we're really on the side of Walter because we really feel he ought to be with his parents, and therefore, we are acting in his best interests. Initially, I thought they'd be much more reasonable than they turned out to be.

I can easily say I'm not a contributor to the ACLU. I would say an organization like that would serve a useful purpose provided it wouldn't go to the left as far as it does.

For example, why doesn't the ACLU undertake the defense of human rights in the Soviet Union? Take one individual and take his case to the World Court. Not once have you seen that.

One thing is certain: it was not PR for me. I've handled many other significant cases, including the Bakke reverse-discrimination case, so publicity was not my aim. I have more legal work than I can do and, in fact, the bank which I direct requires much time.

My commitment was because of my personal experience and my knowledge from Europe. I was definitely convinced that if Walter went back, he would never see freedom again. That was the bottom line. There were attempts to paint this as a hard-line, right-wing ideological position, as though my and others' experience with to-talitarian rule somehow disqualified us from defending Walter.

It always upset me that the ACLU challenged Walter's right to act in his own interest, even though he showed the same maturity that the ACLU would have exercised if it had been confronted by the same set of circumstances that he faced—forced return to a totalitarian society.

While the ACLU took the position that Walter's destination was not a matter of anyone's concern, the flat truth was that an orga-nization such as the ACLU does not even have the right to exist in the Soviet Union—where Walter would surely have been taken if the ACLU had prevailed.

From the very beginning, Jay Miller belittled Walter's intellect, in effect arguing the acceptability of politically punitive measures based on intellectual attainments.

I said to myself, If I don't do everything I can to help this young man I will have a guilty feeling the rest of my life.

This was a commitment not only to Walter as a person, but to a principle I knew was at stake: I wanted to demonstrate to the people of the United States what the Soviet Union is all about.

From a legal point of view, I was hoping we would get the chance to put the Soviet Union itself on trial. That was the whole thing. I wanted to put on witnesses like Pyotr Vins, the Ukrainian Baptist, Valentyn Moroz, the Ukrainian nationalist, and Alexander Sol-zhenitsyn, the Nobel Prize novelist, and lawyer Ilya Kamenetsky, and others. But it didn't happen.

I kept telling my colleague Henry Holzer, of the Brooklyn Law School, "It's not Walter who's on trial; it's the Soviet system we've got to put on the stand. If we could have their own people testifying at a trial like this, revealing what life is like over there, it could help everybody."

I tell Ukrainian émigrés, "It's your job to speak about it, explain it, because people who live here don't understand. They haven't lived there or sampled it. You've sampled it and you appreciate what life is like here, and we need people to speak about life there. By doing this, we can bring about change."

FROM VIRGINIA EGEM'S DCFS INTAKE SUMMARY

July 30, 9:30—Court hearing. After all-day testimony and debate T.C. [temporary custody] still stands on Walter.
12:00—Attempted to speak to Mr. & Mrs. Polovchak. . . . Parents' attorney [Richard] Lifshitz and [Richard] Mandel [representing the ACLU] would not let me talk to parents. They stated there was no time, even though I explained that Juvenile Court is not an adversary proceeding and that DCFS clients are parents as well as children.

chapter thirteen

THE JULY 30 HEARING

I didn't understand a lot of the legal work and back-and-forth that went on in the hearings that lay ahead. Much of it was technical, way over the head of a regular American kid of twelve, much less an immigrant with hardly any English.

Even though it all got translated, the delays and arguments made it rough for me to follow. Many of the lawyers' complicated fights seemed to have nothing to do with whether I was going to have to go back with my parents.

One thing was clear from the start of the July 30 hearing: my parents' lawyers weren't out to do me any good. They wanted me back with my mother and father—period.

Mr. Kulas and the lawyers with him wanted to show that Natalie and I were out of control and needed to be supervised by the state. The lawyers for my parents argued the opposite. Judge Mooney had to sit through it all and he got a little short-tempered from time to time. To tell the truth, I didn't blame him. I only hoped he didn't blame *me*.

There were a number of interpreters, one telling my parents what was going on, another giving Natalie and me the blow-by-blow. We also had Cousin Walter, who was nearly as good as Mr. Kulas at keeping things straight in both languages.

Judge Mooney, a bald guy in glasses, kept pretty good

track of things. To me, he was someone who would protect me.

My father was so mad at me all the time now that all he could do was stare or scowl at me. Mostly, he didn't look at me and I tried not to look at him, either. There was nothing to see except his anger. Natalie was just as mad back at him.

Sometimes he interrupted the action by breaking in with his own comments, and when my mother testified, he fidgeted a lot, as if he wanted to tell her what to say. He didn't want her to speak up on her own.

Lots of reporters milled around outside the courtroom and came inside to keep notes on what everyone said. They tried to get me to talk outside, but the same rules applied as before: I couldn't say anything to anyone.

JULIAN KULAS

The July 30 hearing was the formal start of the struggle that stretched over the next six years. I realized the ACLU had little interest in reconciliation or compromise. It wanted to send the child back to Ukraine with the parents.

That first day, I had a reminder of the strong Soviet interest in the case: Pyotr Prilepski was sitting right there in the audience. He told reporters he was only an interested observer, but his presence should have made it perfectly clear to everyone that the Soviets were more than just "interested."

Seeing him there, I wondered what must be going through the minds of the Polovchaks, especially Anna, the mother. There was no way they could feel anything but trepidation in the presence of this Soviet official. Such worries would overcome any requirements to tell the truth under oath.

The ACLU lawyers were Richard Lifshitz, Richard Mandel, and Lois Lipton. They got right to their attack, announcing within moments of the start of the hearing that they had filed legal motions challenging Judge Mooney's temporary order putting the children in Cousin Walter's custody. They passed these documents to us and asked for a quick decision by the judge.

Their motions declared that the MINS petition violated the parents' rights to privacy, family sanctity, and due process under the

U.S. Constitution, and claimed the Illinois law setting up the MINS provisions was unconstitutional "in that it presumes that the child beyond control of his parents is automatically in need of supervision."

Further, they said the law "unreasonably interferes with the liberty of parents to direct the upbringing of children, including the parents' right to *determine the residence of said child. . . .*"

The petitions argued that while the parents had been present at the emergency hearing two weeks before, "their physical presence did not amount to actual presence since they were not informed of the nature of the proceedings, nor provided with an impartial interpreter nor represented by an attorney" as the law required. They said no proper evidence was presented to support a temporary custody order, and said the parents had been barred from giving testimony.

The parents had signed affidavits swearing the same thing. Prilepsky also had signed accompanying forms saying he had accurately translated the affidavits into Ukrainian for the parents.

Rick Michaels, the young assistant Cook County prosecutor who was representing Walter with me, asked that the ACLU provide written legal citations supporting its petitions for dismissal. But Mandel demanded a decision immediately. He said he believed the MINS law was "unconstitutional on its face."

This riled Judge Mooney. "What? Would you let them run at large and self-destruct?" he demanded of Mandel. "We hear five thousand of these cases a year in this court. We try to reach out and help. The whole thrust of the Juvenile Court Act is contrary to what you are telling me. . . . This is the law of Illinois. . . . You are implicating that we are taking a twelve-year-old away from [his] parents without just cause. . . ."

Mandel pressed his point, but the judge said his interest was "to determine what is in the best interest of the minors and their parents. The idea is to return them to their parents as quickly as possible. Now, I don't want this hearing to be delayed by a lot of irrelevant argument."

"I don't believe the United States Constitution considers it irrelevant . . ." Mandel retorted.

Mary Ellen Nash, a lawyer who was serving as the children's legal guardian by order of the court, told the judge that the children admitted to being uncontrollable and were ready to put themselves in state custody.

"I have fully advised [them], explained their constitutional rights, in the Ukrainian language," I told Mooney. "The minors are aware of the consequences of their admission. They understand their rights against self-incrimination, their right to being confronted by their accuser, their right to a trial.

"Further, they have been advised that one of the consequences could be separation from their parents until the age of twenty-one. They have made these admissions voluntarily and without coercion."

While Lifshitz entered an objection to all this, Mooney called the children forward.

"Natalie, do you understand the English language?"

"I understand, but don't speak well," she said.

"Walter?"

"A little bit."

Mooney then had the interpreter tell the family, "Usually in cases like this we place the minor under the supervision of the court and assign a probation officer to work with the minor and the family with the view toward . . . preserving and strengthening the minor's ties, minor-family ties. . . .

"In other words, the whole purpose of these proceedings is to eventually reunite the mother and father, son and daughter. . . . The order I enter is temporary just to see if we can work things out. Tell Natalie and Walter the idea I have in mind is [to] eventually return them to their parents. If at all possible. . . ."

The interpreter repeated this to the children, and then reported to Mooney their answer: "Your Honor, the answer is if they will not be returned to Ukraine."

At this point, Anna Polovchak, the meek, quiet, dominated wife, struggled to say something.

"Your Honor, my client, Mrs. Polovchak, through the interpreter just said she would like to ask five questions of the court to help her understand what is going on," Mandel said. The reporters stirred with interest.

"I do not know what these questions are," said Mandel. "Normally, I would not make such a request at this time, but because of the language problem, I'm asking your discretion. . . .

"Although I do not think the questions she has to ask are relevant in an orderly proceeding, I would appreciate it if you would try to answer them.

"Some you may not be able to answer because they are ultimate facts, but let her ask her questions, get an answer . . . basically because of her unfamiliarity [with court proceedings]."

Mooney peered at Mrs. Polovchak. "Mother, you have some questions you want to ask me?"

Mrs. Polovchak stood and read from a sheet of paper while the interpreter translated.

"I would like to know who really—who tells the children what to do?" she began, her face taut with emotion and the strain of addressing a judge for the first time in her life.

"The children the parents, or the parents the children? Who really conducts the life? The parents of the children, or the children of the parents? And, I know that the children would be promised golden mountains, all kinds of gifts."

I couldn't let this falsehood stand. I lodged an immediate objection.

"My son was promised golden mountains, and he was brought closer to them and now he wants to conduct the life of the parents," she persisted through the interpreter.

Mooney looked at her quizzically. "Well, the law as I read it to you shows that . . . the emphasis is on the family life, the children and the parents living together in peace, in freedom, and the ideal expressed in our Constitution, the pursuit of happiness."

"I still have other questions to ask here. The second question—"

"It is not a question as I see it of the children dictating to the parents or the parents dictating to the children," the judge broke in tartly.

"The children have certain responsibilities to the parents, obedience and many things that are within reach," the judge continued. "Such as emptying the garbage, maybe doing the dishes every once in a while. But primarily, going to school. And the parents have the responsibility of the care, custody, control, and the discipline of the children. So, that's the law here."

I tried to keep the discussion from going much further, but the judge was very curious about her views. "This whole case is unusual because of the translation problem," he said. "That's why I'm allowing a great deal of latitude here."

"Are we parents . . . [to] lose our rights because of the six months we are staying in the United States?"

"You are not losing any rights at all," replied the judge. "What you have done, though, [is] you and your husband called the police when the boy ran away. Right? And then the police found the boy. They acted at your request. Nobody invaded your privacy. So, then the boy was found; and he was brought to court because we felt there was a problem that may need to be resolved. That is it."

Mrs. Polovchak was undeterred. "Is there a law in the Constitution of the United States [that says] a twelve-year-old boy can be taken away from his parents and be influenced so the parents have no custody over him? Is there such a law?"

"No, not in the Constitution," said the judge. "However, under the Juvenile Court Act under the State of Illinois, there is the act under which we operate. Under certain circumstances, a child may be taken from the custody of his parents if it is in the best interest of the child."

Since Prilepski was there, I doubted she had dreamed up these questions all by herself and I said as much.

"I wrote the question in my house all by myself," Mrs. Polovchak replied. "There was no lawyer to help me with the question."

"What is the next question?" Mooney asked.

"Whoever destroyed the family of Polovchak?" demanded Mrs. Polovchak. "I want the court to show it."

"Well, as far as the family of Polovchak, it hasn't been destroyed," said the judge. "We have taken your son and put him in temporary custody pending this hearing."

"Who took apart the family of the Polovchaks? Who should be responsible?"

"I think you started when you called the police reporting your son missing," said the judge, his patience beginning to fray.

"Our child was taken away and was absent for a whole week, so naturally we had to turn to the police to help us to get back the child," Mrs. Polovchak argued.

"So, the police turned to the court for help," retorted Mooney. "They thought you needed more help—period. That's what this is all about. . . . All right, Mrs. Polovchak, is that the last question now?"

"I have another one. I have a very big question. The sister of my husband talked my son in by buying, giving many, many, lots, promises of different type. She is the one who lives in California. And the son of another sister who lives in the—"

"I object to this type of testimony," I broke in. "This is not a question. I think she is testifying before the court, before the proceedings have commenced. She is making statements of fact, Your Honor. I don't think this is appropriate at this time. She asked to pose five questions to the court. And I see these are statements."

"You finished, Mother?" the judge inquired.

"No—"

"—Well . . ."

"They belong to the Baptist—" Mrs. Polovchak resumed her attack on Cousin Walter.

". . . She is talking about in-laws and relations," said Mooney. "Now, that has nothing—Would you tell her that has nothing to do with the matter before me right now . . ."

"I was talking about it only because these were the people who took my son away from us," said the mother. "Walter Polowczak took him away, and this is why I wanted to talk about it. He is a cousin."

"I see," said Mooney. "I think that this takes care of all of your questions, and I hope you feel a little better now. I hope I answered everything I could."

"Thank you very much for it," said the mother.

A little later, Anna Polovchak took the witness stand herself and was questioned by assistant prosecutor, Rick Michaels, representing the children on behalf of the state.

Michaels focused on the events of July 14, when she had come home from work to find Walter and Natalie moving out.

"I asked Walter, 'Walter, where are you going?' " Mrs. Polovchak testified under oath.

At that moment, she looked bewildered, lost, and hurt, probably just as she must have the day her son walked out. As I watched this, I felt a twinge of deepest regret at what had happened to her. Walter, who was sitting next to me, looked at her calmly. His face was serene, offering no clues as to his feelings.

" 'Let your heart not hurt because of the fact that I'm leaving,' " she recalled Walter telling her. " 'I'm going away. It is my business. It is my business.' "

"Did you give your son permission to leave and not stay in the family apartment?" Michaels asked.

"I didn't tell him anything," Mrs. Polovchak answered. "I only asked him, 'Where are you going, son?' After that, they left."

I felt unhappiness, disappointment. Maybe even frustration. Mrs. Polovchak's inertia grated on me; I found myself upset by her inability to deal with her husband. Even assuming that *someone* must make decisions in a family, and there needs to be a semblance of agreement, this woman continued to be so neutral even though there was plenty of reason to believe she would just as soon have stayed here.

Next, Rick Michaels called Cousin Walter to the witness stand. After a few questions, the cousin began recounting the events leading up to the children's flight.

"She asked me where was I taking little Walter. I responded that I was not taking him anyplace. If he was going, he was going with his sister. That I was not tying him down. I was not forcing him to go to do anything. . . .

"She asked Walter where he was going. He responded something to the extent he was going where he wanted to go. . . . That was the basic response. I just walked away. . . . Little Walter said that he was going where he wanted to go, and I left so I did not hear if anything else happened."

"Was there any way that Mrs. Polovchak could have stopped you . . . from taking Walter's things physically?"

"If her son didn't want to go, I would have never attempted to take him," Cousin Walter replied.

Under questioning by the ACLU's Mandel, Cousin Walter said he had not called the parents to inform them that their children had come to stay with him in his new apartment. "You never contacted them?"

"No, I did not."

He also said he had taken the children to the Baptist church, despite the parents' objections.

"Did you talk to him at all [about] where he would sleep if he moved in with you?"

"No, I did not."

"Did you tell him he could move in if he wanted to?"

"I did not tell him. . . . I do not recall making that statement to him."

"Did you tell him he should ask his parents if he wanted to move in with you?"

"No, I didn't."

"Did you tell him to talk to his parents if he wanted to move in with you?"

"I told him many times before that he should always talk to his parents."

"Did you talk to his parents then?"

"I did not."

"Why didn't you?"

"I had no reason to."

"You had no reason to talk to the parents of a twelve-year old you were having move in with you?"

"I was moving by myself."

"You had Walter with you, didn't you?"

"He came with me, right."

"Did you have any reason to talk to his parents Sunday night to tell them that Walter, twelve years old, was sleeping over at your house?"

"No, I did not feel so."

"Did you feel you could control Walter? Is that why—"

"I—No. I don't."

"Do you want Walter to live with you?"

"That is an irrelevant question," Cousin Walter replied determinedly.

"I asked you, do you want Walter to live with you?"

RICK MICHAELS: Objection, Your Honor. Irrelevant.

RICHARD MANDEL: His motive in taking Walter.

MICHAELS: . . . I object. All this is irrelevant. If counsel would learn what his case is about he might be better in his cross-examination.

MANDEL: Thank you, Mr. Michaels.

JUDGE MOONEY: Objection is sustained.

MICHAELS: Thank you, Your Honor.

At this point, the first serious legal clash of the hearing erupted. It began when the ACLU attorney expanded on his reasons for questioning Cousin Walter so closely. In an unexpected twist that I regretted then and still regret, I found myself forced to oppose the ACLU, which wanted to explore the question of destination— it began asking Cousin Walter about "Russia."

I had already agreed with the state's attorneys, whose support I needed to get a positive MINS ruling, that we would try to keep the issues in the case narrowly focused on matters usually addressed in a Juvenile Court hearing, avoiding the larger political dimension that my Ukrainian heart ached to explore.

MANDEL: How do you feel about Russia?

MARY ELLEN NASH: Objection, Your Honor.

KULAS: Objection, Your Honor.

MANDEL: Your Honor, I think it is relevant.

MICHAELS: We have a petition of a Minor in Need of Supervision, runaway. I don't know what his motives are. They are certainly not relevant to this proceeding. Now, I ask you—I don't [ask] what you know about Wisconsin. We are talking about cases over here [in America]. Let's keep this in line. A minor ran away from home.

MANDEL: It is not a case—

MICHAELS: How do you feel about Chicago?

MANDEL: Did he run away or was he taken away? Was he influenced away? The minor's statement to the police, which is in their file, says he left because "I do not want to go back to the Ukraine." Does this twelve-year-old have that right? That is the issue before this court to decide.

MICHAELS: I object to all counsel—it is totally irrelevant.

MANDEL: I would object to this man interrupting.

KULAS: What counsel is trying to do is make this a political case. This is not a political case. It is a MINS.

SHERIFF: Order in the courtroom, please! One at a time.

KULAS: He should address himself to the issues of the MINS case.

MICHAELS: This is far beyond the scope of the examination of this counsel. Counsel wants to call witnesses to prove something else.

RONALD MAIMONAS (assistant state's attorney): I object to this line of questioning of this witness at this time. It is irrelevant, beyond the scope of our direct examination.

MANDEL: The police report states the reason the boy doesn't want to go to the Ukraine. This is certainly relevant to whether he has run away. . . . We are not talking about Wisconsin; we are not talking about Wilmette or Park Forest or any other place. We are talking about whether the influences—whether this boy is a Minor in Need of Supervision, whether this twelve-year-old can determine where he wants to live and if he can, well, that means he is beyond the control of his parents and a Minor in Need of Supervision.

I think it is perfectly relevant that the person who physically took this boy out of the apartment, that we get his views on the Ukraine and the returning to the Ukraine and whether he had any influence.

MICHAELS: First of all, counsel misstated the evidence quite clearly. This witness stated quite clearly he at no time, in any way, shape or form took the minor respondent from his home. He said the minor respondent came with him. He is very adamant about that. Counsel is attempting to misstate the evidence once again. He does that very well. I think the Court understands the evidence.

Secondly, in terms of the other issue about [motivation] of people to whether these people are runaways or not in fact their motive is totally unimportant. In fact, if they have motives, that's more evidence that in fact they're beyond the control of their parents. They have left home for a reason. That is what this is about.

In the scope of examination, Walter Polowczak, the witness on the stand, is quite clear, consistent about events that took place, certain times, certain dates. He has testified to that. And his feelings about the Ukraine or any other place on this earth are totally irrelevant, way beyond the scope of that direct examination. If counsel has another issue that he wishes to bring in, he will have adequate opportunity to do that. . . . It is beyond the scope of this examination at this time.

JUDGE MOONEY: After listening to this extensive argument, perhaps we can put this whole matter into context. . . . The question [is] whether or not it would be in the best interest of the children to return them to their parents' custody, control, dismiss these petitions and with the understanding that immediately they would be taken with parents back to their home from whence they came, in the Ukraine.

Now . . . the matter before me is to determine whether or not these are in fact Minors in Need of Supervision under the Juvenile Court Act.

So, at this point in time, any matter having to do with the best interest and the children returning to Ukraine will be reserved until the dispositional hearing unless there is a finding at the adjudicatory hearing. Your objection is sustained. Move with your entire case.

MANDEL: For the record, I would like to point out why I believe it is relevant.

MAIMONAS: Objection. Haven't we had enough on this? If counsel wants to make an offer of proof, this is a sidebar [bench conference]. If counsel has true legal points to make, let him make it to the court, not to the stands. So, let him make a sidebar.

MOONEY: As a matter of fact, I was hopeful you would finish with this.

MANDEL: I'm just about done.

MOONEY: Finish. I ruled on this question, and I think it is entirely improper for you to reopen the matter once the court has ruled. I told you, the Ukraine or living conditions . . . in their former home is relevant at the dispositional hearing, do you understand me?"

MANDEL: I understand that it is relevant at the disposition. I also believe it is relevant—

MOONEY: I said it is not! Now, are you the judge, or am I?

MANDEL: I—

MOONEY: If you are the judge, then perhaps we will recess, assign it to you to do the hearing.

MANDEL: All I want to do [is] put on the record why I believe—

MOONEY: On the record.

MANDEL: I believe it is relevant at this point to see if he is beyond control, if in fact . . . this man influenced the children not to go to live with their parents because of his prejudice against the Soviet Union and the Ukraine. . . . Then, I think it is relevant in determining if this child . . . whether the twelve-year-old is beyond the control under these circumstances. Not on disposition, but on the findings that are before you. Is he beyond the control? That's why I believe it is relevant.

MOONEY: You made your record, now proceed.

MANDEL: That's all the questions.

MOONEY: Very well . . .

Natalie was put on the witness stand next. Rick Michaels asked her about the days just before she and her brother left their parents.

NATALIE: I recall that my cousin left the house that evening [Saturday, July 12, two days before Walter left]. But me and my brother were home sleeping that night. And my father was screaming and arguing, why are we taking away his son.

In the morning my cousin asked me, "You want to go church?"
I said, "Yes, I want to go up to the church."

Sunday morning, my cousin called me up, asking would I like
to go to the church. I said yes, and my brother also said he would
like to go to church.

My cousin came . . . stopped the car one block away. I left with
my brother and went there and went with him to church.

MICHAELS: Now, at that time did you tell your brother Walter
that he had to go to church with you?

A: No, I didn't tell him. I just asked him does he like to go,
if he likes it is fine. He can go.

Q: [Did] Walter [go] to church with you and Cousin Walter
that day?

A: Yes.

Q: After church, what if anything [did] you then do?

A: After that I told my cousin I would like to go home, and
he took me home to the address on Fullerton Avenue. . . . I did
want to go home and pick up belongings.

Q: What happened when you went into the house . . . ?

A: I came home and started gathering my belongings. My
father disconnected the telephone. And I started walking down.
He walked right after me. I got on the bus and he followed me and
said, "I want back my son, give back my son to me."

Q: . . . Where did you spend the night?

A: I slept in the . . . new apartment.

Q: Now, did your parents . . . give you permission at any
time to go and live other than [in] their house?

A: My parents never told me so other otherwise.

JULIAN KULAS: Yes or no. Was that the answer?

MOONEY: Would you repeat that question?

KULAS: Your Honor, the answer was, "My parents never told
me yes or no." The translation was given—I think it should reflect
the proper translation.

MICHAELS: Did you have any conversation with your brother
about whether or not he would stay at 5025 West Byron?

NATALIE: I asked him at that time, "What do you want to do?
If you want, you can go back to your parents. If you want, you
can stay here. I'm not going to chase you out. It is your life and
you have to decide."

Q: Did Walter say anything to you at that time?

A: "I don't want to go and live with my parents. I want to live with you."

MANDEL (cross-examination): You said that . . . on several occasions your parents said that you were not to take Walter with you? Is that what you said?

A: Yes, I did.

Q: When did these conversations start?

A: At the time when they started applying or making out documents to the Soviet Union and that means—

Q: In other words, when they decided to go back to the Ukraine these conversations started? Is that what you're saying?

A: Yes.

Q: And how often did these conversations take place?

A: Maybe once or twice, because I didn't want to go back to Ukraine. So, they didn't start working on documents for me.

Q: Was your cousin Walter present when these conversations took place?

A: Not the cousin, but my brother. With me and my brother. Not with cousin.

Q: Cousin wasn't there?

A: No.

Q: When did your cousin Walter first tell you that he rented an apartment?

A: When my father started to threaten that he will kill us, he decided to take an apartment, and I decided to go with him.

MANDEL: Your Honor, I move the answer be stricken as nonresponsive.

MICHAELS: Exactly responsive. It is perfectly responsive to the question.

MANDEL: The question was, "When did your cousin Walter first tell you that he was renting an apartment?" That can be answered with a date, not a speech.

MICHAELS: Objection.

MOONEY: It could be a date or occasion. She recited the occasion. Objection overruled.

MICHAELS: Thank you.

MANDEL: When did you and your cousin start talking to Walter about whether Walter would leave or not?

NATALIE: I told my brother Walter that Sunday morning [while] going to church that I'm not coming back to this place because of the conditions. I cannot stand it any longer. And at that point he says he is going with me and if I wouldn't take him, he will come on the bus to join me. . . .

. . . [On Saturday night] my father was slamming windows and screaming and screaming that he wants to kill my cousin. This was the reason why my cousin left the place and went to the new apartment.

MANDEL: When did you first tell brother Walter that you were moving into Cousin Walter's apartment?

A: When my cousin Walter told me he is moving, and I said, "I'm moving with you." My brother said, "I'm moving, too." And I said, "You can't do that. You have to go back to your parents and live with them." And he answered, "No, I want to live or go where you are going."

Q: Did Cousin Walter tell you that if you decided to stay, he would help you stay?

A: No, he didn't tell me that 'cause I hadn't decided anyway to stay here. Maybe he did say it to my brother.

Q: . . . Did brother Walter say that Cousin Walter told him that Cousin Walter would help brother Walter stay?

A: Yes, my brother told me that.

KULAS: Natalie, you testified that on Sunday when you left home, your father followed you. . . . Did he say anything to you?

A: Yes, he swear to me. He was saying ugly words to me . . . whore.

KULAS: Did [Cousin Walter] ever ask you to leave your home?

A: No, he didn't. I asked him. I told him that I wanted to leave.

Q: Did he make any promises to you?

A: No.

Q: Did he give you any gifts?

A: Gifts, no.

Walter was brought to the stand next and sworn in. He looked fresh and interested, a nice contrast to the grim and tense faces elsewhere in the courtroom.

In a series of brief answers, the child sketched in the events of the weekend he and Natalie fled the parents' house. From my point of view, the key parts of his testimony centered on his astonishing determination to leave his parents. Here is some of the testimony, with Rick Michaels asking the questions.

Q: Did [Natalie] ever tell you to leave your parents' home without their permission?

WALTER: No.

Q: Did your cousin Walter ever tell you to leave your parents' home without their permission?

A: No.

Q: When did you decide to stay at the apartment on Byron Street?

A: I don't recall that.

Q: Did Walter or Natalie tell you you should stay on Byron Street that night?

A: No.

Q: Did your cousin or Natalie tell you that you should go home to your parents' house?

A: They didn't chase me out, but they told me if I want to, I can.

Q: Do you remember going to your parents' apartment on [July 14]?

A: Yes.

Q: For what purpose did you go . . . ?

A: I went to get my things.

Q: Did you see your mother in the apartment that day?

A: At the very end, when I had packed already my belongings.

Q: Did she say anything to you . . . ?

A: Yes. She asked me where I am going. . . . and I answered, she should not be concerned about it.

MANDEL (cross-examination): Walter, when was the first time you talked to your cousin Walter about staying in the United States and not going back to the Ukraine with your mother and father?

A: I don't recall.

Q: Was it a long time ago or just recently?

A: No, just recently. Maybe two months ago.

Q: And what did your cousin say to you when you talked to him about that?

A: No, he didn't say anything about it. He just asked if we want to go back.

Q: And what did you say to your cousin?

A: In the beginning, I didn't tell him anything, because I didn't really know myself if I wanted to or I don't want to.

Q: When you decided that you did not want to, when you first told your cousin that, what did he say to you?

A: He didn't say anything.

Q: Did [he] ever tell you that if you decided to stay, he would help you?

A: No, he didn't try to convince me to stay, but he said if I do, he will help us.

Q: Did your aunt in California talk to you about staying?

A: No, she didn't talk to me about it.

Q: Did [Cousin] Walter's mother talk to you about it?

A: No. She said I have to go back.

Q: But Cousin Walter said you did not have to go back, is that right?

A: No, he didn't say anything about it.

Q: But he said that if you stayed, he would help you, is that it?

A: No. He didn't try to convince us to stay, but he said if I do, or he said, if we do, he will help us. . . . If we want to, he should help us.

Q: Now, is the reason you don't want to be returned with your parents now because you don't want to go back to the Ukraine, is that the reason?

A: That is the reason, and also is, I don't care about it. They don't talk to me. . . .

Q: Your father was unhappy here after he left the Ukraine, isn't that right?

A: Yes.

Q: Now, on Monday the 14th, when you went back to the house to get your clothes, did you tell your cousin Walter you wanted to take your clothes before you went back to the house?

A: Yes.

Q: And Walter knew that you were planning on going back to his apartment with him that day, didn't he?

A: No. He said—No, he didn't order us. He said that if we want to come back, we can come.

Q: When did you tell [Cousin Walter] you wanted to go with him?

A: Sometime Friday.

Q: Friday before he left?

A: I told him Friday that I wanted to go with him.

Q: That was before your cousin even moved out of the apartment, is that right?

A: My father said that he would kill him.

Q: Is it true that you first told Cousin Walter that you were going to move in with him on the Friday before you moved?

A: Yes.

Q: Now, if your cousin Walter said you could not move with him, would you have stayed at home?

A: I would have gone anyway somewhere.

Q: Where would you have gone?

A: I would have gone somewhere.

Q: When your mother asked where you were going, and you said, "It's not your concern," had you talked to Cousin Walter about that, about what you were to tell your mother if she came home?

A: No.

Q: Did anyone tell you not to tell your mother or father where you were after you moved to [Cousin] Walter's house?

A: No.

Q: Did your cousin tell you to call your mother and father to say where you were?

A: He said if we wanted, we can call. He didn't prevent us from calling.

KULAS: Walter, you know that you are in court and you are to tell the truth?

A: Yes.

Q: And are you telling the truth?

A: Yes, I do tell the truth.

Q: Walter, did you have a conversation with your father about going back to Ukraine?

A: Yes.

Q: What, if anything, did your father tell you?

A: He said I have to go back and I said I don't want to.

Q: Did he tell you what would happen if you didn't go back?

A: No.

Q: Walter, why did you run away from home?

A: My parents don't like me, because they don't talk to me, and I was afraid they would take me back to Ukraine.

Q: Walter, did your father ever tell you that he would call the police if you didn't go?

A: I was told by my father that if I didn't go, he would pay the police a hundred dollars, they would tie me up, put me on the airplane, and send me back.

Q: Walter, did your cousin Walter promise you anything?

A: No.

Q: Did he make any offer of gifts to you?

A: No.

MANDEL (re-cross-examination): Walter, didn't your cousin promise you that if you left, you could live with him?

A: No.

Q: Did he say that you could?

A: No. He said, "If you don't want to go, I'll take you to my place."

KULAS (re-cross-examination): Walter, if the judge felt that this matter should be completed here today, and we would all go home, would you go back to your parents?

MANDEL: I object. That's irrelevant.

MAIMONAS: That's the issue.

MOONEY: I will allow the answer.

KULAS: If the judge decided [to] conclude this case today, would [you] go home today?

A: No.

Walter was the last witness for the day. The hearing then turned to arguments between the ACLU's Mandel for the parents and Rick Michaels and me for Walter.

Mandel opened by sharpening his attack on Cousin Walter. ". . . There is no question that Cousin Walter and his two friends took a twelve-year-old out of his house without the parents' consent . . . [perpetrating] what is basically a quasi-criminal act. . . . When you take custody from someone, you're violating certain rights, and it is the same as a criminal act, in effect. . . .

". . . The major issue is it's uncontroverted that [Cousin] Walter subverted Walter Jr., to break up the family, tear down the fundamental rights of the family to stay as a unit. . . . If there is any[one] beyond control, it is Cousin Walter [who] has aided and abetted the violation of this act. There is no question about it. . . .

"If this child is beyond the control, he is beyond the control with the aid of Cousin Walter, and Cousin Walter is committing an act in violation of the laws of Illinois in aiding and abetting this child. If this child is violating the law, Walter is the man who is violating other laws even more.

". . . That is why it is ludicrous for the state to say this [boy] is beyond control. He is beyond control solely because Cousin Walter has permitted him to leave the home, provided the apartment for him. . . . And, no, he may not have urged little Walter to stay, but saying constantly, 'If you decide on your own to stay, come to me.' That in effect is what [Cousin] Walter is saying, and that is not beyond control, even wearing the blinkers the state wants us to wear."

Mandel continued his attack. "The issue is the son does not want to go back to the Ukraine, therefore he is beyond the control of his parents. That is the issue before this court. And the Supreme Court of the United States on similar issues on many occasions [has] said that parents have certain rights, and the state has no right to interfere.

"Does the state have a right to ever interfere with the parents whether they want to move to Alabama . . . South Africa . . . or to the Ukraine . . . ?

". . . The state is trying to say we are going to deprive the parents of their rights to this child without proving anything wrong with the parents. . . ."

Mandel summed up: ". . . Walter's rights are being violated as much as the family's if he is declared a Minor in Need of Supervision."

Michaels called this argument "ridiculous," reviewed the testimony, and concluded, "The court heard evidence from four witnesses, including one of the clients of Mr. Mandel, that Walter Polovchak on his own two legs, carrying his own belongings, walked out of that home. . . . That's the situation that the police found when mother called and told them her son had left home without her permission and he could be found someplace else. And that's the situation we are asking this court to intervene in. . . ."

Michaels argued that if the court dismissed the MINS petition, "it means that Walter and Natalie are free to go anywhere they want, without the supervision or custody of any person. . . . If this court finds, as Mr. Mandel is urging, that it has no jurisdictional basis, it can't order anything. It can't order them to go with [Cousin] Walter. It can't order them to go home with the judge. You can't order them to do anything, unless there is a basis for it. . . .

"[Walter and Natalie] have testified [that] on July 19, their intentions were never to return to that home. That clearly says they are not within the control of their parents . . .

"And, therefore, the state comes to this court and says, 'Well, we've got a seventeen-year-old girl. We've got a twelve-year-old boy. And we've got two responsible adults without the authority to direct their activity.' And the law says that's not the right idea. Our law says that's not the right idea. Our law says we are supposed to have somebody who directs the activity of twelve-year-olds and seventeen-year-olds in the state. We don't like the idea of them just being on the street. Unfortunately, that happens to many. . . .

". . . This court better get involved, because we don't like them showing up in [Chicago serial murderer] John Wayne Gacey's crawl space. We want to make sure they're given the proper protection and custody that a child needs. . . .

"If sending these children home to their parents only means they're going to run away again, then the court's intervention is not going to accomplish the basic purpose and policy of the act, which says we're here to provide adequate care and guidance to children in this state. . . .

"We found these two young people out of control of their parents, and all we are asking this court to do is to find simply and clearly, because all of the evidence is consistent in this case. There's not one bit of inconsistency in this case. . . ."

I finished the arguments for the children, pointing out that "it was the parents [who] brought these children to these United States, and it took many months, in fact, about two years of efforts to bring them to this country. And these children, in great anticipation to live in the United States, have decided that they would rather stay in the United States than go back, because they have acquired many new friends, and they certainly know the difference between life in a free society and life in a restricted society. . . .

"Your Honor, children are not chattel. Parents are responsible for bringing the family together. That is true. And I think that the parents also should be sensitive to the needs of their children. And, of course, they are obligated also to act in the interest of the children.

". . . It would not be in the interest of the children and the parents to change the custody from the state to the parents. . . ."

"I believe we have all exhausted our arguments," said Judge Mooney.

However, Mandel returned to the question of the juvenile statute's constitutionality, and went on to say, "The purpose [of the Juvenile Court Act] is to preserve and strengthen the minor's family ties whenever possible, removing him from the custody of his parents only when his welfare, or safety, or protection of the public cannot be adequately safeguarded without removal. His safety is not at issue. The only thing at issue, does he go back to the Ukraine with his parents or not? That is not an issue of welfare or safety of the child."

The judge agreed with Mandel that part of the Juvenile Court Act was vague. "I would like to see that clearly defined by the Supreme Court." He encouraged Mandel to bolster his arguments with legal citations.

Then Mooney finished the hearing back where we started: "But for today, it is a question of whether or not the minors are in need of supervision."

However, he made no ruling. Exhausted, we adjourned knowing we would all be back before him in a few days. This was far from over.

chapter fourteen
THE THIRD HEARING—
PART I

From Virginia Egem's Intake Summary

August 11:00—Home visit to 5025 W. Byron . . . to talk to children re visits with their parents. Both children expressed strong fear of serious repercussions if Walter returned to parents and thus to the Ukraine. At this point both refuse to talk to father—agree to see mother. Walter states he will kill himself if returned home.

August 4, 9:30—Court hearing. T.C. [temporary custody] now on Natalie also. . . .

WALTER

The days between the two big hearings passed the way a summer is supposed to for any American kid: I ate ice cream and hamburgers and lazed around with Mike Marian. The weather was great—lots of blue sky, plenty of sun, and big clouds rolling around above. I stuck to my cutoffs and T-shirts. We'd sit on our bikes out in front of Cousin's apartment, go up and down the block, just have a good time together.

The TV crews came around now and then, tried to get me to talk to them, then took off. I didn't talk to them.

I guess the only real difference between me and most twelve-year-olds was that I had a bunch of adults for friends as well, who had as much time to spend with me as I could want. *I* was their job. Pretty dull work for them but I didn't mind.

The bodyguards were real easy to get along with. They didn't drink, they didn't get mad at me, they didn't scream or shout. They were pretty relaxed. It was the first time I'd ever seen grown-ups, big guys, act like this.

Just being around them, I was beginning to relax. What I liked most was that you could predict how these grown-ups were going to act. Nothing unexpected. They were real steady the way they did things. They didn't mind laughing with each other. They treated Mike Marian okay, too. Life got peaceful. The truth was—and this isn't too hard to say—it was a lot better than having my dad around.

They were good to my cousin Walter, too. They accepted him. More than that, they liked him. This was a change from my father. Since Cousin Walter was sort of a godfather to me, I was real sensitive to how they were going to treat him.

I never heard from my parents during this time, and I never tried to call them. There was nothing I wanted to say to them, and I know my father had nothing much to say to me. If he heard my voice, he'd just get mad. So it was better that we didn't talk.

One day, some people came from the Illinois Department of Children and Family Services to talk with Natalie and me. They meant the best, asked some questions about how I wanted to live and what Natalie wanted to do with her life. It didn't seem like they were nosy or prying for anyone else, just friendly questions about us. They even had an interpreter along who wasn't bad in Ukrainian.

The thing they really wanted to know was how I got along with my parents, asking all sorts of questions about this, and talking about a possible reconciliation. I knew Mr. Kulas favored it, and I didn't want my parents to disappear, either. Sure, my father and I had plenty of differences, but I never wanted the kind of fight we had gotten into.

I said what I felt inside: "I'm not going to live with them if they aren't interested in staying in America. I'll kill myself if I have to go back."

I had thought these words to myself plenty of times, and they didn't sound like anything special in my head. But when I said the words to these visitors there was a silence. They looked real surprised and uncomfortable. For a long time after that I didn't try to think about what I had said. It made me uncomfortable, too.

During these days, Mr. Kulas explained what might happen in the next hearing. He said nothing had been settled by the first one and that Natalie and I might be asked to testify again. I didn't mind.

Judge Mooney had been friendly enough. I didn't like the lawyers for my parents, but they hadn't done any harm to me in the first hearing. In a way I was looking forward to it, and in a way I wasn't. But I wanted to get things settled, once and for all.

When we went to court the next time, on August 4, I was dressed up in my good clothes again and feeling a little strange.

We went inside. The place was packed with all kinds of people once again and I felt weird with all those eyes on us. I couldn't figure out why half of them were there. Just curious, I guess. But still it gave me a funny feeling. Especially when I recognized the Soviet diplomat Pyotr Prilepski, sitting there in the audience. He'd really latched on to my parents.

The deputy sheriff told us to rise, Judge Mooney came in, sat down, and the hearing began. First, my father testified. Seeing him on the stand, moving around in the chair, angry and upset, was an unpleasant experience.

Then I was asked by my parents' lawyers to get up and answer questions from them. They had already asked me some questions last time, but I think they wanted to trip me up in some way. I was careful in answering. I couldn't ask Mr. Kulas or anyone else for help, but I knew I was safe as long as I kept everything short— and didn't tell any lies. That's what Mr. Kulas had told us, and I didn't forget his advice.

The third surprise was when a psychiatrist got on the stand to testify why he thought I was just a little, rebellious kid who didn't deserve anything much better than a good spanking. This man, who had never talked to me for even a single minute, said that I ought to go back to Ukraine with my parents.

If he had ever lived there, he would have known enough to say something else. But it didn't matter—once he had his say, the damage was done.

The best way to tell it is just to use the transcript of the hearing. You can see how everyone got mad, changed, calmed down, and went on. It began with Mr. Mandel, the lawyer hired by the ACLU for my parents, questioning my father.

RICHARD MANDEL: Before you left the Ukraine, did Walter, your son, want to come here with you?

MICHAEL POLOVCHAK: The parents were going, and he went. He wanted.

Q: While you lived in the Ukraine, did you ever have any problems with Walter, such as with the police or his running away?

A: No. No. That couldn't be. No. I had no trouble with the police, with court, or with anybody else. I'm the first time in court.

Q: Did Walter ever run away?

A: That was never the case when Walter would run away. There might have been some little problems with neighbors. That's all.

Q: When you first told Walter that you were thinking about returning to the Ukraine, what did your son say?

A: The first time, he said, "I don't know."

Q: When was the first time Walter said that he did not want to go back to the Ukraine?

A: At the time when I applied for document for return . . . about two and a half months ago. I don't recall exactly.

Q: Did Walter give you any reason why he did not want to return?

A: He said it's nicer here and therefore he wants to stay here.

Q: Mr. Polovchak, will you please say what Cousin Walter told you when you told him you were going back to the Ukraine with your family?

A: He said, "That's your business."

Q: What else was said between you and your nephew concerning your son Walter's return?

A: My son said that he does not want to return.

Q: Did you ever have any discussion with Cousin Walter concerning Cousin Walter taking your son away from the house?

A: We did not have any discussion about him taking my son away. I like to tell the truth.

Q: Do you love your son Walter?

A: And who wouldn't like a child? It's part of your family.

MANDEL: Did he say "like" or "love"?

INTERPRETER: "Like."

Q: Why do you want your son to return with you and your family?

A: For the love of a child. For uniting the family. My wife raised him and brought him up till the age of twelve. And this is why we like to be together.

I'm responsible for my children. If he will be taken away, where is my responsibility? I am the father, after all, and am responsible for my son, and for my family.

RICHARD MICHAELS (cross-examination): Mr. Polovchak, when your son Walter and your daughter Natalie moved out of your home [on] Fullerton, did they have your permission to leave?

A: Nobody knew. I wasn't home, I was at work. And my wife just came at the time when they were leaving. I didn't have the slightest idea. I didn't know anything about it till my wife told me when I came home. I was at work at the time.

JULIAN KULAS (cross-examination): Mr. Polovchak, isn't it a fact that when you decided to return to the Soviet Ukraine, you wanted to go by yourself at first?

A: I didn't know if the government there will accept us without our child.

Q: Was it your intention to go back to Ukraine by yourself?

A: How could I have planned to go back by myself . . . ? I planned to go back with my family and not to divide the family.

Q: Mr. Polovchak, you have testified that you liked your children. May I ask you, did you take Walter to a movie at any time during his lifetime?

MANDEL: I object. We never went into that on direct [examination]. It's way beyond the scope of direct examination.

RONALD MAIMONAS: They are talking about love and what they did for everybody. This seems to be relevant to the love question.

JUDGE MOONEY: This is a civil matter. Overruled.

MICHAEL POLOVCHAK: [I go] to work at two o'clock. [I come] back at one o'clock. And [I] naturally [want] to take in some sleep.

Mrs. Polovchak goes to work. She comes back. She has to make some preparations for the next day. And . . . the child, you see, also was supposed to be taken to school. And then we were supposed to pay a strange woman, a strange person for bringing the child back from school.

KULAS: That's not responsive to the question. My question

was, if he ever has taken the child to the movies during the twelve years of his life.

A: In our country, the school has movies provided. They're providing movies for the children. All the child has to come to the mother is ask for money to go to the movies. They go. But when the children are small, they are not allowed to leave in the evening to go anyplace.

Q: Mr. Polovchak, your son Walter loves the game of soccer, football, is that correct?

A: [I] worked. [I] had to start at five o'clock in the morning to drive a bus. Then [I] would come home. And [I] had to relax. [I] didn't know. [I] didn't know if the child did go. There was the mother to see to it that the child goes places.

Q: Did [you] ever buy a football for the boy?

A: He could buy himself. He was getting money, as much as he needed.

Q: Mr. Polovchak, did you ever go see your child play on the team?

A: I was working and I didn't—I was working, also—[going to] different places. So I didn't always have the time to. . . . There are schools in our country. And the schools are taking care of all those things and arranging different things for the children.

Q: Did you, in the past twelve years, take a vacation from your job?

A: I was taking [one] every year. They are giving vacations every year, twenty-eight or thirty days of vacation.

Q: And did you [leave] your town during these vacations?

A: No, I didn't go, because during vacation I had to work around my house. I had plenty of work to do. And I had to stay home to work around my house.

Q: Mr. Polovchak, isn't it a fact that you have left on numerous occasions to other parts of the Soviet Union?

A: I didn't go anyplace except to Czechoslovakia once.

Q: Did you go to Moscow?

A: I did go to Moscow because when I started working on the [emigration] document, I had to go to Moscow. There was no interpreter. I had to go to the American embassy. There was no interpreter. . . . One thing is I had to go to Moscow.

MANDEL: Your Honor, I would like to object to the relevancy at this point of this whole line. What is culturally done in the Soviet

Union and culturally done in the United States, I think, is irrelevant. Whether the mother takes prime responsibility there and no longer does here, I don't see what the relevancy is as to whether Walter is beyond the control of his parents. Whether they went to vacations and soccer games, those items are certainly not relevant to [Minors in Need of Supervision] beyond the control [of parents].

KULAS: Your Honor, the counsel for the parents has asked the question if [Michael Polovchak] loves his children. And I think part of the love for the children is attending to the interests of the children. And certainly, any child that takes an interest in baseball, or soccer, or football, it's very significant to show if that love existed. I also am leading into other parts to dispute Mr. Polovchak's statement that he loves his children.

MOONEY: The objection is well taken. I think both sides have equally balanced the matters which are not germane to this issue before the court. . . . At this point, we have a balancing of non-germane matters, and I think it's time we got into the matter before the court, so [the] objection is sustained.

KULAS: Your Honor, may I ask the witness about his conduct immediately prior to the children leaving the home, which might answer some of the questions [about] why the children are beyond control of the parents?

MOONEY: That would be germane.

KULAS: Mr. Polovchak, starting in about April of this year, did your sister take you out of Chicago on weekends?

A: Yes. We did go.

Q: . . . This year, did you and your sister, her husband, and of course your wife go to Rockford, Illinois, for the weekend?

A: We were going only to the place where they live, where they are building a house.

Q: But it's also a resort, isn't it?

A: No. I don't know. I was told there was some kind of a camp where children are coming.

Q: . . . During all these weekend trips, you would leave Friday and come back Sunday night, is that correct?

A: Yes.

Q: Did you ever take your children with you?

A: I took once my child. I went with mother, that was my wife. And we took our child once. We came there, and my brother-in-law asked our son, "What do you want me to buy you?"

And I said to him, "Come with me to church." He didn't eat. He didn't talk the whole day, only because mother asked him to go with her.

Q: But that's the only time that you took Walter . . . ?

A: That was only once because the other times, he didn't want to go with us.

Q: When you left for those weekend trips, did you ever leave money [for] the children?

A: Please ask my wife. I give her the money I earn, and she manages, and she gives what is needed.

Q: Were you ever concerned that the children would have proper care during this weekend, these weekends?

A: The children didn't eat. The mother would say, "Eat." Why wasn't the police called and asked why isn't the child eating? Why was I asked only in court . . . ? Why did no one come to ask us questions concerning the children during the six months and why was they waiting till now for the court hearing to ask us all those questions?

MANDEL: Your Honor, I think the witness has caught exactly what this is. [Kulas] is trying now evidently to prove neglect, not Minors in Need of Supervision. And there is no neglect petition here. . . .

MOONEY: . . . That's true. . . . All you have established is that the parents went on a few weekend trips with their relatives and left the children with someone else. Period. That's all.

KULAS: Mr. Polovchak, you indicated that you had a conversation with your son about returning to the Soviet Ukraine, is that correct?

A: I talked to him, and I told him there is a law that you are supposed to be there where your parents are going to be.

Q: And did you not, in fact, tell him if he would not return that you would call the police, that they would tie him up, put him in an airplane and take him back?

A: I told him that the need will be, I'll turn to the police because you belong with your parents. And you children are supposed to go with their parents.

So he said, "Oh, I know the police can be paid off here." And I said, "If the need will be, I'll pay the police."

Q: Mr. Polovchak, you had some written communication with your sister, Anastasia Junko, in California, did you not?

A: What do you think? What are you talking about?

Q: Did you write letters to your sister in California?

A: Of course. I did write.

MANDEL: I object. This is way beyond the scope of any direct examination. If he wants to put some letter on, he can put it on later on rebuttal.

MOONEY: What is the purpose of this questioning?

KULAS: Well, I think there is some evidence here as to the intent of the father to have the sister take care of the children while he intended to return to Soviet Ukraine.

MOONEY: Well, that's germane. You may inquire along those lines.

KULAS: . . . After arriving in Chicago, did you write letters to your sister in California?

A: She was writing to me, and I had all the letters she wrote to me.

Q: And did you write letters to her?

A: I did. Why wouldn't I write? I did write.

Q: In those letters, did you tell her anything about the children?

A: Yes. I did write to her, if my family would be divided, I'll be forced to return by myself.

Q: Did [you] write the letter before [your] son ran away?

A: My sister wrote to me, "You take a place, pay rent, go with your children to a rented place. I'll pay for the rent. I'll pay for the food." I still have the letter in my possession.

I was struggling, sleeping on the floor. I would still be willing to sleep on the floor.

Q: . . . Isn't it a fact that in the letter to your sister, you offered to her that Natalie should go and live with her in California?

MOONEY: That's a question that can be answered yes or no.

A: Yes.

Q: Isn't it a fact that in your letters to your sister, you have indicated that Walter might be attending school in California and live with her in California?

A: Never. I didn't even allow him to go there. She wrote to me asking if the children can come to her. I wrote back, "Our daughter can go, but not our son."

MANDEL: Your Honor, again I'm going to object to the relevancy of whether this is beyond the [issue of Minors in Need of] Control. It just goes on and on.

MOONEY: Yes. I think we better limit this.

KULAS: The last question, Your Honor. Mr. Polovchak, did you tell your sister that you didn't care if the children went with you or not?

A: I didn't say that. I told my sister if she wants our daughter, she can have her.

MARY ELLEN NASH: Did you ever, while your cousin was living with you, Cousin Walter, tell them that they could stay there?

A: No. What could I have said? We were together. . . .

Q: Between July 14 when the children left your home, and today's date, did you ever tell the children to come home?

A: You mean after they left? After they left our house . . . ? I couldn't find them. I found them through the police. . . .

Q: At the police station did [you] tell [your] son to come home?

A: [At] the police, they were questioning him, "Why did you leave? Why did you leave?" Nobody asked me anything.

Q: Did [you] tell [your] son to come home?

A: Of course. Mother told him. Our child told him.

NASH: I have no further questions, Your Honor.

Next, my parents' lawyers put Sergeant Leo Rojek, the policeman who had arrested me three weeks earlier, on the stand. Another ACLU lawyer, Mr. Lifshitz, got him to tell what had happened that day, and then asked him what I had said when Sergeant Rojek asked me why I'd run away.

LEO ROJEK: [Walter] stated that his father intended to go back to the Ukraine, but that was not his intention. He wanted to stay in this country because he had found a new school, has new friends, and has a new bicycle, and found that this country has more opportunity for him than the Ukraine.

I was the next witness. One of the things I had learned about testifying in a courtroom was that you could tell the truth but, depending on the way the lawyers asked the questions, it might sound like something else. I went up to the stand hoping that the truth would sound the way I knew it actually was.

chapter fifteen
THE THIRD HEARING— PART II

Before I was called to the stand, the ACLU lawyers got into a big argument with Mr. Kulas and his team about whose witness I was: whether I should testify as a witness called for my parents or against them—an adverse witness.

Mr. Kulas wanted me to be an adverse witness to my parents, and that was good enough for me—then I wanted it, too. But I was going to say the same things no matter who asked the questions so it didn't make any difference to me one way or the other.

I figured the only person in the whole courtroom who really had something to hide was Pyotr Prilepski. If he got put on the witness stand, Mr. Kulas surely had a few questions for *him*.

Through all this, I think the biggest thing in my mind was that I wanted to get the hearing over with and go back home, where I was safe. I feared that by the end of the hearing, I would be sent back to my parents.

Finally, I was brought to the stand. After a few questions from Mr. Mandel about where I lived in Chicago and how long I'd been here, he asked me about life in Ukraine.

Q: And did you go to school when you lived in the Ukraine?

A: Yeah.

Q: And did you have food when you lived in the Ukraine?

This started another fight and in the end, Lifshitz and Mandel got the judge to agree to my testifying as though I were working for my parents. Why wouldn't they just let me be a witness for myself?

Judge Mooney peered at us through his glasses. "I permitted a certain amount of testimony about his life in the Ukraine at the request of his own attorney, until it balanced with what you people did," he told Mandel. "And then, as a matter of balancing the excesses, I guess, I cut it off.

"Did you have some pertinent points to develop about his life? That is of interest to the court, too, the life before coming here. After all, he's been here only six months of twelve years."

Without answering the judge directly, Mr. Lifshitz began questioning me. He asked me things like whether I lived with my parents in Ukraine, did they provide food and clothing for me, and had they taken care of me. I answered yes to all these questions, because that was the basic truth—if you took out all the fighting, the running around, the tears, and the father almost never being there.

Q: Before you came to the United States, how did you like living in the Ukraine?

A: No.

Q: You didn't like it?

A: No.

Q: Why didn't you like it?

A: Because there aren't many things to be bought there. And if there is something, you have to pay three times its value. And also, there is a Komsomol. You have to go through Komsomol.

My parents, my sister, and other relatives and Ukrainians in the courtroom knew what "Komsomol" meant: the Communist youth group that checks you out for party membership when you're a teenager. Prilepski sure knew what it was. Natalie had belonged to it because she wanted a good job. A lot of people were in Komsomol for that reason. It was a powerful organization with plenty of ways to keep people from going their own way in life.

The blank stares of the judge and the opposing lawyers made it easy to see that they didn't know anything about the Komsomol. To them it was something that lived on Mars, and just about as interesting. It made me wonder why the judge and the ACLU guys all thought they knew so much about life in Ukraine that they could decide whether I ought to go back there.

Q: Walter, do you like the United States?

A: Yeah.

Q: Why?

A: A lot of food. Because there's a lot of food here. And you can buy many things. And it's also good to go to school here.

Q: Walter, why did you run away from home?

A: Because I was afraid that my father would take me back to the Soyuz.

JULIAN KULAS (cross-examination): Walter, during the twelve years of your life in Ukraine, did your father ever take you on vacations?

MANDEL: I object, Your Honor. There is nothing on direct examination on that.

KULAS: You asked him about food. A man does not live by food alone.

JUDGE MOONEY: Objection sustained.

RICK MICHAELS: I object on Mr. Kulas's behalf. Counsel's examination was based on this young man's life and whether he liked it or didn't like it in the Ukraine prior to coming to the United States. And it has to do with how his parents cared for and gave him custody during that period of time.

I believe that counsel has a right on cross-examination to go into these areas. And it seems to me that it is directly relevant and directly within the scope of their direct examination. . . .

MOONEY: That question was asked and answered through the father on the basis of your interrogation.

KULAS: I understand, Your Honor. However, the father was very vague in his answers.

MOONEY: . . . Well, all right. If it's to clarify the record for that purpose, then I can admit his answer. . . .

KULAS: Walter, when you lived in Ukraine, did you see your father every day?

A: Maybe twice a week.

Q: And was this at all times like that?

A: Yes.

Q: Did your father take you anyplace, to a soccer game?

RICHARD LIFSHITZ: We object to this. You allowed him to go into that to clarify one answer. Now he's trying to open the whole thing up again.

MOONEY: I want to limit this whole line of questioning because the matter before me, if I ever get to it, is to decide whether or not a factual basis has been established [for approving a MINS petition].

KULAS: I want to establish the parents' life in relation to this child—I think it's very relevant to show what kind of relationship he had with his parents.

MOONEY: That's been established. The point in fact is, are these children now Minors in Need of Supervision? Are they, on the 4th day of August, 1980, in Chicago, Illinois, Minors in Need of Supervision?

That's the only issue before me. That's the only one I want to decide. And from this point on, that's the evidence that I'm going to permit . . . to assist the court in making that determination, and nothing else.

KULAS: I have no further questions of this witness.

I got down from the witness box and joined the crowd in the courtroom. The next witness was a psychiatrist who was going to testify for my parents, which meant he would be against me. All in all, I didn't expect anything much good to come from him.

There were times in all this testifying and hearings that I really felt depressed, wondering whether I could actually win against my parents. It seemed to me that every time Mr. Kulas wanted to get down to the real situation, the lawyers for my parents found ways to stop me from telling the story, or made me or Natalie or Cousin Walter sound like we were lying.

I know I didn't understand how the law works. But sometimes in these hearings, it seemed like a fence or a wall. Sometimes, I thought, the law got in the way of the truth. Maybe I'm not supposed to say something like that, but that's how it seemed to me.

The psychiatrist was an older man named Littner. He told the judge he'd won a lot of awards for helping kids.

Although the doctor hadn't talked to me, didn't know anything about me or my family, or how we had lived in Ukraine, he talked like he knew all about us, like he'd been living with the Polovchaks for a long time.

This was hard to figure out: I'd never seen him before but he was able to tell the judge why I had run away, what I was supposed to have been feeling and thinking, and a lot of other things the doctor didn't know anything about.

Mr. Mandel set this up by talking about a "hypothetical," a made-up situation that seemed on the outside like the fight between me and my parents. But it wasn't anything like the real story. Here's what Mandel told the psychiatrist were the facts:

MANDEL: . . . Walter's decision to leave home was based upon the fact that his parent had decided to go back to the Ukraine; his cousin Walter was willing to allow him to live with him; his cousin Walter and his sister Natalie assisted Walter in leaving his parents' home; since leaving, Walter has resided with his twenty-four-year-old cousin and his seventeen-year-old sister; Walter's parents love him; Walter's parents have never physically or emotionally harmed him; Walter's parents' decision to return to the Ukraine is based on their desire *to do what is best for the Polovchak family*; Cousin Walter, who lived with the Polovchaks, told Walter that if Walter did not return, Walter could live with him.

Now, based on those facts, do you have an opinion based upon a reasonable degree of medical certainty as to whether Walter's parents can control him despite Walter's desire to remain in the United States?

DR. LITTNER: Yes, I do have an opinion.

Q: And what is that opinion?

A: That Walter's parents could control him.

Q: And upon what do you base that opinion?

A: Walter's action of defying his parents is related to actions, an act rather, of a child rebelling.

A twelve-year-old child usually will go with his parents, no matter where they wish to go. That will take priority over any other desire that the child has.

If a child rebels against that particular issue, the child is not making an independent judgment. What he is doing is reacting to what the parents are saying, reacting to what the father is saying. And in effect, therefore, the father is controlling what the child is doing.

It is negative control, but it is still just as much a control as though the child were to say yes.

Q: Doctor, do you have an opinion based upon a reasonable degree of medical certainty as to whether the behavior of Walter in leaving his home with his twenty-four-year-old cousin and his seventeen-year-old sister indicates that he cannot be controlled by his parents?

A: . . . I do have an opinion.

Q: And what is that opinion?

A: It does not indicate that.

Q: And what is the basis for your opinion?

A: His cousin's willingness and his sister's willingness to let him stay with them puts an aura of respectability on this, as though it were an independent judgment of the child. All it is doing is providing the child with a rationalization for rebelling against his parents.

If the cousin and his sister were not in the picture, Walter might do something like locking himself in the bathroom and refusing to come out.

It would be of the same order of rebelliousness against a request by the parent. So that the existence of the cousin and the sister I do not think would change the ability of a parent to control Walter.

Q: Now, Doctor, do you have an opinion, based upon a reasonable degree of medical certainty, as to whether Walter's conduct as described in the hypothetical is harmful to his welfare or is a danger to the public?

A: I do not believe that it is a danger to the public. But I think that his decision, if implemented, would be very destructive to Walter.

Q: What do you mean by "his decision, if implemented"?

A: If he were allowed to *not* go back with his parents, Walter would be harmed. The longer that he would be separated from his parents, the more harm would be done to Walter.

Q: Please elaborate on the type of harm you are talking about that would be done to Walter.

A: As I see it, Walter is rebelling. This is his answer to something that is bugging him. Something is worrying Walter, either about himself or about his relationship with his parents. His answer is to rebel against what his parents wish. . . .

. . . That is not a mature way of dealing with a problem. It is a way of avoiding the problem. That's what rebelliousness amounts to. . . .

Hearing this, I almost wanted to walk out of the courtroom and go home. Something was bugging me all right—the thought of going back to Ukraine. The doctor didn't want to admit that, so he made up a lot of reasons why it couldn't be true. But what he said next really got to me. He treated me as though I were some kind of animal that couldn't think for itself. His idea was to punish me by ignoring my "rebellious act."

A: . . . If we go along with this rebellious act, we are only saying to Walter, it's all right for you to not deal with whatever is bothering you. You can avoid it by an act of rebellion. That condones immature behavior in Walter.

Q: . . . Do you have an opinion as to whether removal of Walter from his parents will be harmful to him both in the short range and the long range?

A: Based on my experience with twelve-year-old children who are separated from their parents, they are harmed psychologically by the separation. The longer the separation takes place, the more harm is done. And if it is a very prolonged separation, the harm psychologically to the child becomes irreversible.

Q: When you stated that Walter's conduct, within a reasonable degree of medical certainty, as described in the hypothetical, did not indicate that his parents could *not* control him, will you please explain a little more of what the basis of your opinion was on that.

A: If Walter had wanted to run away, he would have done what runaways do. He would have disappeared. Runaways do not wish their parents to know where they are.

This is not what Walter has done. If anything, Walter has made very certain that not only his parents but an awful lot of other people know where Walter is.

This is not a runaway. This is an act of defiance. It is a provoking of the parents in order to elicit some kind of response from the parents. Elicit, as I heard some notion about being tied up and being put on an airplane. To a twelve-year-old child, that is an act of love. That proves to the child that his parents care. It's not the way adults react. It is the way a child reacts.

Walter, as I see it, is trying to find something from his parents. To do this, it means he is under the control of the parent.

Q: . . . Do you have an opinion . . . based on the facts of the hypothetical, as to whether a twelve-year-old has the maturity to make decisions on whether or not he should live or not live with his parents?

A: No twelve-year-old, as far as I am aware, has the intellectual or emotional capacity to make such a decision.

Q: Upon what do you base that opinion?

A: A thousand or so children that I have seen in private practice, the four thousand or so children that I have been consulted on in the child welfare agencies, which deal all the time with separation of children.

To me, this doctor was weird. He didn't like me any more than my father did. Maybe less. But he didn't even know me. Mr. Michaels went after him on cross-examination.

MICHAELS: . . . Would it make a difference if Walter's parents did not love him?

A: That's inconsistent. If they didn't love him, they wouldn't want him to go back with them. They'd say, "Thank God, we'll get rid of this brat."

Q: Would it make a difference if there was another motivation for wanting Walter to return with them other than love?

A: Such as what?

Q: Such as the government of the Soviet Union would not allow the parents to return without their son, who is on the same visa.

A: To my way of thinking, I don't think it would make much difference whether the government insisted that the condition of their returning be that the twelve-year-old come along.

Q: Doctor, I just gave you a hypothetical reason that they might want him to come back other than love. And you have indicated to me that you didn't think that would make a difference.

A: I can think of another reason. A father may not love his son, but believe that a family should be together. To me, that would be a perfectly valid reason for his wanting his son to come back with him.

Q: . . . If the fact that Walter's parents love him were not true, but if they wanted him to return for some of these other reasons . . .

A: My answer would still be the same.

Q: Doctor, one of the bases of the hypothetical was that Walter was never emotionally harmed. Is that a significant factor in your answer?

A: No, it's not a significant factor.

Q: . . . Would you have an opinion as to whether or not it might be harmful for Walter to be forced to return to his parents?

A: Yes, I have an opinion. It would be harmful if Walter were *not* forced to return to his parents. It would be harmful to Walter.

Q: Doctor, could you tell us what types of decisions, if any, a twelve-year-old would normally be mature enough to make for himself concerning his life?

A: He is mature enough to know what foods he likes and what food he dislikes. He is mature enough to be able to be angry at his parents, to be able to love his parents. He is mature enough to know whether he is doing well in school. He is mature enough to have some idea as to why he might not be doing well at school, if that were the case.

These all have to do with very direct issues that Walter is confronting, not with a global issue as to where he should live.

Q: Do you think that a twelve-year-old would have the maturity level significant enough to be able to determine the difference between living in Chicago, Illinois, and living in Sambir, Ukraine?

A: He would have the maturity to compare living standards. However, a decision that he would make as to where he would live, he wouldn't have that maturity, although he might spout words like "freedom," "better food," and things like that.

If he were to use those sorts of things, they would all be rationalizations to try to deal with the question of where he would live.

Q: But he certainly would be able to compare living standards in two rather diverse places, is that right?

A: That's what I believe.

Q: And would he be able to form some opinions as to which he preferred or didn't prefer?

A: At one level, he could say I like the ice cream better here than I like the ice cream there. Or, I like the theaters here better. He could certainly know and be able to make an opinion on issues like that.

Q: Would he be able to understand issues such as the educational program in a society?

A: He could compare the excellence of the teaching [here] versus the excellence of the teaching there, yes. But when he starts to use these comparisons to explain where he wishes to live, they are just pure rationalizations.

Q: . . . You indicated that normally a twelve-year-old would go to live wherever his parents wish to live, is that correct?

A: He'll go with his parents wherever they wish to live. Yes.

Q: And would it therefore be somewhat unusual for a child to defy his parents over that issue . . . ?

A: No. I have seen many children who have defied their parents over that issue.

Q: Would it be unusual for those children to leave their parents' home rather than move?

A: In some of these cases, I have seen that's what they have done. In each one of them, when I have had a chance to do a full evaluation, the problem always was not the rationalizations they gave, but some inner worry that the child had about himself and he was trying to solve it in a very irrational way by not wanting to move, or running away, or something like that. . . .

. . . [Walter] is at a point, twelve years of age, where he is taking his first steps towards independence. Preadolescents and adolescents typically at this point have trouble with that beginning. . . . And so there is a lot of rebellion that goes on at this age in adolescents and preadolescents. It's normal.

If a child is allowed to rebel and get away with it, one of the results is that he may grow up and deal with all future problems by rebelling rather than solving them. He will rebel and defy. That would be one of the consequences of separating Walter from his parents around an issue of rebellion.

KULAS: In your opinion, Doctor, [is] a twelve- or thirteen- or fourteen-year-old child in a position to make comparisons as far as some of the basic freedoms of that individual, of a child?

A: I do not believe that a twelve- or thirteen- or fourteen-year-old child is in a position to make such a comparison with regards to such basic issues as freedoms.

MARY ELLEN NASH: Dr. Littner, if you were told that a twelve-year-old child had gone so far as to threaten to kill himself if he had to return to his home, would that change your opinion as to whether a twelve-year-old child should make a decision to return or not return home?

A: All such statements would say to me that this kid is really in trouble. Somebody should find out what is upsetting him so much. I doubt very much if that had anything at all to do with the issue of returning home.

Q: If you were told that a parent in a given family had done several things, such as chasing a seventeen-year-old daughter to a bus and calling her a whore in public, had run around a house slapping and screaming that he would kill a family relative, would you consider whether or not that might affect the return of a child to that house?

A: None of the things you mentioned would change my opinion.

Q: Would returning a twelve-year-old child to a home where his parents lived, against the child's will, cause some emotional harm to the child?

A: It would cause some superficial harm to the child, but not as much harm as would be caused by not returning the child.

Q: Is it possible that a child returned to such a home would run again?

A: It's certainly possible depending upon the circumstances. But the facts that I have heard would not cause me to think of Walter as a runaway.

After a lot of arguing, the lawyers for my parents allowed Mr. Michaels and Mr. Kulas to ask some questions of their own psychiatrist, Dr. Robert Bussel. But as I listened, only one question really stood out:

KULAS: Doctor, if a parent would say to a child, "If you don't go with me, I will call the police, they will tie you up and put you in a plane and send you back . . ."—in your medical opinion, is this an act of love from the parents . . . ?

DR. BUSSEL: Not as normally construed, love.

Q: Would you consider such a statement a threat to the child? Would it instill fear in the child?

A: I should certainly think so.

After a few more minutes, the doctor was excused. No one else had anything to say. I was tired. Listening to the long fights, paying attention when I could to the translations, and watching the back-and-forth left me worn out. Everyone else looked the same way—beat.

The judge wanted to get things over with. "All evidence is in on the question of factual basis for the pleas of Minors in Need of Supervision heretofore entered by the minor respondents, Walter and Natalie Polovchak," he said. "Very well."

He leaned forward. What's next? I wondered.

"He wants to make a decision in your case, right now," whispered

Cousin Walter. My heart skipped a beat. Natalie and I exchanged glances. Would he send us back?

"The lawyers will make their last arguments," my cousin said. "Then the judge decides."

I had my one big hope: that Mr. Kulas, Mr. Michaels, Mr. Maimonas, and Mary Ellen Nash would win. They *had* to win. If they didn't, I was ready to take off for good. And this time, no one would find me. I was sure of that.

Judge Mooney nodded at Mr. Michaels.

"The proponent of the issue has the burden of going forward," said the judge.

Rick Michaels rose to make his final statement on my behalf.

chapter sixteen
THE JUDGE'S DECISION

1

Rick Michaels looked through the piles of notes and files on the table in front of our lawyers. He seemed tired, and so did everyone else in the courtroom.

Mr. Michaels kept it short. "Walter [and] Natalie [have] testified that if they were forced to return to their parents, they would leave home. Natalie and Walter . . . are beyond the control of the parents. . . . They refuse to live in the Polovchak home. . . . They are Minors in Need of Supervision under Section 24 of the Juvenile Court Act.

". . . It is obvious that in order to provide care, custody, guidance and discipline, some intervening force must be taken. We [ask] this court to make findings of MINS and adjudicate these minor respondents wards of the court."

He sat down. The reporters scribbled in their notebooks.

Then it was Richard Mandel's turn. I knew the chief ACLU lawyer for my parents wouldn't have anything good to say about us. But I had no idea he would try to make it sound like World War III.

"The evidence is that Cousin Walter brought two friends to the house, helped Natalie and Walter pack up and move. . . . There is no question [Walter] left. . . . [But] I do not think that is what 'beyond the control' means.

". . . When a twelve-year-old stands and says, 'Fine, I don't want to move with you,' that does not mean he is beyond control. Particularly in this case, where there is a twenty-four-year-old cousin who gives him all sorts of encouragement. . . .

"[Cousin Walter] gave him every opportunity, including packing him, driving him away, not telling the boy to call his parents for five days, keeping him away . . . giving him a place to live. That's certainly not beyond the control when Cousin Walter enters into it. I think that is the key fact."

At the time of this attack on my cousin, I was just a little kid from another country. Most of the best things in my new life had been brought to me by my cousin. So when I heard all this, I was mad and upset.

Even now, years later, I feel angry about this powerful lawyer's attack on my cousin. While my parents and I lived and suffered with our problems down through the years, he found other things to do.

"The real issue is Walter and his cousin now do not want Walter to go back to the Ukraine," Mandel went on, "and does the state have any right to interfere with the family decision between the parents and their twelve-year-old? Parents contend no. . . . But that's what the state is trying to do, butt in on the life of the family . . . and they cannot. . . .

". . . What is 'beyond the control'? . . . How many times have children acted defiantly? My children, your children. They are beyond control momentarily. That doesn't mean 'beyond the control.'

"In this case, you have the added influence of Cousin Walter aiding and abetting the child to act defiantly. . . . Walter is trying . . . emancipation from his parents only because 'I do not want to go back to the Ukraine. Therefore, I want to be emancipated.' . . . But our legislature said no to twelve-year-olds. . . .

". . . At the start of this case [Judge Mooney said] . . . this court [and] the state can . . . interfere with the family and remove a child from the custody of his parents only when his welfare or safety or protection of the public cannot be adequately safeguarded without removal.

"The state has not proven one fact of that. They have not been able to prove that Walter's welfare is harmed if he goes back to the Ukraine. We have no right to impose values on that. I don't want to go back to the Ukraine. I don't want to live there. I never have been there. I have no intention. Most of us do not, but to say that Walter's welfare is damaged because he is going back where he lived twelve and a half years of his life . . . There is no proof of damage to Walter's welfare . . . to the state, society. . . .

"The state cannot . . . intervene on behalf of a twelve-year-old being defiant of his parents. . . . Judges are not left at large to decide in light of personal and private notions. . . . You cannot interfere in bringing up children.

"I think there is another . . . very important point that the Supreme Court has said . . . the burden of proof is on the state in defending the constitutionality of a MINS statute. . . .

"They said that the freedom of personal choice in certain family life matters [is a] fundamental constitutional [guarantee], and when there is a statute that attacks [this freedom], that it is presumably unconstitutional and the state must uphold it. . . .

"In order to find wardship, you would have to find that Walter is beyond the control, if we ever know what it means. . . . The state hasn't proven that by its own witness, [who] said he is not beyond the control.

". . . There is not one bit of evidence the state has put in that it is in the best interest of the minor and the public to be made a ward of the court. And you cannot make a finding of wardship unless you find both of these items. There hasn't been any evidence nor could there be any evidence that [it would be in] the best interest of this child— in fact, Dr. Littner testified that it is *harmful* to the child.

"In conclusion, I would like to point out there isn't a paper, a person, or a politician, or anyone in the past two or three years that hasn't been saying the state is not Big Brother. The state cannot interfere with the sanctity of the family except for very, very solid reasons.

". . . A twelve-year-old saying 'I am defiant and I don't want to go back' does not give the state the right to interfere. It doesn't show he is beyond the control. It doesn't show it is in the best interest of the child or society that wardship be decided.

"I think the world is watching this case. It wasn't our bringing it. The state and Mr. Kulas started bringing media in. It wasn't my people. You are put on the spot by the state and the Ukraine community and everyone is watching you. The world is watching you, Judge, to see if the state is going to interfere."

He sat down.

Now it was Mr. Kulas's turn.

"Your Honor, [Illinois juvenile law] says parents should not retain custody of a minor if the court determines that [it] is contrary to the minor's best interest," Mr. Kulas said. ". . . Evidence shows that Walter left home of his own volition. Evidence shows there was conversation between Walter and Cousin Walter. And at no time did the cousin indicate to Walter that he should live with him. The evidence further shows, Your Honor, the father raging, angry, slamming the door . . . cursing, using vulgarity.

"He was chasing [his] daughter . . . to the street, screamed at Natalie and even called her a whore. We also have testimony that the father left these children alone for . . . many weekends since April. . . . Your Honor, if it wasn't for the cousin . . . in fact, you should be grateful for the cousin. He has taken care of these children during [the father's] absence. . . .

"I'm sure everyone is cognizant of this case. This case has received considerable publicity. Mr. Mandel indicated I brought the media into this matter. That's absolutely incorrect. In fact, when I first came to visit the child at the police station, the media was there. I was not aware of that fact.

"I have never called a news conference. The ACLU, when they decided to get into this, called a news conference to announce what they would try to highlight interest in this case. But, I would like to submit to this court, in view of this extended publicity and Walter's statement in court and to the media—that he [prefers] life in the United States to life in the Soviet Union—has caused considerable embarrassment to the Soviet Union.

"We see this in the Soviet press of recent days. In fact, much embarrassment. If Walter chooses to return, he would be a marked man. . . . I believe he would not be permitted to attend the best schools. I believe his fellow students would be avoiding him. I believe he would not be permitted to hold the best job [or have] the best housing.

"Your Honor, by granting custody of Walter and Natalie to the parents and by permitting the parents to take him to Ukraine, against free will, would indeed slam the gate of liberty forever for these children."

Mr. Kulas finished. Natalie and I wanted to clap for him.

Next came Mary Ellen Nash, who was there for DCFS as our legal guardian, what the court called Guardian ad Litem.

"The question before the court today . . . is whether or not Natalie and Walter Polovchak are Minors in Need of Supervision. That's a very simple question, Your Honor. . . .

"The minors have admitted that they did run away from home. . . . Their reasons for leaving home are immaterial to this court at this time. They may be material during a dispositional hearing, but at this time, the only thing the court has to consider is whether or not the minors left without the permission of their parents.

"Anna Polovchak testified that when she came home from work and found Natalie and Walter packing their things, she asked where they were going. Walter replied, 'Don't worry your head about it. I'm going elsewhere.'

"The children left. The father asked—demanded—of Natalie that she return Walter to him. Neither Natalie nor Walter returned.

"The father was at the police station when [Walter] was brought in. And the father could not or would not convince the minor to return home with him. Walter and Natalie have consistently said they will not return home.

"If they return home, Your Honor, they have said they will run and the purpose and policy of the Juvenile Court Act is not only to keep families together, but to protect children against their own acts which might hurt them.

"And that is exactly the case here, Your Honor. Natalie may be seventeen years of age and may be able to take care of herself if she runs away. Walter is twelve. . . . It is possible from his testimony that he could fend for himself. But I would ask the court whether or not this would turn out like many other Minors in Need of Supervision cases that we see, where a child is either harmed on the street or turns to crime in order to support himself. Particularly if there is no one, no family member and no member of the community, willing to give the child help. I believe that Mr. Mandel's argument [asks that] no one should have helped these children and no one should have stood up for these children when they ran away from home.

"However, I think that would be a disservice to all children [who] wind up within the purview of the Illinois courts. I think we have a duty to protect them. Thank you."

Though I didn't know her at all, she really seemed to care about us—the children.

Rick Michaels made a final statement for us, ending by saying,

"Clearly, it is in the best interest of these minor[s] if this court intervenes in their lives, make[s] certain they are under care and guidance of responsible persons. . . . The state is not seeking to remove these children from the parents' home. They removed themselves. The state is seeking to [establish] control over these children. . . . We didn't find the children in the parents' home. Not to find MINS under those circumstances is to say their behavior is appropriate and this court will not intervene. . . ."

Judge Mooney said, "It was clear to me from the beginning, when I placed Walter under temporary custody of the state, that this case was going to be handled as I would any other MINS case I have handled in the last year, and that comes to over five hundred.

"They are going to be given the same due process that I give any other runaway youth. They will be given the same equal handling with the same idea in mind—to first of all, return them to their parents and family unit at the first opportunity. And that's the law. That's what I'm going to follow. . . ."

He ordered some social workers to come see us, saying he wanted "periodic visits at home" between my parents and us.

"I noticed the [little] brother here today, going over and playing with his brother and sister. That's good. I don't want to tear this family apart. I want to make certain it is in the best interest of Walter and Natalie when I finally rule in this case."

He took all of us in with his stare. "So I think now, the finding of MINS . . . is going to be entered in each case. And there will be adjudication of wardship here based upon all the evidence that I have heard. . . . Everyone seems to forget [that] on July 19th, I did what I had to do. . . ."

I looked at my sister, at Cousin Walter, and Mr. Kulas. It sounded as though the judge were about to rule for us.

But the lawyers suddenly gathered up their files and papers and headed for the door to the judge's office behind the courtroom. There was going to be some kind of private meeting back there. The hearing still wasn't over.

JULIAN KULAS

Judge Mooney was on the edge of making the most important decision of the case but he still had some things to hear that he did not want aired in open court. So with the court stenographer along to keep a record, we continued the hearing in his chambers.

"I have one comment," Mandel began. "I think that it goes into this whole thing. I don't think anyone doubts that the cousin, Walter, has this tremendous involvement in young Walter's—"

"Objection," broke in Ron Maimonas, one of the assistant state's attorneys. "We doubt that. We don't know. . . . Counsel is always assuming things."

"I'm going to ask guardian about that," said the judge. Then he turned to us all. "I will tell you why, now that they are wards of the court. I want to make sure they are in the best possible placement."

"Our feeling if these children ran off—" Mandel resumed, but the judge interrupted.

"[Cousin] Walter may be the *best* influence," he said. "I don't know, but I know that I would prefer an older person, adults or something. That's my own idea."

Mandel argued even more heatedly against leaving the children with Cousin Walter. "If it wasn't for Walter—there was encouragement."

"He told me he would run away again," Judge Mooney commented. "That's enough for me."

"Two guards have guarded him for two weeks," Mandel persisted. "They can guard him at his [family] home for that matter. . . ."

The conversation moved to the idea of placing the children with Maria Gusiev, Michael Polovchak's sister, and her husband. "Maybe I'm a little old-fashioned," said Judge Mooney. "I would like a secure elder aunt or uncle. . . ."

Mandel took after Cousin Walter again. "Could we have protective orders to keep [Cousin] Walter out of this. . . . Walter having been a problem."

"I object," said Rick Michaels.

"Walter is a pretty bad guy," Maimonas said sarcastically. "He supported him, and room and board for six months. He seems pretty terrible so far."

Judge Mooney took exception. "I don't believe I can enter such a finding today," he told Mandel. "No way. . . . They ran to him, and he took them in. I will tell him not to try to influence the children in reconciliation with their parents."

The discussion turned to finding a Ukrainian-speaking psychiatrist for evaluations of the family, when Richard Lifschitz reopened the ACLU's basic attack.

". . . We are still contending there was no hearing [July 19th] . . ." he declared. "I'm suggesting . . . that the court consider the possibility of returning the children to the parents under a court order that they not flee home. I believe that if the court orders them not to, they won't."

"I'm going to do that, as I said," Judge Mooney replied, "as soon as I can after the clinical [evaluation], after certain investigations. . . ."

The judge asked Virginia Egem, the social worker, to discuss possible guardians.

"I see no reason why they should not remain [with Cousin Walter]," she declared. ". . . The children are safe, happy, and secure where they are right now. I can't give a recommendation about a home which I haven't been given the opportunity to investigate."

But the parents, said Mandel, "do not believe Walter is . . . neutral. They feel he has disrupted their family, and [Cousin] Walter's mother [Maria Gusiev] has sided with her son. . . . [The parents] feel relatives have influenced their child to be apart from them. They want neutral. They want the child back with them. That's their choice.

"They don't want to have Cousin Walter continuing to do things like take him . . . against their will to the Baptist church. The parents don't like that. They were worried about [Cousin] Walter driving a car. He was in two accidents. They disapprove Walter's influence on their son, and that's why they are very much against where he is staying.

"The Immigration and Naturalization people are still here. They will guarantee the people aren't going to flee, go back. Nothing can happen. [There is] no urgent and immediate necessity, I think, to remove them from the home. . . ."

The judge peered at the ACLU men. "Will you guarantee his

personal safety?" he asked. "He is not your client. You are not worried about him, no. The Guardian ad Litem worries."

This was Mary Ellen Nash. "I certainly can't guarantee that either child will remain in the parents' home," she said.

I got into the discussion. "My concern is for the safety of these children, and the evidence we have heard is obvious that the father goes into those moments of anger. . . . I think it would be really ill advised at this point to return these children to the parents. I think the children feel comfortable with [Cousin] Walter. They can communicate. They learn. There is no great generation gap as between the aunt and the children."

Virginia Egem said Walter had told her several times "he will commit suicide if he is returned home."

"Walter told you that?" the judge asked.

"Yes, sir."

"You would testify to that under oath, wouldn't you?"

"Yes, sir."

"That's enough," said Mooney.

After more discussion, we all returned to the courtroom. "Will somebody translate for the parents here, please?" the judge asked. He addressed the parents.

"It is my decision that . . . if at all possible, the children will be placed with your sister and brother-in-law, who live in Chicago. And that Walter, the cousin, will not be continuing to be in charge with the responsibility, although he has done a good job. . . .

"Now, three times each week, it can be seven, I want them to visit their parents at their own home. Parents' home, or if the parents want to go with the aunt or uncle, either way."

INTERPRETER: There is a question from the father. Should I answer?

JUDGE MOONEY: What is the question?

INTERPRETER: "Why [can't] children stay with us, why is—"

MOONEY: We want to make certain they don't run again, that's why. I'm afraid the next time if Walter runs, he may not run to Cousin Walter. He may run someplace where he will be harmed. And Natalie may be harmed.

I want when you two . . . when they get together, I want them to be happy with their home so they will stay. No longer to run. Then you can do whatever you want. The court will walk away. That's what it is all about.

The interpreter spoke up again. "The father has a very important question he insists that I should ask."

"Yes?" said Mooney.

INTERPRETER: "I didn't hear anything about the court giving back to me my child."

MOONEY: I will repeat it once more. You heard it, didn't you . . . ? As soon as I can, you will get both children back. It is up to you. It is up to him to work with the children so we can get this family together. That's what we are all about. Court is recessed.

WALTER

The judge walked out, and the courtroom broke out in noise. People hugged Natalie, grabbed me. Reporters clustered around. I felt almost numb, but I was smiling. I couldn't keep it off my face, no matter what Mr. Kulas had told me.

Natalie and Cousin Walter were the same way. I didn't want to look at my parents, but I stole a glance at my mother. She was looking sad and quiet. My father's face came into my sight. He looked real angry.

2

FROM VIRGINIA EGEM'S INTAKE SUMMARY

[Aug. 4 entry, continued] Children to be moved from Cousin Walter as per Judge Mooney as ACLU claims he exerts undue influence on children. This takes place in Judge Mooney's chambers. . . . I am still denied access to Mr. & Mrs. Polovchak by ACLU.

Aug. 6, 3:30—Visited Mr. and Mrs. Gusiev. Mr. Gusiev stated that Walter and Natalie should never be returned to their parents or to the Ukraine. They also stated that Mr. Polovchak was a liar and would lie under oath. I did not think the home would be suitable for the same reason the ACLU did not think Cousin Walter's home suitable. Contrary to DCFS policy of attempting to reunite families. This would be my recommendation to the Judge through written report. . . .

Aug. 7, 9:30—Court. Court orders still stand, attempt to visit family three times a week. Judge expresses disappointment that

Gusievs not to be used. Judge requests DCFS find "neutral" foster home where parents speak Ukrainian and English, as soon as possible.

2:30—Visit with potential foster parents Mr. and Mrs. Bylen. Very pleased with this family. Seem as "neutral" as possible concerning political issues. Seem sincere as foster family. Want to provide normalcy for the children.

4:30—First home visit at 3624 W. Fullerton with Mrs. [Michael] Polovchak. . . . Mother cried when she saw Walter, barely spoke to Natalie. Embraced Walter, not Natalie. Mother expresses severe headache. Asks if youngest son can go along to Cousin Walter's house when children go home. I agree—children should have opportunity to visit with their little brother. Mother is vacillating. Would like to stay in U.S. and have Walter and Natalie with her, but feels she must go with her husband.

Aug. 8, 11:00—Visit with Mr. Polovchak. Visit was supposed to take place at [parents' apartment]. [But] INS agents informed me that [parents] apt. is a security risk (people on the roof next door and "suspicious" people on the street). Meeting is to take place at 10 S. La Salle, at Mr. Mandel's office. . . .

. . . Meeting with father a disaster. The children quite upset. . . . Walter quite upset by the meeting. . . . Father yelled throughout entire visit. . . .

Aug. 12, 11:30—. . . Both children extremely upset. Mr. Polovchak screams again for entire visit. . . . Both children crying by the time we [leave].

Aug. 14, 12:00—Visit with both parents. . . . Again Mr. P. screams entire time. Yells at Natalie. . . . Walter states will not visit father anymore. Mrs. P. will not speak, only comment from her is Walter needs a haircut. Both children ask mother to stay in U.S. Mother says she goes with father. Father says he doesn't care about Natalie or what she does but Walter is coming home.

Aug. 15, 9:30—Court—gave Judge Mooney oral and written report—Judge orders children placed with Bylens and . . . asks that children be moved to foster home as soon as possible. . . .

4:30—Placed Natalie and Walter with Mr. and Mrs. [Jaroslav] Bylen. Both children crying, but cooperative.

Aug. 20, 9:30—Problem [at] home—Mr. Polovchak now has phone number and is harassing foster family.

Aug. 21—Cousin Walter called to inform me that Natalie had called him stating that her father is continuing to call the Bylen home. The children called him back, asking him to leave them alone. The youngest child, Michael, got on the phone and said father has a gun. . . . Natalie states that mother says father has a gun and will use it. . . .

Aug. 26, 3:30—Visit with foster parents and the children. The children were not willing to visit with their parents. Finally they agreed to visit if their parents would not scream at them as they had on past visits.

4:30—From the time we walked in the door until we left—both parents screamed at the children. Natalie was interpreting and stated that her father said he did not want her back at the house or to visit him at all. Walter also stated that his father said he only wanted to see Walter from now on and not Natalie. It was a very hostile visit and both children stated they would not return to their parents' home.

Aug. 27, 2:00—Clinicals with Dr. Nabolotny with the children. . . .

WALTER

Cousin Walter knew the Bylens from church. I think I might have seen them there once or twice, but I didn't know them at all.

One day in August, we simply got moved over to their house— me, my sister, my clothing, her clothing. When we arrived, the Bylens were so friendly, I never thought of them as strangers again. They were saying things like "Here, Walter, do whatever you want . . . sleep, sit around and watch television, whatever. We just want you to feel at home."

They were real nice, trying to be good "parents" to us even on the very first night we were there. The Bylens treated us like we were their own real children.

"Feel at home," they said, smiling and showing us around their house. They only wanted to help us.

Feel at home . . . but I couldn't feel at home. Even though they were Ukrainians, spoke the language real well, had immigrated from our country the same as we had, and knew it as well as we did. They understood how we felt about our parents and why we wouldn't want to accompany them back to Sambir. But I still felt out of place there, even though I didn't want to.

You just don't barge into someone else's lives, move into their home, eat their food . . . live with them . . . and not feel strange. It made me feel tense and unhappy.

About this time, the government decided that I was safe after all, and cut back all the bodyguards, and then finally removed the last one, too. I was sorry to see them go: I had really gotten to like them, and I learned a lot from them. I was nervous for a while without them, but after a few days, I quit worrying about it.

chapter seventeen
LEGAL UPS, LEGAL DOWNS

Our new life settled down for Natalie and me, and the rest of August moved by pretty fast. I didn't know it, but at the same time, the legal fight was getting harder. Sometime in that first summer of my escape from Ukraine, Mr. Kulas got important help from a lawyer in New York State named Henry Holzer. He wasn't a friend of Mr. Kulas's or anything, but Mr. Holzer's wife got interested in the case, and then both of them helped us out—sight unseen.

ERIKA HOLZER

I was working on my novel *Double Crossing*, which is about heroism and the Communist threat, when I heard about this little boy in Chicago who had stood up to the Soviet Union. I was horrified at the prospect of what would happen to him if he were ever taken back there. I was writing a syndicated column at the time, "One Woman's Voice," and decided to try to help out by writing about the case. So I called Julian Kulas, introduced myself over the phone, and we began talking.

The conversation went on for quite a while, as we discussed the legal questions. I'm a lawyer, and the case was very interesting, but I'm not an expert in the kinds of issues it raised. So after we had talked for a while, I introduced Julian by telephone to my husband, Henry, a lawyer and law school professor who is a specialist in individual rights.

I wrote the column and Henry began helping Julian. That's how it began for us.

HENRY MARK HOLZER

As a lawyer for almost thirty years and a teacher of constitutional law at Brooklyn Law School since 1972, I've had a longstanding interest in international affairs and individual rights. I used to represent Ayn Rand, whose philosophic theory was rooted in the notion of individual rights. This appealed to me greatly and still does, and I've always been highly sensitized to those kinds of issues.

My wife and I were both very taken with the drama of what had occurred, that a twelve-year-old boy would defect. She talked to Julian, and then he and I began to talk. It became apparent to me that he and the Polovchak children were in for a very long legal haul.

They were going to be in very deep water legally and constitutionally, because the resources of the ACLU were going to outgun them. The Chicago ACLU were old hands at constitutional litigation and Julian was not. So I started giving him advice on the phone, as much as I could.

My values are what you would call pro-freedom, pro-individualist, anti-Communist, anti-collectivist. So I wanted to do everything I could to help, but I also did not want to be horning in on Julian's case. This was never a question of fees, because neither Julian nor I ever sought to be paid, even though he, especially, spent thousands of his own dollars on the case. It's that I just don't like to louse up somebody else's arrangement.

Sometime during that first summer, Julian was asked to appear on a New York radio program in connection with the case, and he couldn't go. He called to ask if I would do it for him. I said I'd be happy to, but now this ambivalence I had came out.

I said, "Look, on one hand, I'm delighted to help you out. On the other, I don't want you to think I'm horning in on this. If they ask, what shall I tell them my connection is to the case?"

"Well," Julian said, "how would you feel about co-counsel?"

That made it official. I was happy to be *de facto* and *de jure* co-counsel, because the idea of a twelve-year-old who defects from the East appealed to me greatly. One doesn't get a chance to stand up for one's principles that often, let alone in that dramatic and unusual a way—helping defend a child against totalitarian Soviet rule. My values got me into it, and kept me in it for five and a half years.

Julian and I spoke on the phone two or three times a night. The case permeated our lives. There literally was not a day that went by that something didn't come up, or that I wasn't thinking about it. We eventually had seven separate cases going; I was playing a transcontinental chess game. I'd get an idea and call Julian to say, "Do this," or "Let's do that." It went on like this for years.

Separately, Julian and I both reached the same idea of putting the Soviet Union itself on trial. This stemmed from the fact that at the core of the case was the unwillingness of the boy to return to a terribly tyrannical system. Whatever the legal issues, this core remained intact and powerful, there for all to see, whether the case was styled a political defection, a domestic MINS case involving a runaway, or a constitutional case aimed at exalting the federal grant of asylum over the state's custody arrangement, through the supremacy clause of the U.S. Constitution. The actual unwillingness of the child to return to his homeland stood forth, however it was styled legally and procedurally.

To the extent that the parents and the Soviet system were asserting a claim on him, the nature of that which sought him—the tyranny of Soviet rule—was very much involved.

Julian, my wife, and I are concerned in a very broad way with East-West issues, and any opportunity to expose, publicize, and publicly condemn that system is one we would very much want to take advantage of. So here was a dovetailing of avocational interest and proper management of a very important lawsuit. If the opportunity had arisen, we could have done a very good job of putting the USSR on trial—a show trial in the best sense of the word. I think this is one of the things that the other side began to understand and didn't very much like. At a certain point, they began to drag their feet.

The ACLU fights parental rights every day of the week, and so in this case, you want to ask, if they so much believe in children's rights in such issues as opposing notification of parents in abortion cases, how come they don't believe a twelve-and-a-half-year-old, who has received asylum from the U.S. government, is entitled not to return to the Soviet Union, the most damnable place on earth? To me, the only answer to this question is that the ACLU has a different agenda. It was founded by Communists and fellow travelers, and they have become increasingly radical and have a very clear social and domestic agenda, as well as an international one. The onus is on them to explain clearly why they wanted to give the child back to the parents, who they knew wanted to go back to the USSR. It isn't enough for the ACLU to simply invoke the standard of parents' rights.

More than that, I think they were doing the work of the Soviet Union. In his sworn deposition, ACLU lawyer Harvey Grossman denied knowing if Pyotr Prilepski was a KGB agent. . . .

EXCERPT FROM GROSSMAN DEPOSITION

KULAS: Did you know that Peter Prilepski was a KGB agent?

GROSSMAN: I didn't know that then and I don't know that now to the extent that your question assumes that to be the case. I don't know that that is a fact at this point in time, either. I dealt with Mr. Prilepski as a consulate—as a member of the consulate and that's all.

HENRY MARK HOLZER

John Barron, the *Reader's Digest* specialist on the KGB, said the job Prilepski held at the Soviet embassy was typically a KGB position. So here you've got the Roger Baldwin Foundation of the ACLU, devoted to civil and individual and children's rights, perhaps consorting with the KGB to destroy a small boy, and, at the least, ship him back to the Soviet Union.

At the least, the child would face reeducation; at the worst, his life would be ruined. He would be marked as an enemy of the people. So the ACLU was at least hypocritical in this.

I wanted to save this boy and, tactically, everything was subordinated to that goal, including the series of delays that ensued over the years that prevented us from ever bringing the case to a full trial. But I also had my own agenda.

Walter's case offered the opportunity to make a statement to the world that there are people in this country who know and understand the difference between a free, democratic society and a totalitarian Communist state, and will do whatever they can to save one person.

There was nothing I could do when the Soviet sailor Simas Kudirka was sent back to his ship in that notorious case. But I vowed that if I ever had an opportunity to do anything in a situation like this, I would do it—for me as well as for him.

Walter provided that opportunity. I did it for me, my vows, what I believe in. The worst of worst cases was that the government, press, ACLU, would all gang up on us and we would have to run— hide Walter. I had contingency plans for just that. I never told Julian, because he would be the first person the authorities would seek. For his protection, I wanted him to know nothing.

Julian and I built a real bond, a relationship good for all time: we went through a war together. It was very draining emotionally, but there is nothing we wouldn't do all over again if the need and the cause were there.

One of the remarkable things is that no lawyer in this nation of lawyers ever offered to help. Not one person said, "If there's anything I can do, let me know." We did it all ourselves. If we had been defending a kid whose parents were trying to take him back to South Africa, we'd have had Jane Fonda, Ramsey Clark, Ed Asner, and others helping out. But this just involved parents who wanted to take this child back to the totalitarian Ukraine. Nobody did a damn thing to help. I don't understand it.

HARVEY GROSSMAN, ACLU ATTORNEY

Just a week before I arrived at the Illinois ACLU, the adjudicatory hearing took place at which Walter was found to be a MINS.

As I saw it, it seemed as if Juvenile Court was being used in a manipulative way to get a political result allowing Walter to stay here. It was that simple.

I'd been a Legal Aid lawyer for many years before coming to Chicago and had done a fair amount of juvenile work. I was quite familiar with policies regarding runaways—and Walter clearly didn't fit into the classification of a child against whom Cook County or its state's attorney normally would have taken formal action as a first-time runaway.

We rightly saw that the state's Juvenile Court Act was being tortured by the intervention. In fact, this is almost exactly what the Illinois Supreme Court said in its later ruling upholding our case: that it was unprecedented to have state action in a first-time runaway.

I guess it's a little confusing knowing what entity of government should be concerned with the welfare of children in such circumstances. Clearly, that needs to be identified, and there needs to be that sort of intervention. In Walter's case, it's hard to say who that should have been or how that should have occurred. But the Immigration and Naturalization Service doesn't seem terribly well suited to inquire into the welfare of a child, as the Seventh Circuit opinion later indicated. While state juvenile authorities seem more capable, it's hard to carry out these responsibilities in terms of a MINS.

[Walter's attorneys] could have tried to have it considered a neglected-child case instead, trying to make the point that the parents wanted to try to take Walter into an atmosphere injurious to his welfare. I don't think as a legal approach a neglected minor would have been any better, but I think at least it would have focused on what his lawyers thought—that he could be subjected to harm.

Instead, they wanted to try to bootstrap that into the second stage of the juvenile hearing, the dispositional hearing, where rules of evidence don't apply, and really put on a horror show. But it never took place. I don't know who made those decisions, but I think it was primarily the assistant state's attorney.

Under the guise of saying Walter was a MINS, the parents would first lose their rights, then, in a proceeding where there were no rules of evidence, face a confrontation in which they would be accused of subjecting their child to harm, because people would have testified for Walter that there was a pattern of reprisal on the part of the Soviet government with regard to political figures.

Our clients found themselves in a situation where their child had been taken away from them on an emergency basis, which the Illinois Supreme Court said never should have happened. Then, when they sought an immediate hearing, the judge refused to hold it, and instead converted it into a regular adjudicatory hearing.

At that point, it was very hard to relate to Walter as a political figure. I'd done his deposition and asked him why he wanted to stay here, and it was really the same old parody: he had friends, he liked his school. But not that he was struggling for his freedom, or wanted religious freedom, or wanted to grow up in America or feared persecution.

The final DCFS report depicts the family as still functioning at that point. There also are psychiatric reports, examinations done for our clients that have never been seen by Walter or his lawyers. Dr. Littner and a colleague met with Walter and the parents on numerous occasions in group conflict sessions. The psychiatrists' conclusions were basically supportive of the parents' position.

We had Michael go through several clinical evaluations with a Ukrainian-speaking psychiatrist to make sure he was okay, and he was. I can say there was no pathology, no problem, and a great sense of sympathy and understanding that he would feel the way he felt.

The asylum grant to Walter was equally unique and probably as troublesome as the juvenile proceeding. My reading of the depositions of federal officials suggested there was a great deal of paranoia by them—notions of kidnapping, clandestine plots, and so forth. Ultimately, they went back to the State Department and asked them to remove the security watch because nothing had ever happened.

In fact, local INS officials didn't want to grant asylum, but did so on orders from Washington. We never tried to dislodge it substantively, even though there had been a great deal of deceit in how the asylum proceeding was carried out. For example, Walter's immigration papers don't reflect at all the whereabouts or existence of the family in the United States.

Walter's attorneys, I'm sure in good faith and intending to assist their clients, mischaracterized our intentions, in an effort, I presume, to create strong public opinion and in the interest of getting a strong response from federal officials, who obviously were quite sympathetic to them once Reagan came on board.

Our federal suit never sought the forcible return of the child. It just wasn't so. From the time they went back to the Soviet Union, we had an agreement with the parents that we would never do anything other than return them to their status quo. The intention of these suits was only to eradicate unconstitutional conduct, to wipe the slate clean, and they would always have to start over from base one with their child.

The state suit did exactly what we sought: it vacated all those orders and returned him to the status quo. And if you look at all the briefs we wrote, and decisions from the federal case, that obviously was our position.

All we were saying is that the order had to be vacated because of the unfairness.

Whether Walter could have legitimately proved an asylum claim was not a specific issue in any of the cases. We would never have represented the parents in a substantive proceeding of that nature. Our retainer agreement specifed as to the federal side that all we'd do was challenge procedural due process. They understood that we would not file a lawsuit on their behalf that would result in or require the forced return of their child.

But we never made this position public. We never wanted to say how limited our suits were, because we didn't want to give Walter a blueprint for fighting his parents. From day one, that was part of our problem. We thought that if we were vocal, we would tell Walter exactly what he needed to do to win and we didn't want to intervene into the family situation that much. In addition, we're clear on this in the press, we're always talking about conciliation.

We never said Walter would be forced to go to the Soviet Union. We said that the results of the federal suit would be such that the parents could come here and talk to him, and if they could convince him to go to the Soviet Union, then that was a family matter.

Now, I don't think Anna and Michael Polovchak resolved issues with their children the way I would want to do with my children. But on the other hand, I don't have the right to tell them how to do that.

We tried very hard to get the family into counseling, paid the bills for it, but it blew up after a few visits. Part of the problem was that Julian refused to sign a stipulation that this counseling was to be off the record. I don't fault him for that. I think Julian did an extraordinary effort to assist the kid. I might not have done what he did in the way he did it, but I don't question his intentions, or the extent of his energy and commitment.

It was very difficult to get Michael into counseling anyway. He always thought it was just more of the court case. Based on discussions I've had with psychiatrists who deal with other east Europeans, his attitude is not that unusual, particlarly for the men—concrete, nonabstract-thinking, everyday practical-Joe guys.

My impression of Michael is that . . . the economic system or form of government under which he lived was an irrelevancy to him. The question to him was simply, as a workingman, what was his job and his pay—how did his family live every day?

He did not have a refugee mentality, he did not come here to suffer to increase the living standard of successive generations, which is what I think of as the refugee mentality. At the same time, Michael thought he was going to get rich . . . right then and there improve their standard of living.

We'll never know if family counseling would have succeeded or not. In this instance, it could not go forward because of the legal impediments, and that's not unusual. It's a terrible, terrible thing that happens in Juvenile Court all the time. By the time you get to Juvenile Court, you no longer have flexibility to do the kinds of things that families often need to do to solve their problems.

I found Judge Mooney to be an untalented judge, very removed from everyday realities of parent-child relations, ineffective in the case. The assistant state's attorneys pretty much ran his courtroom. That's also not uncommon.

I guess we were concerned at that point that whatever its outcome, the dispositional hearing would destroy the family, because what the other side wanted to do was to establish a pattern of persecution. But Walter would never fit within that. In fact, Walter had not been granted asylum on the basis of persecution, but solely on the basis that he wanted asylum.

At the time he sought asylum, in July 1980, it was the State Department's policy that any East-bloc national applying for asylum got it, because the very act of asking could bring persecution if he was sent back to his home country. Three months after Walter received asylum, State abandoned the policy forever.

Meanwhile, Walter's side had a bootstrap opportunity: how would the Soviets know you had applied for asylum? "The press." How would the press know? "I told them today." So it became a very difficult proposition for the parents. We frankly didn't care whether he had asylum or not. Asylum was an irrelevancy to us for a very long time.

But when the departure control order was issued on the basis of asylum, that's when it became a problem.

JULIAN KULAS

Although there were many different hearings in many different courtrooms over the next five years, the ACLU's tactics and performance never really varied from the early hearings. Rather than detail each separate case and court appearance, I think a couple of these exchanges from late summer 1980 accurately portray the ACLU's views of Walter and the issues throughout our long confrontation. Here are several, drawn from my files, with some of the discussions abridged for clarity:

On August 7, 1980, the civil liberties unit challenged the possibility that the children would be placed with the Gusievs—which hadn't occurred. They'd read a story in the *Chicago Sun-Times* quoting Dmitri Gusiev saying things critical of the USSR.

Richard Lifschitz for the ACLU said he wanted the hearing "in light of the definite bias of the aunt and uncle towards Walter not returning to the Ukraine.

"Because of that, we are requesting the court not place Walter with his aunt and uncle, and return . . . him to his parents . . . [or] place Walter in a neutral foster home.

"However, our primary relief which we are seeking is that Walter be returned to his parents. The basis of that is this court's statement on August 4, that the court is desirous of reconciling Walter with his parents. We feel it would be appropriate that this court order Walter be returned to his parents' home, since there is very little chance that Walter would run away. . . .

". . . Since this proceeding has begun, [Walter] has been accompanied by two Immigration officers wherever he goes. We feel that those officers could ensure that Walter not run from his parents' house.

"Further, we would ask the court to order Walter not to leave his parents' house. . . ."

Arguing for the state, Rick Michaels complained that Lifschitz "misunderstands both the law . . . and the orders entered by this court. . . . The fact that this petition only involves Walter and not Natalie shows . . . the parents' real purposes."

I told the judge that I was not opposed to moving the children from Cousin Walter's, but that I could not agree to return them to their parents.

During that session, the judge mentioned that he had read a *Sun-Times* article that reported from the Soviet Union how a grandmother had abducted one of her own grandchildren to keep him from accompanying the family to the West, which the granny apparently opposed.

The Soviets required only that the ten-year-old child sign a form expressing the wish to stay in the Motherland, and it would be allowed.

"Apparently, a declaration is all that's necessary over there," Judge Mooney remarked, inferring the diminished powers granted parents and the ease and speed with which the USSR accepted even a very young child's declaration of fealty.

"I can't respond to what is occurring in the Soviet Union," said Lifschitz. "What I am concerned with is what is happening to Walter."

To my mind, the exchange made perfectly clear what the ACLU was unwilling to admit—that they didn't care or understand what life was like in the Soviet Union, despite Walter's willingness to run away from home to escape it.

"Walter is still in his cousin's home," Lifschitz said. "There was clear evidence presented to this court that Cousin Walter would do everything he could do to keep Walter from returning to the Ukraine."

"That was not the evidence," I broke in.

". . . The longer he remains with his cousin," Lifschitz argued, "the less likely it is that any chance for reconciliation will occur. . . . Every day that goes by which Walter is out of his home is damaging to Walter. . . ."

"Why do I try a case on Monday and retry it on Thursday?" Judge Mooney said wearily.

"Your Honor, because there are new facts," Lifschitz said.

"There are no new facts that I have not heard," the judge replied. "You are repeating yourself."

"Your Honor—"

"And the next time, I am going to hold you strictly to procedures, and I am not going to entertain frivolous motions. . . ."

Then Harvey Grossman repeated the ACLU's objections.

". . . Continued placement of Walter in the cousin's home is contrary to the intent of this court to achieve reconciliation, and indeed is contrary to what we are trying to do on behalf of the parents," Grossman said. "And that is why we are here today. Continued placement with the cousin creates family tension."

Carol Amadio, a lawyer representing DCFS, rebutted him. "Your Honor, before the court ever made orders for visitation, the department tried on numerous occasions to get the family to visit with the children, and the [parents] refused. . . .

"This kind of continued stirring of things is making it very difficult for us to implement any kind of reconciliation. The parents have got to recognize the fact [that] it is difficult for children to be moved around over and over. And we are trying our best to effect a placement that will be satisfactory for the children. We are also considering the family—the reconciliation problem has to do with Walter. But they have got to be willing to recognize some needs of the children, and I don't think they're doing that. . . ."

". . . The issue for the Polovchaks is . . . that the child continues in the custody of Cousin Walter," Grossman said.

". . . The child is not in the custody of Cousin Walter," said Virginia Egem, the caseworker. "He is in the custody of DCFS. We are at the point now where we are looking for a placement for him—an appropriate placement. Until we find one, he will, with the court's permission, remain with his cousin."

". . . We should be addressing ourselves to both children, and not Walter alone," I reminded.

"We can't forget Natalie," agreed Judge Mooney. ". . . She was a ward of the court, too. A seventeen-year-old girl, notwithstanding the fact that the parents aren't concerned about her, and her remaining in the United States. We are. She is our ward. We have to look after her."

RICHARD LIFSCHITZ: Your Honor, I would just like to say again, the parents are concerned about Natalie . . .

JUDGE MOONEY: . . . They're not concerned about her staying or going back.

LIFSCHITZ: They are concerned.

MOONEY: Well, they said no.

LIFSCHITZ: That's not true. They are concerned. However, they have decided that this is what she is going to want to do, and they will respect her decision and allow her to do it. They don't want her to stay. But this is what she wants to do. And they are willing to respect that decision.

JULIAN KULAS: This is contrary to the evidence presented in court.

JUDGE MOONEY: It's contrary to all the evidence I have heard. Maybe you attended a different case?

On August 15, we were in court on the same issue again. At that hearing, the judge discovered what I had learned weeks before—that Walter was extremely nearsighted and the parents had never done a thing about it.

The ACLU evinced no knowledge of this and more or less tried to paper it over. They didn't offer a word of concern or sympathy for the child, who had spent years, it seems, unable to see very well. They didn't find a single pleasant word to say to the DCFS social workers who, having discovered the problem, quickly set about helping Walter.

The issue came up when the judge unexpectedly asked Virginia Egem, the caseworker, "How is the health of these children?"

EGEM: They seem to be just fine, Your Honor. Except Walter has an eye problem.

MOONEY: Yes? What is that eye problem?

EGEM: Very poor vision. Twenty-eighty and I can't remember the other.

MOONEY: Poor vision?

EGEM: Very poor. But we got glasses. We are waiting for them.

MOONEY: Well, how long has he had that eye condition?

KULAS: That has been in existence for a long time, Your Honor.

MOONEY: But he hasn't had any corrective lenses?

KULAS: No. He has never been provided any. There was never any attention given to it. In fact, I think Natalie has some problem with vision as well.

EGEM: We are going to take her next week.

MOONEY: So you are getting glasses for Walter?

EGEM: We ordered them yesterday, Your Honor. It is going to take ten days.

MOONEY: Twenty-eighty did you say?

EGEM: Real bad. I was in the room. He can hardly see the wall.

MOONEY: Oh, for goodness sakes.

HARVEY GROSSMAN: It might be the root of the problem.

MOONEY: How is it that the parents didn't discover it?

GROSSMAN: I have no idea.

LIFSCHITZ: Your Honor, we had no knowledge this was an existing condition. I have no basis to know that. And for Mr. Kulas to say they were aware—

KULAS: The father told me about it.

LIFSCHITZ: Judge, I don't see any point in going into depth on this issue.

MOONEY: Don't you tell me what I am going to inquire about in a hearing like this.

LIFSCHITZ: I am not trying to tell you anything.

MOONEY: They are wards of mine.

LIFSCHITZ: Fine.

GROSSMAN: Your Honor, I would be happy to find out what the actual situation is surrounding it and inform the court.

MOONEY: Every time I inquire about something that is a little sensitive to you, you say, "I don't think it is proper to go into it."

GROSSMAN: Your Honor, I think it is a natural response for an advocate, since our client was being quoted through Mr. Kulas. I apologize to the court. But that definitely put the discussion in an adversary context for us. We are representing our clients here today.

MOONEY: I don't know whether we are representing anybody but the best interest of all the parties. . . . It is not intended to be adversary.

GROSSMAN: Your Honor, I understand that. But the best interest is determined by us representing our clients, and Mr. Kulas is representing his clients and you are the one who determines best interest. What we do is act on behalf of our clients. . . . I don't mean to insult the court in any way, shape, or form. But when Mr. Kulas quotes our client under oath, naturally, we are going to respond.

MOONEY: Very well. If you insist on making it adversary, I will treat it as an adversary proceeding.

GROSSMAN: I do not mean to treat it as an adversary proceeding. I am explaining my position. . . .

The tone and nature of the wrangling among us never really changed through all the years to come.

Perhaps nothing that happened in all the five years of the legal battle spoke more forcefully to this point than the ACLU's surprise move on November 5, 1980, when without warning, the ACLU lawyers demanded that the case be removed from Judge Mooney's jurisdiction and sent to the Illinois Appellate Court.

The parents' lawyers invoked a procedural rule that sets a ninety-day time limit between the first day a Family Court judge establishes temporary state custody over a child and a full hearing and disposition of that case.

Since many of the delays had been caused by the ACLU lawyers themselves, I felt this was an unfair tactic. In one of those reversals that often occur in legal proceedings, we found ourselves arguing against the appeal on the grounds that it would only cause further delays in finally deciding the case.

The ACLU, on the other hand, was determined to press its sudden appeal. It won. Judge Mooney relinquished the case, and it was kicked upstairs in the Illinois state judicial system to the Appellate Court.

HARVEY GROSSMAN

Taking it out of Juvenile Court prevented a zoo in Juvenile Court—which already was a zoo. The kind of dispositional hearing that Walter's lawyers wanted, put on without rules of evidence, would have just been out of control. Walter would have become so scared and intimidated and would have thought that his parents were such bad people to try to do that to him that his parents were convinced that the hearing would be so destructive, there was no point in having the hearing.

The other point was, why endure that kind of hearing if the

Juvenile Court, in the first instance, had no jurisdiction—as clearly it did not, as the Illinois Supreme Court said.

JULIAN KULAS

The irony, of course, is that the ACLU's move opened the door to a series of further delays in the case. We lost a number of decisions in the ensuing years, but the delays themselves took on a life of their own, adding month after month after month to the procedural and legal battle.

With each passing day and week, Walter got older. The magic number—age eighteen—steadily approached. No lost legal decisions could slow time's passage.

Neither the Holzers nor I ever bought the ACLU's argument that in taking the parents' side against Walter, it somehow was upholding individual rights against government intervention. We weren't alone in this view.

For example, one day in 1981, I received a letter from the ACLU of New Jersey, seeking my help in a case it had taken on behalf of a sixteen-year-old Chilean boy who wished to remain in the United States instead of accompanying his parents back to Chile.

". . . I understand that your client, Walter Polovchak, was deemed eligible for permanent residency," wrote Lin Fulcher, a New Jersey ACLU legal assistant. "I am hoping that this will be of some help to our client.

"This ACLU affiliate has taken the position that our case is one of children's rights, a different stance than that taken by our Illinois affiliate, as you certainly know. . . ."

I was happy to send them some of our briefs, and wondered if the Illinois ACLU would ever come to its senses. It never did.

chapter eighteen
DEPARTURES—
BUT NO GOODBYES

1

I celebrated my thirteenth birthday on October 3, 1980, at a party given by Mr. Kulas, Cousin Walter, and some of the people who had helped me. The ACLU made a big deal about the fact that my parents weren't there, even writing almost two years later in their official report on the case:

"As Michael and Anna watch the evening news on television, they see Julian Kulas, a Baptist minister, and people they do not know celebrate Walter's thirteenth birthday at a party at a restaurant. The parents have not been told of the party. They must wait for their one-hour weekly visit to give their son his presents. As the weeks go by, their visits with their children become increasingly strained."

My father had done plenty of things for me since I'd been born, but giving presents to his family wasn't something anyone would remember him for. The ACLU tried to make out that my parents were just like parents in a storybook. It wasn't true.

The truth is that by the time of my birthday, my parents and I seemed to disagree about everything. Under the court ruling, we had "family visits" each week, all of us groping around for something to talk about that wouldn't get somebody mad. Despite help from DCFS social workers, these visits never solved anything.

I felt myself drawing further from my parents. I was suddenly starting to grow more, getting bigger than my own father. I don't think he liked this very much. It made the differences between us seem even greater. Also, I was getting along in school on my own, with no help from my parents because they still knew almost no English, and the list of things they didn't like was pretty long, from Big Macs to rock music to movies—even most of the TV shows I watched. What did we have together?

I played soccer with a boys' team and there was in my mind the memory that my father had never kicked a ball around with me. Even Mr. Kulas, who worked all the time and had a family of his own, didn't mind playing a little soccer with me from time to time. All it took was a ball and a piece of lawn or field. You could even dribble a ball on the sidewalk or in an alley. So I resented my father trying to pass himself off as someone who really cared for me, when he spent no time with me.

One Saturday, Mr. Kulas took me to a Notre Dame football game. The press showed up and some of the grown-ups gave me gifts. I didn't know what in heck was going on out on the field— you couldn't see the ball half the time and the players really beat up on each other. Even now, American football remains pretty much a mystery to me. But what was I going to tell my father about this weekend? However little I knew, he knew even less.

There was something else as well, much more important than football or soccer, or maybe anything else good that happened to me that fall—my new glasses. They helped me so much—I hadn't had any idea of how much I'd been missing before!

Now I could see everything in a room without squinting. I didn't feel so funny, because I could see what other kids could see. And now I had glasses, just like a lot of them did. Some of the things I'd been uncertain about, that sometimes made me want to kick myself, or wonder why I was so stupid, just went out of my life. For good. If I had never had the guts to run away, I might still be trying to get by without glasses, and wondering what was wrong that made me seem so out of touch.

It wasn't my parents or the ACLU I had to thank for this improvement. It was the state caseworkers who found out what was wrong with my eyes and knew how to fix it. I didn't know how to talk to my father about this, but I was pretty sure I knew what he'd say even if I had brought it up with him. So that was another example of the resentment I felt.

Pretty soon, I was thinking about contact lenses, because they could make my vision even better. They didn't exist for everyday people in the Soviet Union. My parents had never heard of them, so how could I talk to them about contacts? But Cousin Walter knew, and so did Natalie, Mr. Kulas, and the Bylens, as well as plenty of other Ukrainians who had come to America and managed to build themselves a good, new life. I wanted the same for myself.

So all the time I was growing, they were staying the same.

Christmas and New Year's 1981 came and went. Nineteen eighty had been full of surprises, and 1981 was filled with them, too. I didn't look back. I looked ahead. It was lucky I did.

On January 19, Natalie reached the magic number—eighteen! She didn't waste any time: on January 25, without telling any of the DCFS caseworkers, my sister moved out of the Bylens' house and returned to Cousin Walter's. The Bylens understood, but Walter, Natalie, and I were very happy . . . my sister was *free*!

EXCERPTS, JUVENILE COURT OF COOK COUNTY
SOCIAL INVESTIGATION, NATALIE POLOVCHAK
DATE DICTATED: 2/26/81 OFFICER GOGGIN

---

1) On 1/19/81, the child became eighteen years old.
2) On 1/23/81, the minor moved to the home of her cousin without permission of her temporary custodian, DCFS.
3) Subsequent view of her self-placement with Cousin Walter reveals his willingness to care for her. Natalie wishes to remain with her cousin, asserting that she no longer needs the care of foster parents.
4) Natalie has applied to the CETA Program for part-time employment while studying for a GED Examination in June.
Child's Statement:
    Natalie stated to this officer that when she was originally placed, with her brother, Walter, in the temporary custodial care of Mr. and Mrs. Bylen . . . it was to be for a short period of time. However, it has gone on for a period of over three months and Natalie felt uncomfortable staying there. She said she likes the Bylens, but did not want to remain in a foster home. She added that she has said all along as soon as she was eighteen years old she would . . . go

live with her relative, Cousin Walter. She did in fact state this to this officer several times. She added since she had made this clear, it should be no surprise that she acted on this. She feels that at the age of eighteen, she does not need to be in foster care nor does she need to be under the custody of DCFS. She added that she has her life fairly well mapped out at this point, has plans, and with the temporary help of her Cousin Walter will be able to take care of herself. . . .

At this time, Natalie has no intentions of returning to live with her parents. She stated unequivocally that she will not ever return to Russia and in addition, should her parents decide to remain in the United States, it is doubtful . . . she would live with them. Natalie feels that it is in her best interest, at this point, to live with Cousin Walter. Cousin Walter stated to this officer that he is totally agreeable to giving Natalie whatever financial assistance she may need at this time. . . .

[Her] relationship with her cousin is very good. They have a close family relationship that seems to be based on friendship and mutual respect. . . .

The girl has become much more assured in her self-evaluation and her ability to handle her living situation. Natalie has made a couple of firm decisions concerning where she wishes to live, and her future, and [it] appears that she has used mature judgment. . . .

Mr. and Mrs. Polovchak in previous interviews have indicated they felt Natalie was old enough to make her own decisions in so far as remaining in the United States is concerned. . . . Despite the obvious strain and problems that have developed in Natalie's relationship with her parents, she does continue to visit them. Within the last few months, it would seem that her relationship has in fact improved with mother and dad and there are some positive signs that there will be a continuing thaw in their relationship. . . . There is less arguing and more family rapport. This does not necessarily mean that there will be smooth sailing from here on, but it does show that there has been some progress. . . .

Natalie's relationship with her brother Walter continues to be very close. She is still very concerned about the outcome of his case in court and is going to remain close to him. She has no plans to leave the city until her brother's case is resolved.

Recommendation and Plan:

This officer feels that Natalie at the age of eighteen is showing an ability to make and act upon mature adult plans. It is recommended that Natalie be allowed to pursue her own course of action in life. . . . It is apparent that in the very near future, she will be able to care for herself independently. She should be allowed to make her own decisions.

P. O. Goggin 2/27/81

WALTER

If anyone deserved a birthday party, it was Natalie—the first Po-lovchak kid to make it all the way to freedom in America!

Once again, she had led the way for me. My sister was a great example for sticking with something, no matter what the odds. She looked out for herself, but she had looked out for me, too, and I owed her a lot. All I hoped was that I'd someday get free myself.

And once again, Cousin Walter was there for us, ready to give whatever help was needed. This was the man the ACLU tried to paint as some kind of horrible enemy of my family, trying to tear it apart.

The truth was different from the way they made it out to be. Even though my father went on and on about how Cousin Walter was destroying his family, my mother and father didn't say much when Natalie moved back with my cousin.

My parents knew they had tried to pin things unfairly on Cousin Walter, and when they couldn't change Natalie's mind, they gave up and treated her okay—the first time in years—because she was completely beyond their power. Maybe I'd get there someday.

But all this changing around was nothing compared to what happened in August that year. Two shocks.

I'd gone to a soccer camp up in Baraboo, Wisconsin, west of Chicago, and was having a pretty good time there, working out, improving my game. I hadn't paid attention to the court cases or any of it for weeks. Nothing had happened to change any of the legal fights, so I just forgot about them. I hadn't heard from my parents, either. We'd had a visit early in the month, then I went off to camp and that was it. I was happy.

Around dusk on Wednesday, August 12, one of the camp officials found me and called me into his office. He was calm and sort of sad-looking. "Your parents have gone back to the Soviet Union," he said, just like that.

"*What?*"

"It's true. I just got a telephone call from Mr. Kulas."

"*They're gone?*"

"Yes. They left Chicago Monday night on a train for Washington, and they flew out of Washington today at five P.M. our time."

"Did—did they say anything . . . did they say goodbye?"

He just looked at me.

I felt numb all over. My mind was stunned. I felt like crying. *My parents had left and never even said goodbye? Not even a phone call?*

I just stared at the man.

"Now, it's okay . . ." he began.

I looked at him some more. I didn't know what to say. I think I felt embarrassed—for my mother and father.

I wondered if Natalie and Cousin Walter knew. The camp official said there would be some calls later.

They were on their way back to Ukraine without me!

The whole situation started to whirl inside my head. Why had they gone? Why hadn't my mother even said goodbye?

I went out of the office and wandered off by myself. I felt like an orphan. If they really wanted to make it hurt, my mother and father had succeeded.

There were calls later that night from Natalie, Mr. Kulas, and others, but there really wasn't much to say. It took me a long time to understand why they acted that way. On the one hand, I knew why they had given up. But not to even say goodbye . . . that part was the toughest for me.

When the press found out about it, they went wild. Pretty soon there was a helicopter rattling around over the camp, taking videotape. There were headlines all over the place. It was hard to realize that I'd never see my mother again.

HARVEY GROSSMAN

That was the year Michael and Anna became so depressed. They lost faith in the system. Ultimately, they left.

They became increasingly depressed, increasingly disenchanted with the legal system. We had filed an appeal from Judge Mooney's original ruling, but the Illinois Appellate Court delayed a decision for months. Of all the delays, that was the most destructive we encountered in the case. It did a great deal of damage to the parents.

To begin with, it's almost impossible for them to think about a legal system in which individuals prevail against the government. So they were very distrustful of the process from day one. They never had any faith in the system from day one.

And when the Juvenile Court appeal dragged on and on, they became more frustrated and things got much worse for them. They had been talking about going back, and ultimately that's what they told us they were going to do.

Among the two or three scenarios floated by Julian and Holzer was one that the parents didn't really care about the kids, but since Walter was on the father's visa, Michael had to take the kids back because the Soviets wouldn't let them back in without everyone who had been on their visa. This wasn't the case. The parents genuinely loved Walter and didn't want to be separated from him just because they wanted to return to their homeland.

But the parents' departure unquestionably undercut their position that they wanted their kids to go back with them.

I think they had no faith in our being able to get Walter back— either at that time or later. And so to them the situation was, they and their other child were being held here in some sort of circumstance beyond their control and they couldn't win anyway. They unquestionably had lost faith.

We knew it was coming. I didn't want them to leave; I told them it would be harmful to their case. We established we would not continue to represent them unless they agreed to return to the United States to engage in any further proceedings—and in fact exercise custody and guardianship over their child if we were able to secure that for them.

They agreed, and that's why we continued to represent them. They always had to come back to get the benefits of any case that we did for them.

Why didn't they say goodbye? They had become totally alienated by then. The family visitation was no good. By that time, Walter had become convinced, I think, that he was going to be tortured and jailed if he returned to the Soviet Union, and once he became convinced and believed it, I don't think there really was any way to restore any kind of harmony to the family.

HENRY MARK HOLZER

About the same week that the Polovchaks were quietly getting ready
to leave America without saying farewell to the children they couldn't
live without, I made an extraordinary discovery. I was talking by
telephone with an assistant federal prosecutor, Nancy Needles, in
the office of the U.S. attorney for the Northern District of Illinois.
This has always been one of the most powerful and visible federal
prosecutors' offices in the country.

The ACLU had gone into U.S. District Court with a suit challenging the grant of asylum to Walter. Nancy said she was calling
me to inform me that in connection with the suit, she had just
worked out the custody arrangements for the children between the
U.S. Attorney's Office and the ACLU. I was astonished that such
negotiations had been going on.

I just played nice and dumb and listened politely while she talked.
She said, "I'll send you a copy of the letter. It says that if the
parents win custody of Walter from the State of Illinois, the federal
government will stand aside and let the parents take him."

This was devastating news. It meant that despite the sovereign
grant of political asylum from the State Department to a twelve-
year-old who was a sure target of reprisal in the Soviet Union, the
U.S. Attorney's Office was ready to sell him out.

The very idea that the U.S. attorney would agree with the ACLU
to stand down on defending the asylum if the state courts gave
custody to the parents is something I still don't understand.

Following up the telephone conversation, Needles, in letters to
Julian and me on August 5, informed us on behalf of Dan K. Webb,
the Reagan appointee as U.S. attorney, "Our intention is to file
this agreement with the court on August 24. . . . It is requested
that the terms of this agreement remain confidential until its entry
or until you take some formal action to preclude its entry. . . ."

I got on the telephone, made a lot of calls, talked to a lot of
people on Capitol Hill. Roger Simon, a *Sun-Times* columnist, wrote
a column making the deal public, under a strong headline: U.S.
ASYLUM FOR WALTER: A SELLOUT? It appeared the day after the Polovchak parents flew off to the USSR. It was the first major piece.

"This is a sellout," I was quoted as saying. "The United States is abandoning him. It is horrendous."

I wrote to Reagan's new Attorney General, William French Smith, telling him in part, "If the federal government reneges on the asylum which it granted to Walter Polovchak thirteen months ago, the United States will be sending an unmistakable message around the globe: America's promise of safe haven cannot be trusted; our grant of asylum, rather than being unconditional, irrevocable, inviolate, is instead ephemeral, temporary, suspect. . . ."

I talked with Bob Novak and he wrote a column, the gist of which was that William French Smith's Justice Department was not being as Reaganite as it should be.

Ed Meese saw the column the day it appeared, and the very same day, I got a call from the Justice Department. Somebody there wanted me to know there had been a terrible mistake on my part, that I didn't understand what had happened because this thing had only been a proposed, tentative, preliminary, nonbinding draft of something that needed to be discussed . . .

I said, "That's very strange—what do you do with the formal letter that's been written?"

And they said, "Oh, we'll change it." They had just reversed themselves.

From then on, they committed themselves to protecting the asylum of Walter, and they did pretty well. For example, Webb, the Reagan appointee in Chicago, later told the Appellate Court of Illinois: "The grant of asylum is an integral part of this country's immigration law, international law, and the foreign policy power of the [chief] executive. . . . The judiciary is foreclosed from nullifying or subtracting from that grant. . . ."

Ever after that first episode, I never really trusted them again. Anybody who was capable of doing what they did once was capable of doing it again.

Julian was completely unused to this kind of thing, let alone the dishonesty of it all.

When the parents went back to the Soviet Union, I told Julian, "This is the turning point. From a tactical point of view, whatever rationale they had, they have just made a colossal tactical blunder. It's one thing to try for custody when they were in Chicago and quite another thing to try it from the USSR."

Beyond that, there is no doubt that the parents discredited themselves by leaving without saying goodbye. I think the mother certainly wouldn't have done that—whatever she was, she was a mother. But apparently, they were controlled by others.

In late October, Justice came through by granting permanent residency to Walter, a stronger form of precitizenship status. It strengthened Walter's situation, and, as it turned out, not a moment too soon, either.

JULIAN KULAS

It was very interesting and instructive to see how the Soviets handled the return of the Polovchaks to Soviet territory.

"I am crying for my children taken away from me," Tass, the official Soviet press agency, quoted Anna as saying. It was surely true that she was crying and that she probably had convinced herself that the courts had taken the children away, but the statement quickly descended into fantasy.

"Courts in the United States are a parody of justice," she said. "I know that Walter wants to come back home, but he is being prevented from doing so."

She described the home visits arranged by DCFS as ordeals in which Walter was delivered to her door by "two extremely gloomy characters. They hardly allowed him to speak. Walter was extremely lukewarm, somewhat senseless, as if not alive. They surely poison him with narcotics. It is quite clear that they detain him by force."

Michael Polovchak was quoted as saying that he was offered money and a house if he would participate in organized anti-Soviet activities. "I refused and they took away my children for that," he supposedly said. "I will continue to struggle and not be quiet until they return my children to me."

This was exactly the kind of propaganda that the Soviets were capable of making from this terrible situation. Once again, they demonstrated that distorting truth was more important to them than any other consideration. When it came to propaganda, they really didn't care what happened to Polovchak or his wife—or his children, for that matter.

The parents' abrupt departure opened several doors for us. In mid-November, with Walter now fourteen and beginning to really look his age, Anastasia and John Junko petitioned the Cook County Circuit Court to adopt Walter.

"We allege the parents have deserted and abandoned Walter, and that they have not shown any interest in Walter and his well-being . . ." they wrote in their court papers. This was the kind of sharpening of the issue of adult responsibility and child welfare that Walter's situation centered on. Henry and I felt no qualms backing the Junkos in their efforts to give Walter a stable home within the Polovchak family in America.

As the year came to a close, however, there was one more shock in store for us.

In the last week of December, the Appellate Court of Illinois overruled Juvenile Court Judge Mooney by a 2–1 vote and ordered Walter reunited with his parents.

The majority judges, Helen McGillicuddy and William White, confined themselves to the question of whether or not Walter had been properly removed from the Polovchaks' custody the previous year—and found he had not. They said they could see no cause for Mooney's finding that Walter was "beyond his parents' control."

"We believe that Walter's health, safety and welfare were not jeopardized when he absented himself from the family residence," they wrote in their opinion. "Walter was in no physical or mental danger as his needs were being met by his sister and cousin. Viewed in its simplest terms, the situation . . . [was] one of family discord caused by a child's disagreement with his parents' decision to return to their homeland. We have serious doubt as to whether the state would have intervened in this realm of family life and privacy had the parents' decision to relocate involved a move to another city or state. The fact that the parents had decided to move to a country which is ruled under principles of government which are alien to those of the United States of America should not compel a different result.

"Whether the minor may be entitled to political asylum in this country is an issue that should be decided by another forum. The Illinois MINS statute should not be utilized as a subterfuge to achieve such a result.

"We hold that under the facts presented, the trial court's determination that Walter was beyond the control of his parents was against the manifest weight of the evidence. Walter's single act of leaving the family residence after learning of his parents' decision to return to their homeland was an exaggerated manifestation of parent-child conflict and was not sufficient to bring him within the jurisdiction of the [Juvenile] Court. We further find that Walter, having gone to live with his sister and cousin, was not placed in a situation of grave danger such that he required care and guidance from the State."

It was a strongly worded decision, but the split vote gave us cause for hope. Looking for positive signs, Henry and I were gratified at the minority dissenting opinion of Judge Daniel J. McNamara, who called "unwarranted" the finding that the juvenile laws had been used as a "subterfuge." He wrote that Walter's act of packing up and leaving right before his mother's eyes "was the act of a boy beyond the control of his parents."

All this was beside the point. We had been defeated for the moment, and we faced the path of appeals.

First, however, there was an immediate step to be taken. On New Year's Eve 1981, I asked the Justice Department to issue a Departure Control Order, alerting all Immigration and Border Patrol agents that Walter was not to be allowed to leave the country.

Barely a week later, the order was issued, and prosecutor Dan Webb told the media: "I, as U.S. Attorney, will do everything I can to see that Walter remains in this country."

Harvey Grossman denounced all this as "further governmental interference with the Polovchak family's internal affairs." He vowed the ACLU would not give up its fight to reunite Walter and his parents. "The federal government does not have the constitutional authority to affect parental custody through its immigration laws."

This was a high moment for the ACLU, which had succeeded in its effort to win an important round for the parents. Yet there were numerous ways to appeal the Appellate Court's ruling, and Henry Holzer and I set out to do just that. The only thing the 2–1 decision meant to us was that we had more work to do.

Absolutely nothing was going to deter us from keeping Walter in the country. Not even the sudden return of his father.

2

COUSIN WALTER

When the parents left, the shock for all of us was severe. But it was also true that their departure made many things a lot easier for us as well, because we didn't have to worry about the fights, the arguments, the real stress of facing Walter's father in court and in the family meetings. They all just stopped dead. We had a lot more time and the kids were able to grow up a lot.

At the same time, the parents' departure unexpectedly delivered a very important legal advantage to Mr. Kulas and Mr. Holzer. They quickly began saying that in order to properly prepare their case, they needed to have a detailed interview, under oath, with Walter's father. But how could that occur, since the parents were now back in the Soviet Union?

No way. Mr. Kulas and Mr. Holzer couldn't get to Ukraine, and we all knew it would take the Soviets months, maybe years, to bring themselves to approve a visitor's visa for Michael Polovchak. So our lawyers asked for such a deposition—one of the best delaying tactics ever. Each day that passed without Mr. Polovchak here to give his deposition was a day to the good for Walter—one less day to go to the magic moment when he turned eighteen!

Then we learned that Mr. Polovchak would come back in April 1982, and spend a few days in Chicago to give his deposition. We put our heads together and thought what this meant for our fight. After a lot of talking, we realized that here was our chance to solve this mess once and for all. We could take the initiative and make clear to the father when he arrived that he had much to gain by agreeing to drop his attempt to get Walter back to Ukraine. He could be the hero, issue a statement saying his heart was breaking but he realized that for the good of his child, it was time to drop the fight and reconcile himself to the fact that he was going to have an American citizen for a son.

We knew it was unlikely the Soviets would agree, but it was worth the effort.

When Michael arrived in Chicago, he stayed at a downtown hotel, and he and the children talked by telephone. Natalie spoke with him first—maybe two hours—trying to soften him up before the hostilities of the questioning. It didn't change anything. He was just as certain as ever that he was right. Then it was Walter's turn. He got on the phone and told his father, "Leave me in peace."

WALTER

I was not looking forward to talking to my father or to seeing him again. Even though I missed my mother a lot from time to time, I wanted to be left alone by him. That's the way it was, so I hadn't thought much about him all those months he was back in Ukraine. When it came to thinking about my father, life in Chicago for me was sort of like things had been in Sambir. He was gone so much of the time that I had learned how not to think much about him when he wasn't there.

Now here he was. After that first night, he, Natalie, and I had a couple of meetings. It was hard. I wanted to find out how Mikey and my mother were, and he told me, but there was so much anger and we were all kind of suspicious of what each other was up to that nothing much really happened or got said.

Maybe part of me wanted my father to hug me and tell me everything was going to be okay, that we could all live together in America. Maybe part of me hoped that was what he had come back to tell me. But he never said anything like that. He just tried to convince me to see it his way. I couldn't.

JULIAN KULAS

In April 1982, word came from the ACLU that Michael Polovchak would soon arrive in Chicago to give a deposition in the case against his son.

By the time he arrived, Henry Holzer and I had prepared thousands of questions we hoped would get at such key questions as the role of Pyotr Prilepski in the custody fight. We also had plenty of things to ask about girlfriends, pornography, and black-market operations in Sambir.

But the man we saw and interrogated was not the Polovchak who had defiantly gone his own way in the world of his choice. This Polovchak was almost pitiful—obsessed, fierce, defensive, evasive to the point of exhaustion. Here is a typical exchange as Holzer tried to get him to acknowledge that he had a relationship with a woman from the Sambir area:

HENRY HOLZER: Do you know a woman named Halia?

MICHAEL POLOVCHAK: I don't know any women.

Q: Do you know a woman named Halia?

A: I don't know any women.

Q: Do you know a woman named Halia?

A: I have answered you, I don't know no women.

Q: Do you know a woman named Halia?

A: I don't know any women.

Q: Do you deny you know a woman named Halia?

A: I don't know any women. They may be women who are named Anya, or Anna, or Halia, but I don't know any.

Q: You don't know a woman named Halia, is that your testimony?

A: I don't know any women, maybe there are some women whose name is Halia, but I don't know any.

Q: You do not—

HARVEY GROSSMAN: He gave you the answer.

HOLZER: He hasn't given me the answer.

GROSSMAN: He said he did not know a woman named Halia.

HOLZER: Ask him if that's his answer.

A: I don't know any women or their names. I went to and from work.

Q: That is not an answer. I'm going to persist until I get a yes or no.

GROSSMAN: Ask for a yes or no.

HOLZER: Please give me a yes or no answer as to whether you know a woman by the name of Halia.

A: I don't know.

Q: Don't know what?

A: What you're asking me about a woman. Five times you asked me.

GROSSMAN: Will you tell Michael that I have instructed him to answer the question yes or no.

WITNESS: I don't know, no.

Q: What doesn't he know?

A: What you asked me, do I know some woman.

Q: Named Halia.

GROSSMAN: Will you tell Michael that I've instructed him to answer yes or no to the question does he know a woman named Halia.

WITNESS: I don't know, there are many women who have different names, I don't know.

HOLZER: I'm going to sit here all year—

GROSSMAN: I'm going to try to get you an answer to the question. Michael, Mr. Holzer has a right to know the answer to the question "Do you know a woman named Halia?" Answer the question yes or no.

WITNESS: I don't know—

GROSSMAN: Tell him I've instructed him not to use the phrase "I don't know." He must answer yes or no unless he doesn't remember.

WITNESS: No.

The deposition took four days to extract, and about the only new thing I heard from Polovchak was his assertion that he had not said goodbye to his children when he left for the USSR the previous year out of fear that an enemy would learn of the departure and interfere in some way. As the final session neared a close, Michael Polovchak got more frantic.

In one exchange with me, he talked of writing some letters to his sister Anastasia Junko.

"Yes, I did write that and I admit that the people who wrote such letters against me trying to insinuate that there was something wrong with me mentally, these people should be put in jail. Yes, the people who wrote those letters can only be put in prison because they insinuated that I was mentally deranged and also had other illnessess, such as syphilis; whereas everyone knew, and there's documentation to the fact that I underwent medical examination before coming here . . ."

At the end of the four days in Chicago, Michael met with the children for about an hour. He told them it was their duty to return to the Motherland. They told him they would never leave America for Ukraine. They embraced and kissed each other on the cheeks . . . and then he was gone.

For all the unhappiness, anger, and anguish he had caused his family, in the end he was a pitiful figure. With the passing of the years, Michael Polovchak has faded from view. Today, he plays no role in the lives of the children who ran from him—and whom he could never bring back home.

Instead, our energies turned toward the complicated matter of the legal appeals. They took years, grinding through the courts with a slow progress that could have been infuriating if it had not been so helpful to Walter.

Everywhere, there were delays. For example, it wasn't until May 1983 that the Illinois Supreme Court, in a unanimous decision, ruled against us, once again holding that Judge Mooney had erred in taking custody of Walter away from the parents.

The justices wrote: "We have been advised that Michael and Anna Polovchak have returned to the Ukraine. It is apparent, therefore, that Walter cannot immediately be returned to his parents, even assuming the federal orders prohibiting his departure from this country had not been entered." If either parent was to return to the United States, they ruled, "Walter's custody shall be given to the returning parent or parents. . . ." If neither parent came back, then the Circuit Court was to handle the matter in the manner "it deems best suited to Walter's needs."

That was a key phrase for it made clear that the state's highest judges had deep concerns for the interests of Walter himself—not only the parents. Even so, the judges found fault with Judge Mooney and the early hearings back in the summer of 1980. "None of the witnesses present, the minor, the parents, or anyone else able to give relevant testimony was examined," they wrote. "Nor did Walter state, as the findings would seem to indicate, that he would not remain with his parents if released.

"Indeed, it is clear from the later proceedings that Walter's obstinance stemmed not from his opposition to being reunited with his parents, but rather from his desire not to return to the Ukraine. . . . It is our opinion that Walter should have been released to the custody of his parents, who were in the courtroom requesting permission to take their son home."

Once again, the ruling went against us, but by the time the judges actually issued their views, Walter was within five months of turning fifteen. He was filling out into a strapping boy with aviator glasses, a shy grin, and relaxed personality. Girls were attracted to him.

Holzer and I went to the U.S. Supreme Court on a request for relief. Time was really flowing in our favor now. The highest court did not make a ruling until February 1984, when, without comment, it denied our petition for review. A blow, for sure. But months earlier, Walter had turned sixteen, and now was just seven months from the ripe age of seventeen—the magic age Natalie had been when the whole controversy first began, and she had been deemed old enough by her parents to make up her own mind where she wanted to live. Now we felt confident that anything short of a direct order sending Walter back to Ukraine immediately would never have enough force to dislodge him. And such an order was unthinkable, anyway.

Even as the magic eighteenth birthday approached—October 3, 1985—troubles continued with the courts.

On July 18, 1985, barely three months before that birthday, a U.S. District Court judge, Thomas R. McMillen, ruled that federal Immigration officials violated the rights of Anna and Michael when they issued the Departure Control Order back in January 1982. The judge asserted that parental rights are "one of the strongest private interests in this country," and that the INS order had "all but negated a parent's right to bring up their children as Communists or Atheists."

"Surely, a minor child of tender years does not have the right to control his own destiny, although in some cases this right is taken away from his parents and given to a court. . . . 'Little Walter' is fast becoming an adult and has spent the last five years in the United States apparently completely removed from any influence or control by his parents. . . ." The effects of this, he wrote, are "perhaps irreversible."

For the ACLU, Grossman said the question of whether Walter would ever want to return to Ukraine was "a matter between Walter and his parents."

When reporters asked me, I tried to sound confident without sounding cocky. "I predicted five years ago Walter would be buying razor blades in Chicago, and he is," I told a reporter. "I'm not worried about the decision. It is only an opinion of one judge."

I immediately filed an appeal with the U.S. Court of Appeals, and on July 29, 1985, a stay of McMillen's order was issued, pending a hearing on motions later that summer. One thing led to another and arguments were not made before the appeals bench until September 9—barely three weeks before Walter's eighteenth birthday.

Like seasoned soccer players who know all the feints, fakes, and tactics of their opponents, Grossman and I once again brought out our arguments and displayed them before the judges. He concentrated on the denial of due process at the very first hearing. I spoke of the possibility of reprisal against Walter should he ever return, offering that as a concrete example of what he had been running from.

On September 11, 1985, the United States Appeals Court, sitting in Chicago, ruled that the constitutional rights of Anna and Michael Polovchak had been abridged when the U.S. Immigration and Naturalization Service issued the Departure Control Order stopping Walter from leaving the country back in 1982.

But the panel also said that U.S. District Court Judge McMillen had been wrong to lift the Departure Control Order without weighing all the consequences of his act—including the genuine threat to Walter if he did return to the Soviet Union.

The judges urged that there be a full trial of the issues before Walter's October 3 birthday—a total impossibility, and they knew it.

At last, Walter would never need to run from anything—or anyone—again.

The stage was set for an extraordinary citizenship ceremony. We had lost and lost—and won everything!

chapter nineteen
AMERICAN CITIZEN!

1

Minute by minute . . . hour by hour . . . day by day . . .
    1980 . . . 1981 . . . 1982 . . .
    Thirteen . . . fourteen . . . fifteen . . .
    When I think of my life as a group of years passing by, it sounds as flat and dull as if I'd never even left Sambir. And maybe that's the way it would have been if I'd stayed in Ukraine—flat and dull. I'd have settled for less from life because there was no other choice.

But every year in America stood as a challenge to me, forcing me to grow up faster and learn far more than if I'd stayed with my parents. So each year in Chicago stood out because it had its own special trials to be faced and overcome. And with every month that I grew older, I was better able to handle these things.

In school I learned how to take the razzing of the other immigrant kids and not to resent it. It wasn't fun for me. When you already feel like a fool because of the way you dress or, especially, the odd way you speak, the insults dig deep. But gradually I learned how to handle this stuff. I thought a lot about why Hispanics and Poles and Oriental kids and black kids—all of us who were strangers to each other and to the rest of America—had to mix it up this way.

After a lot of time, I began to realize that most of them were just as scared or as out of it as I was. Like they were at the bottom of the pile, and they had to have somebody who was even lower in the dirt. So they stuck it to each other, got into fights, ganged up, beat up, tried to make kids around them feel miserable.

Once I saw what was going on, I felt a lot better about myself and my situation. And I got some feeling for what my mother had faced when she came here and tried to start a new life. She was really somebody who mostly wanted to be left alone and not have to face tough problems like learning a whole new language. She had her hands full with my father, and that was enough.

It's too bad she took off and went back to Ukraine before I had a chance to figure some of this out. Maybe we never would have talked about it, since we didn't talk about much of anything between ourselves anyway. But I keep thinking there would have been an opportunity.

That's another part of what the first years in America helped teach me—that unpleasant things are going to happen whether you want them to or not. You're going to have to deal with them when they hit you. There's room for dreams, but you have to be practical and tough enough not to give up if things don't go your way.

That's what the court fight taught me. With the lawsuits, it seemed like every time I turned around there was some new difficulty in my fight. I never lived without the fear that eventually I'd get told I had to go back. I didn't know much about the legal details—they were beyond a young kid like me, for sure. But that didn't mean I didn't worry. . . . I had my own ideas about what I would do if the Russians ever tried to take me, or if the Americans told me I had to return.

But who wants to think like that? What kind of a way is that to live? It's no fun, and that's the truth. You aren't going to get a gun and go off like Rambo, mowing down the people chasing you. I didn't want to have to flee somewhere, go into hiding, play cops and robbers for real. That was dreamland. Things like that don't happen. I had to face up to the situation. I learned to rely on others and to prepare myself—always—for the worst.

I know now that Mr. Kulas and Mr. Holzer had emergency plans of their own to get me away and hide me if the court decisions went the wrong way. But I couldn't behave that way—as if I could flee—during the years that the legal battle went on. I had to treat everything exactly as it happened, without dreaming about some sort of fantastic escape. So my mind got even more practical than it had been.

Each year was marked by something new, something changing for me that would never be the same, no matter what happened to my life. Every day I got one day closer to my goal; each day I was one day farther away from Sambir.

At first, when I was just twelve, I never thought of time this way. When you're little like that, you just don't. You take every day as it comes, and it's real hard to think of anything farther away than a day or two.

But then I was thirteen . . . then fourteen . . . then fifteen . . .

When Natalie moved out of the Bylens' home and went back to live with Cousin Walter, I had to get used to being by myself in the middle of another family's life. For the first time, I missed Natalie. This wasn't only because I felt strange at the Bylens'. The truth was that in the months since we'd left our parents, she and I had really grown much closer. Natalie and I had fought a lot in the years before we moved to Chicago, but after we got settled and decided what we were going to do, we'd been able to put the fights and unhappiness behind us. We had done this together. We had to depend on each other a lot. This was different.

In the first few years in America, Natalie and I *had* to talk about a lot of things, plan how we were going to handle our problems. So we found we could talk about the same things, and discovered we felt the same way about a lot of things, too. I had never realized this.

Now she's married. She has her own life and, as always, is going down her own road. When I think about what's up ahead, I know she and I may never be as close again as we once were. But we have that time of the past, when everything we did was joined. That's something to remember. I'm lucky she was there. She helped me a lot, and I know it. She helped teach me you could overcome unpleasant or sad experiences and move on, making life better by learning how to listen to someone and work things out with them.

If we had stayed in Sambir, I never would have known much about Natalie. She would have gone off by herself, or maybe some-

how would have gotten to America on her own, living with Aunt
Anna just the way she said she wanted to. And there I would have
been, stuck there forever while she found a new life here. I probably
would have only remembered her as someone I'd had trouble with—
and who had trouble with me!

But now, no matter what lay ahead for us, no matter whether
we went separate ways, we had a strong tie that would always be
there. As the years moved along, I understood the value of this
more and more. In ways I never could have figured if I had stayed
with my parents, I grew up in America.

This America . . .

When I first arrived, all I could think of was Jell-O, bananas,
Big Macs . . . it was like a circus of food. As the years passed, I
learned many things that were a lot more important than having
all the food I wanted. I learned how laws were made, how congressmen and the president were elected, how people could speak
up, or write, or pretty much do what they liked.

In Ukraine, people just didn't act this way. Even if they wanted
to, they didn't dare. But here, people spoke what they believed.
There was often a lot of hot air on the television and in the newspapers—it didn't take anyone long to see that. Sometimes, it seemed
pretty confusing. You didn't know exactly what to think about
every big problem. The reporters played up all these differences.

But if you got interested in some issue, like whether the street
in front of the house should be widened, or there ought to be talks
with the Russians, there was plenty of information—probably as
much as anyone could want. There were so many sides to American
freedom.

For somebody like me, who never wanted to kneel on gravel
again as a punishment for going to church, these years in America
have been extra special. I really fell in love with this place. There's
not another country like it anywhere, and there never was. There's
enough freedom in America to fill up three or four Soviet Unions.

I've had no trouble, for example, thinking about getting drafted
or serving in the army if the country needed me. A lot of immigrant
Americans feel exactly the same way—they know what it is like in
most of the rest of the world, and if they have to, they're ready to
fight to keep our country free. I don't know if this makes us any
more patriotic than other Americans. But I know that Americans

from somewhere else have a special feeling for what this country offers.

Slowly, slowly, my eighteenth birthday was drawing closer . . . and closer. . . . Come what may—whatever time of year it was, whatever happened to me in school or out playing . . . another day had passed.

The passage of time sounds good, like something you can count on. But it's also like being in jail—just like a prison sentence. Because you know that you're going to have to wait it out, no matter what happens. That didn't mean I gave up and sat around. I had a life of my own.

I graduated from grade school, then went on to high school. I was no scholar—I got some D's along with the C's and B's—but I got enough good grades to pass, and I was promoted from class to class. Maybe I didn't win any fancy prizes, but I didn't flunk out, either. I knew from Cousin Walter that a diploma and a college degree were tickets to something better than working in a factory. And even though my marks weren't good, much of that was because of the language barrier. I picked up a lot of information in my classes about the way things are done here that you couldn't really put a grade on. It was knowledge that was personal to me, somebody who had grown up in a totalitarian country. As the Soviet way of doing things faded, I became a better American.

Reporters came around from time to time, doing a feature story on the little kid who had refused to go back. But there were fewer stories than in the early years. This was just fine. I was left alone to learn how to become an American.

When they did come, they would take new photos and put them in the paper next to the first pictures the press took of me, back in July 1980. . . . After a few years, even I could see that the little kid from Sambir was slowly fading from sight. *That* kid was from another time, another country.

That's what I believed.

Every now and then, I would go to a special dinner or a reception sponsored by some people who were interested in helping me. Once, I went to Washington and was taken to a hearing before some congressmen. Mr. Kulas and Mr. Holzer had arranged it. (Congressman Peter Peyser of New York had once come out to Chicago to talk to me, and he was ready to put in a special bill to grant me citizenship if I lost all the court battles. Representative Peyser and other congressmen, like Representative Frank Annunzio of Illinois, really stood up for me, and I was grateful that they could.)

I sat in one of the special rooms in the capitol and listened while congressmen and some other people talked about the Soviet Union. One of the men, a Russian who had come to America sometime before, told the hearing that if I was sent back terrible things would happen to me. I just listened to him, keeping my thoughts to myself. But my face must have showed. He had some pretty bad things to say.

Just then Mr. Holzer's wife, who was sitting nearby, reached out, gave me a hug, and said, "Before we ever let that happen, you'll be safe." It was just a great thing for her to do. I felt a lot better after that.

2

After my father's trip to Chicago in the spring of 1982, I heard practically nothing from my parents. I didn't write them; they didn't call. Natalie sometimes sent them a card, and on birthdays I usually received a greeting card from them. That was about it. I knew that Mikey was starting to grow up, and that after a few years, my mother had a little baby girl. I've never met my little sister, but I'd like to. And who knows? It might happen someday. There are surprises.

Still, there were other troubles here. But Mr. Kulas, my cousin, and my sister and others were always there to help. Like the time I threw some stones and broke a neighbor's windows.

It all began when I sort of drifted into friendship with a couple of kids who were bad company. I never decided to join up with them, but I just let it more or less happen.

It was one of the few times in my life that I never thought about much of anything, such as whether heaving rocks at someone's windows might hurt someone inside, or bring trouble to me, or to Mr. Kulas or Cousin Walter. I didn't think at all.

Even after it was over, and the damage had been repaired and I had been scolded and reminded, I still wasn't thinking much. Because pretty soon, I got into much worse trouble: shoplifting.

It was no accident that it happened, but in a way, it was just like an accident—nothing planned. It happened when I got caught holding the bag for some kids, friends of mine who were taking some things in a store. I knew what they were doing and never tried to stop them, much less try to stop myself. I thought I was being smart, showing off for someone else, proving I was such a tough guy.

When the store people grabbed me, I was stunned. An instant later I realized I'd been a stupid jerk. I hated myself. If I could have taken back the few minutes of stupidity and breaking the law, I would have. On the spot. It was like a nightmare—and I caused it all by myself.

All my regrets didn't mean a thing. The store manager was real angry, as well as real pleased he'd caught somebody. I think he was thinking of jail. Second by second, my situation got worse and worse. I don't think I'd ever been so scared. But Mr. Kulas pitched in and rescued me again.

He talked to the people in charge and asked them to give me another chance. He said I'd learned my lesson and would never do anything like that again. Boy, was *he* right!

He got me out of a real scrape that never should have happened. I felt so ashamed, I didn't know what to say to him. I still don't.

When it was all over, I knew I had caused a lot of grief for myself and everybody else. At the time, the reporters were still doing stories about me, and if they had ever found out about this, there would have been headlines all over the world. But Mr. Kulas raced around and managed to get people to keep it out of the news. If he hadn't, the ACLU or a judge would have found out. I might have ended up right back in Ukraine.

Without a thought, I'd made it real easy for my parents or the ACLU to say that living in America without my parents was turning me into a criminal. How dumb I'd been! It had been a real close call.

I felt terrible about what I'd done. I also realized that from then on I had to think about everything before I did anything. To this day, I can't exactly say why I did it. The one thing I'm sure of: it will never happen again.

I learned my lesson.

* * *

Almost as if I'd been looking the other way, October 3, 1985, was suddenly just a few weeks away. My eighteenth birthday!

The reporters started calling again, and I gave a few interviews. There wasn't anything that stood in the way of my goal. Even the final court decision, just three weeks before the day, meant nothing. It came too late. Time really was on my side, after all.

Mr. Kulas, Mr. Holzer, and the others who had helped so much were planning a special swearing-in ceremony for me when I became a citizen on October 8.

The whole affair they had planned was pretty fancy. We were going to fly to Washington, where officials were going to turn a room in one of the U.S. Senate office buildings into a special courtroom so I could be sworn in.

I began thinking what I wanted to say. This was going to be the most important day of my life, and I wanted people to know the truth. I thought a lot about what it was going to mean to be an American. This was my chance to say not only what I felt, but what I *knew* to be true about my new country, my new people, and my life. I had some pretty strong ideas about all these things.

There was something else, as important to me as any of the presents I received that day: a telegram from my parents. They wished me well. This made me pretty sure that they think America is the right place for me.

When we flew from Chicago to Washington, I remembered the airplane flight from Italy to New York way back at the beginning of 1980, when I had promised myself I would never head back the way I had come, from America to Ukraine. I could still remember what I had been feeling that first night when I saw all the lights and cars moving out beyond the airport building. What an exciting place I'd landed in!

That twelve-year-old immigrant had been a frightened little boy. Now I was able to look out for myself. I didn't need the Bylens, or any other foster family selected for me by the state, or Cook County. I could live with Cousin Walter if I chose. . . . I could get a car, a job. . . . As soon as I registered, I could serve in the army—or vote in an election. These were the things I really wanted to do for myself and my new country.

They called it my Birthday Party of Freedom, and dozens of people came to the ceremony at 6 P.M. on October 8. It was held in the Dirksen Senate Office Building, right near the Capitol. The Liberty Institute organized things, and even saw to it that a federal judge from Chicago, Charles P. Kocoras, was flown in specially for the swearing-in.

Natalie and I were dressed as well as we could be. I had a suit on and she was wearing a bright red dress. She looked real pretty, just right for a party. The room was a big one, and to my surprise, there were dozens of people there.

I shook hands with Congressman Jack Kemp, who later would be running for president; Senator D'Amato of New York; Senator Alan Dixon of Illinois; Congressman Robert Dornan of California; and many other well-known people and politicians.

President Reagan didn't come, but he sent a couple of people from the White House, and a letter of congratulation. I was invited to go meet the president in the White House after the swearing-in. I really was looking forward to shaking his hand! But when we finally got over there later, he wasn't able to meet me. A bunch of Middle East terrorists had seized the *Achille Lauro* cruise ship, and the president was dealing with that. We waited about an hour, and an aide finally came out and told us the president would not be able to see me. He apologized a lot, then showed us all around the White House, even into the Oval Office, where we saw Mr. Reagan's desk and a dog that was lying around panting. I thought it was a grand place for anyone to live, especially a president.

We visited the monument to our Ukrainian national poet, Taras Schevchenko, in Washington. He is revered by Ukrainians for celebrating the independence of Ukraine. I remember telling Mr. Kulas, "He sure knew what he was talking about."

But all that came later. The part of the day that really counted the very most was the swearing-in. This was what we had all come for, what I had run away from home for.

Mr. Kulas led off the speakers, telling them a little of my background and how he had come into the case, and how the long court fight had gone. He said he had wanted to put the Soviet Union on trial.

"We had some very credible witnesses, and the Soviet government would never allow the parents to come for a trial, because it would have been the Soviet Union and not the parents that were on trial," he said.

Then he read some of what the judges had written in the last decision that had come just a few weeks earlier, the one telling the lower court to hold a trial rather than just hand me back to my parents.

"We think the judge stepped over the bounds of his discretion in failing to make any provision for the protection of Walter's rights," Mr. Kulas read.

"This court need not be blind to the commonly recognized fact that Soviet citizens who refuse to return to the Soviet Union and who publicly derogate that country are at risk of seriously adverse governmental action if they return involuntarily to the Soviet Union.

"It would seem patently inequitable to force a seventeen-year-old against his will to return to a country where he faced a threat of persecution."

Mr. Kulas smiled.

"We consider this decision important for two reasons," he said. "The first is that the court took judicial notice of the fact that Soviet citizens who refuse to return to their homeland would be persecuted; and that parental rights, although very important, are not absolute and need to be weighed and measured against the rights of the minor."

As he talked, I could *feel* the room grow quiet as each person thought over what he was saying. When he finished, you could hear a pin drop.

Now, there was a feeling in the room of something big happening. All these people, very quiet, the judge wearing a big black robe. People were very still and silent after this.

Then Mr. Holzer talked about how he had gotten involved and reached out to Mr. Kulas.

"Like many of you here today, and countless other Americans," Mr. Holzer said, "for the past forty years I've watched, powerless, while communism has murdered tens of millions of men, women and children, swallowed up country after country, and committed unimaginable atrocities from one end of this planet to the other . . .

". . . This boy's stand against communism, against the Soviet state, against the ruthless KGB, provided me with a rare privilege: to fight them all; to draw a line; to say no; to save one soul; to declare that 'you shall not make Walter Polovchak yet another victim . . .'

"I helped defend Walter Polovchak because in doing so I was defending not only him but also the principle of freedom . . ."

People were very, very quiet. They were listening to every word. We were all somehow pulled together, feeling the same things, believing the same things. I could feel this all around me, and it made me even more confident I had chosen the right words for my brief speech.

Next, Mrs. Holzer stood. "Five and a half years ago, a twelve-and-a-half-year-old kid made international headlines," she began. "After six months in a free country and twelve years in a dictatorship, he let all of us know that *he* knew the difference. He stood up in front of the whole world and, in effect, said, I have a *right* to be free . . ."

I could feel people looking only at me now. I glanced around . . . Natalie . . . Cousin Walter . . . Mr. Kulas . . . Mr. Holzer. . . . We were like a little family of our own . . .

". . . When I thought about the mere possibility that you would be plunged back behind the Iron Curtain," Mrs. Holzer continued, "I picked up the phone and made the call that brought Hank Holzer and Julian Kulas together.

"You know, it isn't often that life offers us an opportunity to stand up and fight for an important principle. I'm very grateful for the opportunity I had to fight for the principle of freedom in the person of a young boy . . ."

Then she recited the poem that's on the Statue of Liberty:

> *Give me your tired, your poor, your huddled masses*
> *Yearning to breathe free,*
> *The wretched refuse of your teeming shore,*
> *Send these, the homeless, tempest-tossed, to me*
> *I lift my lamp beside the golden door.*

Mrs. Holzer turned to me. "Walter, for five and a half years, you've had one foot in that door. Today, you walk through it. Welcome home!"

The feeling of pride and something special grew in all of us there.

I looked around. Here were the people who had stepped forward to help me in my struggle. For most of them, the long fight had meant sacrifice, courage, and caring for me—a kid from Ukraine. It was kind of a miracle.

Now it was my turn to talk. This was my chance to tell all the people here—and anyone else in the country who cared—what I felt about what they had done for me. It was a once-in-a-lifetime chance to say what I felt, and to have people listen. I pulled out my speech and stood before a whole battery of microphones.

"I was twelve and a half years old when I made the most important decision of my life: I told my parents I wouldn't go back to the Soviet Union.

"To those people who thought I didn't know what I was doing and should just do whatever my parents said, I want to set the record straight. I knew what I was doing. After living under communism for twelve and a half years and only six months in a free country, the difference was pretty obvious. I'm Ukrainian Catholic—but in the Soviet Ukraine, my religion was outlawed. Here, I go to church openly. There, you're looking over your shoulder all the time. You can't even go from one town to another without permission. Here, you can go anywhere. The last five and a half years have been pretty tough, but I'm glad I did it and I'd do it again.

"To my family who went back to the Soviet Ukraine, I just want to say I wish you well and hope someday we can be together again. But it will have to be in the West, because as long as I live, I'll never set foot in the Soviet Union."

I looked around as I said that. People were nodding and agreeing with me.

"To all the people who have asked about my future, I want to let them know I'm in my last year of high school and I want to go on with my education. I'm not sure yet about my future career, but I *am* sure of one thing: I pledge here and now that I will be the best American I can be.

"To the brave men and women who came before me, who wanted their freedom and fought for it, I want to say that you made it easier for me and I thank you, especially Simas Kudirka. I only hope I have made it easier for the people, young or old, who come after me.

"To all those who have helped me in my fight to remain free, I will never forget what you did for me and I want to say a special thanks to:

"—the Carter administration, for giving me political and religious asylum even though I was only twelve and a half, the youngest person to ever get it;

"—the Reagan administration, for helping my lawyers defend the asylum;

"—my sister Natalie and my cousin Walter, who stood behind me from the very beginning, gave me love and support, and have been my only family here;

"—all those sympathetic Americans who wrote me and prayed for me and helped me to keep up my spirits;

"—some very special people who cared so much about my right to be free that they made my fight *their* fight—people like Mrs. Erika Holzer, Ludmilla Thorne, Mrs. Natalia Solzhenitsyn;

"—most of all, I want to thank, with all my heart, two men who volunteered much more than their time and legal talent. For without my lawyers, Julian Kulas and Professor Henry Holzer, I wouldn't be here. I wouldn't be free. For five and a half years, they never stopped working and thinking and fighting for me, and I always knew that no matter how bad things looked, they would never let me down. They never did.

"To all of you here today, and to all Americans everywhere, I want to ask you please not to forget the Ukrainian enslaved people and all the other people who are prisoners behind the Iron Curtain, who fight for freedom as best they can and who must not be abandoned.

"Finally, I want you to know that I am very, very glad to be free. I know a lot of people take their freedom for granted, but I don't and I never will.

"God Bless America!"

The judge stood next to me, and Natalie held the Bible. I looked around at the crowd, people I now knew to be my special friends and supporters. They were looking at me calmly, their faces relaxed and smiling at me.

"I hereby declare, on oath, that I absolutely and entirely renounce and abjure all allegiance and fidelity to any foreign prince, potentate, state or sovereignty, of whom or which I have heretofore been a subject or citizen; that I will support and defend the Constitution and laws of the United States of America against all enemies, foreign and domestic; that I will

*bear true faith and allegiance to the same; that I will bear arms on behalf
of the United States when required by the law; that I will perform non-
combatant service in the armed forces of the United States when required
by the law; that I will perform work of national importance under civilian
direction when required by the law; and that I take this obligation freely
without any mental reservation or purpose of evasion: so help me God."*

Strong, old words. There was a moment of silence. Judge Kocoras leaned forward.

"Walter Polovchak . . . it gives me great pleasure to declare you
a citizen of the United States of America!"

The room filled with applause. I held up my certificate of citizenship: *Walter Polovchak, American.*

Suddenly, without a word or a sign from anyone, we were hugging each other . . . all around the room.

Someone's voice began singing . . .

"God bless America, land of the free . . ."

Someone else joined in, and now we all had our hands joined
with each other. . . . People were standing, swaying back and forth,
tears were falling, the song filling the room . . .

> *God bless America*
> *Land that I love,*
> *Stand beside her and guide her,*
> *Through the night with a light from above.*
> *From the mountains, to the prairies,*
> *To the oceans white with foam,*
> *God bless America,*
> *My home sweet home,*
> *God bless America,*
> *My home sweet home.*

We finished and people were hugging and laughing, grabbing
each other and squeezing me tight, too. It was like a wedding, or
the best party I could ever imagine anywhere, right in sight of the
flag, the judge, and the Capitol of the United States.

May God bless these people, I thought to myself. And my parents, too. For they had brought me here, and that had changed my

life forever. They had never understood, but I was sure they would be proud of me just the same.

For all my life ahead, I have one goal and one dream: that I'll be the best American I can be.

So help me God.

About the Author

WALTER POLOVCHAK lives in Chicago with Cousin Walter Polowczak. He is working at a public relations firm and studying for a college degree in telecommunications.

Walter and his sister, who is married and lives elsewhere in Illinois, receive occasional greeting cards from their parents in the Soviet Union. Otherwise, there is no contact between the children and their parents.

KEVIN KLOSE, former bureau chief in Moscow and then Chicago for *The Washington Post*, is an editor on the *Post*'s national staff. His last book, *Russia and the Russians*, was an Overseas Press Club award winner.